ISSUE LABEL
All *Vacation Loans* to be returned by the
FIRST SATURDAY of term
All *Term Loans* to be returned by the
LAST SATURDAY of term

THE ROSE OF
DUTCHER'S COOLLY

HAMLIN GARLAND

AMS PRESS
NEW YORK

Reprinted from the edition of 1899, New York
First AMS EDITION published 1969
Manufactured in the United States of America

Library of Congress Catalogue Card Number: 74-90103

AMS PRESS, INC.
NEW YORK, N.Y. 10003

Contents

ROSE OF DUTCHER'S COOLLY

ROSE OF DUTCHER'S COOLLY

CHAPTER I

HER CHILDHOOD

ROSE was an unaccountable child from the start. She learned to speak early, and while she did not use " baby-talk " she had strange words of her own. She called hard money " tow " and a picture "tac," names which had nothing to do with onomatopœia, though it seemed so in some cases. Bread and milk she called " plop."

She began to read of her own accord when four years old, picking out the letters from the advertisements of the newspapers, and running to her mother at the sink or bread-board to learn what each word meant. Her demand for stories grew to be a burden. She was in-satiate, nothing but sleep subdued her eager brain.

As she grew older she read and re-read her picture-books when alone, but when older people were talking she listened as attentively as if she understood every word. She had the power of amusing herself and visited very little with other children. It was deeply moving to see her with her poor playthings out under the poplar-tree, talking to herself, arranging and re-arranging her chairs and tables, the sunlight flecking her hair, and the birds singing overhead.

She seemed only a larger sort of insect, and her prattle mixed easily with the chirp of crickets and the rustle of leaves.

She was only five years old when her mother suddenly withdrew her hands from pans and kettles, gave up all thought of bread and butter making, and took rest in death. Only a few hours of waiting on her bed near the kitchen fire and Ann Dutcher was through with toil and troubled dreaming, and lay in the dim best-room, taking no account of anything in the light of day.

Rose got up the next morning after her mother's last kiss and went into the room where the body lay. A gnomish little figure the child was, for at that time her head was large and her cropped hair bristled till she seemed a sort of brownie. Also, her lonely child-life had given her quaint, grave ways.

She knew her mother was dead, and that death was a kind of sleep which lasted longer than common sleep, that was all the difference; so she went in and stood by the bed and tried to see her mother's face. It was early in the morning, and the curtains being drawn it was dark in the room; but Rose had no fear, for mother was there.

She talked softly to herself a little while, then went over to the window and pulled on the string of the curtain till it rolled up. Then she went back and looked at her mother. She grew tired of waiting at last.

"Mamma," she called, "wake up. Can't you wake up, mamma?"

She patted the cold, rigid cheeks with her rough brown little palms. Then she blew in the dead face, gravely. Then she thought if she could only open mamma's eyes she'd be awake. So she took her finger and thumb and tried to lift the lashes, and when she did she was frightened by the look of the set faded gray eyes. Then the terrible vague shadow of the Unknown settled upon her and she cried convulsively : "Mamma! mamma, I want you!" Thus she met death, early in her life.

After her mother's burial Rose turned to her father more hungrily than before. She rode into the fields with him in the spring, when he went out to sow, sitting on the seeder box with the pockets of her little pink apron filled with wheat, and her sweet, piping little voice calling to the horses or laughing in glee at the swarms of sparrows. When he was ploughing corn she rode on the horses, clinging like a blue-jay to the rings in the back-pad, her yellow-brown hair blowing.

She talked sagely about the crops and the weather, and asked innumerable questions. Often John could not hear her questions, which were like soft soliloquies, but she babbled on just the same.

"See the little birds, pappa John. They's 'bout a million of 'um, ain't they? They're glad spring has come, ain't they, pappa? They can understand each other just the same as we can, can't they, pappa John?"

John Dutcher was not a talker, and he seldom

answered her unless she turned her eager face to him, and her bird-like voice repeated her question. But it mattered very little to Rose. She had her father's power of self-amusement. In case she got tired of riding about with him she brought her playthings out and established them in a corner of the fence. Her favorite game was " playing horses."

Her horses were sticks of the size of canes, and of all sorts and colors. Each one had a name. How she selected them, and why she selected them out of the vast world of sticks, was a mystery to John Dutcher.

The brown stick she called Dan, the fork-handle, Nellie, and the crooked stick with the big knot was Barney. She had from six to ten, and she never forgot their names. Each had a string for a bridle and they were all placed in stalls, which she built with infinite labor and calculation out of twigs. She led each stick by its halter up to the manger — a rail — on which she had placed oats and grass. She talked to them.

" Now, Barney, whoa-whoa there now! Don't you kick Kit again — now, sir! Kit, you better stand over here by Pete — Barney, you need exercise, that's what you need, — yessir."

She exercised them by riding them in plunging circles about the fields, forgetting, with the quick imagination of a child, that she was doing all the hard work of the riding with her own stout, brown legs. It was a pleasure to John to have her there, though he said little to her.

Often at night as he saw her lying asleep, her long

lashes upon her roughened sun-burned skin, his heart went out to her in a great throb of tenderness. His throat ached and his eyes grew wet as he thought how unresponsive he had been that day. His remorseful memory went back over her eager questions to which he had not replied. Dear, sweet, restless little heart! And then he vowed never to lose patience with her again. And sometimes, standing there beside her bed, his arms closed about the little mound under the quilts, and his lips touched the round, sleep-enraptured face. At such times his needy soul lifted a cry to his dead wife for help to care for his child.

He grew afraid of the mystery and danger of coming womanhood. Her needs came to him more powerfully each day.

When she began going to school with the other children the effects of her lonely life and of her companionship with her father set her apart from the boys and girls of her own age and placed her among those several years older, whom she dominated by her gravity and her audacity. She was not mischievous or quarrelsome, but she was a fearless investigator. She tested their childish superstitions at once.

When they told her that if she swore at God and shook her fist at the sky she would certainly drop dead, she calmly stepped forward and shook her little fist up at the sun and swore, while the awe-stricken children cowered like a covey of partridges.

"There! you see *that's* a lie," she said, scornfully. "God can't kill me — or else He don't care."

She went on exploding these strange superstitious fancies, which are only the survivals in civilized children of savage ancestry.   She stood erect in the door of the school-house when she was eight years old, and pointed her hand at the lightning while the teacher sat cowed and weeping at her desk.

"You said I dassn't," the little elf cried.   "But I dass't, and nothing ain't struck me yet."

Her absolute fearlessness of the things which children shrank from, the dark, and things of the dark, made her a marked figure.   The women of the Coolly thought it due to the lack of a mother's care.   They spoke to the minister about it and urged him to see Dutcher and ask him to try and do something for the child's good.

But Dutcher simply said: "Oh, don't bother the child about her soul. She's all right. I don't bother myself about those things, and what's the use o' spoilin' the child's fun? If she wants to go to Sunday-school, why all right. She'll go where she's interested."

"But, Brother Dutcher, the child is doing outrageous things — heathenish, defying her God."

"I don't s'pose what she does will make any particular difference to God. We understand each other, Rosie and me. Don't worry. If she does anything real bad she'll come and tell me of it. *Chk! Chk!* G'wan, Barney!" He cut the matter short by driving away into the field of corn.

He saw rushing upon him the most solemn and severe trials of a parent. Rose was a sturdy child and promised to develop into a maiden early, and there were a hundred things which ought to be said to her which must be said by someone. He was not philosopher enough to know that she held in her expanding brain the germs of self-knowledge.

He had been passing through a running fire of questions from the child for two years, but these questions now took hold of deeper things, and they could no longer be put aside by saying, " Wait a few years and then I'll tell you." She would learn them elsewhere, if not from him. He braced himself for the trial, which increased in severity.

The child's horizon was limited, but within its circle her searching eyes let nothing escape. She came to Dutcher with appalling questions.

She not only asked him, " Who made God ? " but she wanted to know how she came to be born, and a thousand other questions of the same searching nature. He saw that the day of petty fictions had gone by. The child knew that little lambs, and calves, and kittens did not grow down in the woods. She knew that babies were not brought by the doctor, and that they did not come from heaven.

" Good Lord ! " groaned her father one day, after an unusually persistent attack from her, caused by the appearance of a little colt out in the barn, " I wish your mother was here, or some woman. You do make it hard for me, Rosie. "

" How do I make it hard for you, pappa ? " was her quick new question. " O Lord, what a young un, " he said, in deeper despair. " Come, ain't it about time

for you to be leggin' it toward school? Give me
a rest, Rosie. But I'll answer all your questions —
don't ask about them things of the children — come
right to me always — only don't pile 'em all on me
to once."

"All right, pappa, I won't."

"That's a good old soul!" he said, patting her on
the back. After she had gone he sat down on the feed-
box and wiped his face. "I wonder how women do
explain things like that to girls," he thought. "I'll ask
the preacher's wife to explain it — no, I won't. I'll do
it myself, and I'll get her books to read about it — good
books."

It was evidence of the girl's innate strength and
purity of soul that the long succession of hired hands
had not poisoned her mind. They soon discovered,
however, the complete confidence between the father
and child, and knew that their words and actions would
be taken straight to John as soon as night came and
Rose climbed into his lap. This made them careful
before her, and the shame of their words and stories
came to the child's ears only in fragments.

Dutcher concluded that he should have a woman in
the house, and so sent back to Pennsylvania for his
sister, lately widowed. Rose looked forward to seeing
her aunt with the wildest delight. She went with her
father down the valley to Bluff Siding to meet her.
Bluff Siding was the only town the child knew, and it
was a wonderful thing to go to town.

As they stood on the platform, waiting, her eyes

swept along the great curve of the rails to the east, and suddenly, like a pain in the heart, came her first realization of distance, of the infinity of the world.

" Where does it go to, pappa ? "

" Oh, a long way off. To Madison, Chicago, and Pennsylvany."

" How far is it ? Could we go there with old Barney and Nell ? "

" Oh, no. If we drove there it would take us days and days, and the wheat would grow up and get yellow, an' the snow come, almost, before we'd get there."

" Oh, dear ! " she sighed. " I don't like to have it so big. Do people live all along the whole way ? "

" Yes, the whole way, and lots of big cities."

" Big as Madison ? " Madison was her unseen measure of greatness.

" Oh, yes. A hundred times bigger."

She sighed again and looked away to the east with a strange, unchildish, set stare in her eyes. She was trying to realize it.

" It makes me ache, pappa," she sighed, putting her little brown hand to her throat.

When the engine came in with its thunder and whiz, she shrank back against the station wall, white and breathless, not so much with fear as with awe. She had never stood so close to this monster before. It attracted all her attention, so that for the moment she forgot about the coming of her aunt.

When she looked into the large, dull face of Mrs.

Diehl she was deeply disappointed. She liked her, but she did not love her!

She had looked forward to her coming almost as if to the return of her mother. She had imagined her looking strange and beautiful because she came out of the mystical, far-off land her father often spoke of. Instead of these things Mrs. Diehl was a strong-featured, mild-voiced woman, rather large and ungraceful, who looked upon the motherless child and clicked her tongue. "You poor chick!"

But the thing which had happened was this: Rose had conceived of distance and great cities.

The next day she said: " Pappa John, I want to go way up on the bluffs. I want to go up to Table Rock where I can see way, way off."

" It's a long climb up there, Rosie. You'll get tired."

But Rosie insisted, and together they climbed the hill. Up beyond the pasture — beyond the blackberry patch — beyond the clinging birches in their white jackets — up where the rocks cropped out of the ground and where curious little wave-worn pebbles lay scattered on the scant grass.

Once a glittering rattlesnake lying in the sun awoke, and slipped under a stone like a stream of golden oil, and the child shrank against her father's thigh in horror.

They climbed slowly up the steep grassy slope and stood at last on the flat rock which topped the bluff. Rose stood there, dizzy, out of breath, with her hair blown across her cheek, and looked away at the curving valley and its river gleaming here and there through the willows and alders. It was like looking over an unexplored world to the child. Her eyes expanded and her heart filled with the same ache which came into it when she looked down along the curving railway-track. She turned suddenly and fell sobbing against her father.

"Why, Rosie, what's the matter? Poor little girl — she's all tired out, climbin' up here." He sat down and took her on his lap and talked to her of the valley below and where the river went — but she would not look up again.

"I want to go home," she said with hidden face.

On the way down, John rolled a big stone down the hill, and as it went bounding, crashing into the forest below, a deer drifted out like a gray shadow and swept along the hillside and over the ridge.

Rose saw it as if in a dream. She did not laugh nor shout. John was troubled by her silence and gravity, but laid it to weariness and took her pickaback on the last half mile through the brush.

That scene came to her mind again and again in the days which followed, but she did not see it again till the following spring. It appealed to her with less power then. Its beauty overshadowed its oppressive largeness. As she grew older it came to be her favorite playing ground on holidays. She brought down those quaint little bits of limestone and made them her playthings in her house, which was next door to her barn — and secondary to her barn.

CHAPTER II

CHILD-LIFE, PAGAN-FREE

Rose lived the life of the farm-girls in the seven great Middle-West States. In summer she patted away to school, clad only in a gingham dress, white, untrimmed cotton pantalets, and a straw hat that was made feminine by a band of gay ribbon. Her body was as untrammelled as a boy's. She went bare-footed and bare-headed at will, and she was part of all the sports.

She helped the boys snare gophers, on the way to school, and played house with the girls on the shady side of the school-house; and once, while the teacher was absent at noon, Rose proposed that a fire be built to heat the tea for the dolls.

She it was who constructed the stove out of thin bricks, and set a fire going in it in the corner of the boys' entryway, and only the passing of a farmer saved the building from disaster.

She it was who found the ground-bird's nest and proposed to make a house over it, and ended by teaching the bird to walk through a long hallway made of sticks, in order to get to its eggs again.

She despised hats and very seldom wore hers, except hanging by the string down her back. Her face was brown and red as leather, and her stout little hands were always covered with warts and good brown earth, which had no terrors for her.

Bugs and beetles did not scare her any more than they did the boys. She watched the beetles bury a dead gopher without the slightest repugnance; indeed, she turned to, after a long time, to help them, a kindness which they very probably resented, to judge from their scrambling.

She always urged the other girls to go down to the creek and see the boys go in swimming, and would have joined the fun had not the boys driven her back with handfuls of mud, while they uttered opprobrious cries. She saw no reason why boys should have all the fun.

When the days were hot they could go down there in the cool, nice creek, strip and have a good time, but girls must primp around and try to keep nice and clean. She looked longingly at the naked little savages running about and splashing in the water. There was something so fine and joyous in it, her childish heart rebelled at sex-distinction as she walked slowly away. She, too, loved the feel of the water and the caress of the wind.

She was a good student, and developed early into a wonderful speller and reader. She always listened to the classes in reading, and long before she reached the pieces herself she knew them by heart, and said them to herself in the silence of the lane or the loneliness of the garret.   She recited "The Battle of Waterloo" and "Lochiel" long before she understood the words.   The roll of the verse excited her, and she thrust her nut of a fist into the air like Miriam the Hebrew singer, feeling vaguely the same passion.

She went from Primer to First Reader, then to the Second and Third Readers, without effort.   She read easily and dramatically.   She caught at the larger meanings, and uttered them in such wise that the older pupils stopped their study to listen.

Scraps and fragments of her reading took curious lodgment in her mind.   New conceptions burst into her consciousness with a golden glory upon reading these lines:

> "Field of wheat so full and fair,
> Shining with a sunny air;
> Lightly swaying either way,
> Graceful as the breezes sway."

They made her see the beauty of the grain-field as never before.   It seemed to be lit by some mysterious light.

> "Cleon hath a million acres,
> Ne'er a one have I,"

seemed to express something immemorial and grand. She seemed to see hills stretching to vast distances, covered with cattle.   "The pied frog's orchestra" came to her with sudden conscious meaning as she sat on the door-step one night eating her bowl of bread and milk, and watching the stars come out. These fragments of literature expressed the poetry of certain things about her, and helped her also to perceive others.

She was a daring swinger, and used to swing furiously out under the maple-trees, hoping to some day touch the branches high up there, and, when her companions gathered in little clumps in dismayed consultation, she swung with wild hair floating free, a sort of intoxication of delight in her heart.

Sometimes when alone she slipped off her clothes and ran amid the tall corn-stalks like a wild thing. Her slim little brown body slid among the leaves like a weasel in the grass. Some secret, strange delight, drawn from ancestral sources, bubbled over from her pounding heart, and she ran and ran until wearied and sore with the rasping corn-leaves, then she sadly put on civilized dress once more.

Her feet were brown as toads, but graceful and small, and she washed them (when the dew was heavy enough) by running in the wet grass just before going into bed, a trick the boys of the neighborhood had taught her. She ran forward to clean the insteps and backward to clean the heels. If the grass was not wet, she omitted the ceremony. Dust was clean anyhow. Her night-gowns were of a most sorry pattern till her aunt came; thereafter they were clean, though it mattered little. They were a nuisance to her.

She wore a pink sun-bonnet, when she could find one; generally there were two or three hanging on the

fences at remote places.   She sat down in the middle of
the road, because she had a lizard's liking for the warm,
soft dust, and she paddled in every pool and plunged her
hand into every puddle after frogs and bugs and worms,
with the action of a crane.

She ate everything that boys did.   That is to say, she
ate sheep-sorrel, Indian tobacco, roots of ferns, May-
apples, rose-leaves, rose-buds, raw turnips, choke-cher-
ries, wild crab-apples, slippery-elm bark, and the green
balls on young oak-trees, as well as the bitter acorns.
These acorns she chewed into pats and dried in the sun,
to eat at other times, like a savage.

She ate pinks and grass blades, and green watermelons,
and ground cherries, and blackhaws, and dewberries, and
every other conceivable thing in the woods and fields,
not to mention the score of things which she tried and
spit out.   She became inured to poison-ivy like the boys,
and walked the forest paths without fear of anything but
snakes.

Summer was one continuous and busy playspell for
her in those days before her lessons became a serious
thing, for as she sat in school she was experimenting in
the same way.   She chewed paper into balls and snapped
them like the boys.   She carried slips of elm bark to
chew also, and slate-pencils she crunched daily.   She
gnawed the corners of her slate, tasted her ink, and
munched the cedar of her pencil.

And through it all she grew tall and straight and
brown.   She could run like a partridge and fight like a
wild-cat, at need.   Her brown-black eyes shone in her

dark warm skin with an eager light, and her calloused little claws of hands reached and took hold of all realities.

The boys respected her as a girl who wasn't afraid of bugs, and who could run, and throw a ball. Above all she was strong and well.

c

CHAPTER III

DANGEROUS DAYS

A FARMER'S daughter is exposed to sights and sounds which the city girl knows nothing of. Mysterious processes of generation and birth go on before the eyes of the farm child, which only come as obscure whisperings to the city child of the same middle condition. And these happenings have a terrifying power to stir and develop passions prematurely.

Rose heard occasionally obscene words among the hands. She listened unperceived to the vulgar cackling of old women during afternoon calls. Before her eyes, from the time of her toddling youth, had proceeded the drama of animal life. She had seen it all — courtship, birth, death. Nothing escaped her keen, searching, inquisitive eyes. She asked her father about these dramatic and furious episodes of the barn-yard, but he put her off, and she finally ceased to ask about them. She began to perceive they were considered of that obscure and unmentionable world of sin, with which men alone had proper right to deal.

When the girls of her age in the grasp of some gale of passion, danced about her shouting foul words in the unknowing way children have, she did not take part by word of mouth, though she felt the same savage, frenzied delight in it.

She learned early the signs which pass in the country to describe the unnamable and covert things of human life. She saw them scrawled on the fences, on schoolhouse doors, and written on the dust of the road. There was no escaping them. The apparently shameful fact of sex faced her everywhere.

And yet through it all she lived a glad, free, wholesome life. Her blood was sweet and swift and kept off contagion. Her brown skin flushed with its unhindered current. She dipped into this obscure, questionable world only momentarily, and came back to her father wholesome and happy, except occasionally when some outrageous gesture or word had stricken her into weeping.

Then her father told her not to mind; just be good and sweet herself, and it would help the others to be good too. He blundered sometimes and struggled for words, and talked in grotesque riddles, but she understood his meaning some way and was comforted.

She did not go to her aunt with her doubts and fears for she had heard her say coarse words. Pappa John was her hero and guide. She went to him as naturally as to a mother. It was a noble thing for him to achieve, but he did not know it, and had not sought it. It was indeed thrust upon him. He would gladly have escaped from this part of her education, but as Rose refused to listen to anyone else, John puzzled and disturbed continued to be her timorous guide as a matter of need.

He could not understand her quick perception — something seemed to rise in the child to help him explain. Germs of latent perception appeared to spring up like a conjuror's magic seed, here a kernel, there a tree. One by one obscure ideas rose from the deep like bubbles, and burst into thought in her conscious self. A hint organized in her brain long trains of sequential conceptions, which she had inherited with her sex. She did not require teaching on the most fundamental problems of her nature.

She began to work early, but her work, like her playing, was not that of other girls. As she never played with dolls, caring more for hobby-horses, so she early learned to do work in the barn. From taking care of make-believe stick horses she came easily to taking care of real horses.

When a toddling babe she had moved about under the huge plough-horses in their stalls, putting straw about them, and patting their columnar limbs with her little pads of palms, talking to them meanwhile in soft, indefinite gurgle of love and command.

She knew how much hay and oats they needed, and she learned early to curry them, though they resented her first trials with the comb. She cared less for the cows and pigs, but before she was ten she could milk the " easy " cows. She liked the chickens, and it was part of her daily duty to feed the hens and gather the eggs.

She could use a fork in the barn deftly as a boy by the time she was twelve, and in stacking times she handed bundles across the stack to her father. It was the variety of work, perhaps, which prevented her from acquiring that pathetic and lamentable stoop (or crook) in the shoulders and back which many country girls have in varying degree.

All things tended to make her powerful, lithe, and erect. The naked facts of nature were hers to command. She touched undisguised and unrefined nature at all points. Her feet met not merely soil, but mud. Her hands smelled of the barn-yard as well as of the flowers of the wild places of wood and meadow.

Meanwhile her comradeship was sweet to John Dutcher. He hardly knew his loss of a son, so completely was he companioned by Rose. He had put far away the time when she should wear shoes and long dresses and become a " young lady."

" Let her be, as long as you can," he said to his sister. " She's a mighty comfort to me now, and she's happy; don't disturb her; time to wear long dresses and corsets'll come soon enough without hurryin' things."

CHAPTER IV

AN OPENING CLOVER BLOOM

THERE are times in a child's life when it leaps suddenly into larger growth as the imprisoned bud blooms larger than its promise, when the green fist of its straining calyx loosens in the warm glow of a May morning. Knowledge comes to the child, especially all the subtler knowledge of time, of space, of love, in a vague, indefinite, unconscious way, developing out of the child's organic self precisely as the flower blooms.

This knowledge comes to definite knowledge for an instant only and then returns to the sub-conscious, waiting the next day of warm sun, shining water, and smell of spring. Each time it stays longer, till at last the child can contemplate its own thought and finally express it. These times form real epochs in human life.

One day in June, a party of the school-children, with flashing tin pails and willow baskets, went up into the woods after the wild-wood strawberries. It was late June, and the strawberries of the meadows and uplands were nearly gone. The roads were dusty, the pastures close-clipped.

Merry, bare-footed little creatures! They started forth in the early morning while the dew still flamed on the clover-leaves, and around each corn-hill the ground was still moist. The girls romped and picked wild flowers, the boys threw stones at the chipmunks on the fence, and tossed their tin pails in the air, performing feats of deftness in imitation of the circus-men, whom they had once seen on the green at Tyre.

They entered the forest and kept on up the wood-road until it seemed as if they were explorers. They had the delicious, tremulous feeling of having penetrated into the primeval, where nothing but the birds and animals lived. On past cool deeps of poplar, where the mandrake grew, and the sweet fern spread its magnificent leaves. On until the strawberries appeared, growing in clumps on long swaying stems, pale-scarlet globes of delicious tartness.

They fell to work mostly in pairs. Curly haired Carl kept with Rose, and his sharp eyes and knowledge of the patch enabled them to fill their pails first; then they went about helping the others, whose voices babbled on like streams.

Everywhere the pink sun-bonnets and ragged straw hats bobbed up and down. Everywhere fresh voices. The sunlight fell in vivid yellow patches through the cool, odorous gloom. Everywhere the faint odor of ferns and mandrakes and berries, and the faint rustle of leaves, as if the shadows of the clouds trampled the tree-tops.

There was something sweet and wild and primeval in the scene, and the children were carried out of their usual selves.　Rose herself danced and romped, her eyes flashing with delight.　Under her direction they all came together on a little slope, where the trees were less thick, and near a brook which gurgled through moss-covered stones.

"Oh, let's have our picnic here!"

"All right, let's!"

They made short work of the lunch they had.　Their buttered biscuits were spread with berries and mixed with water from the brook, which the girls drank like the boys — that is, by lying down on their breasts and drinking as the hunter drinks.　Their hunger eased, they fell to playing games.　Games centuries old. Games which the Scandinavians played in the edges of their pine forests.　Games the English lads and lassies played in the oak-openings of middle-age England.

The little ones were ruled out after a while, and the five or six older children (the eldest only fourteen) went on with their games, which told of love.　They joined hands and circled about Carl; they sang:

> "King William was King James's son,
> And from the royal race he run,
> Upon his breast he wore a star,
> Which points away to a conquest far.
> Go choose you east, go choose you west,
> Go choose the one that you love best."

Carl selected Rose, as they all knew he would. They stood together now, holding hands.

> "Down on this carpet you must kneel,

(they knelt)

> As sure as the grass grows in the field.
> Salute your bride with a kiss so sweet,

(Carl kissed her gravely)

> Now you rise upon your feet."

Again they circled, and again a little bride and bridegroom knelt. The fresh young voices rang under the spaces of the trees, silencing the cry of the thrush. The flecking sunlight fell on their tousled hair and their flushed faces. They had forgotten home and kindred, and were living a strange new-old life, old as history, wild and free once more, and in their hearts something bloomed like a flower, something sweet shook them all, something unutterable and nameless, something magnificent to attain and sorrowful to lose.

When they tired of " King William" they all flung themselves down on the grass and grew quiet. Some of the girls made wreaths of flowers strung on grass-stems, while the boys studied the insects under the chips and stumps, or came slyly behind the girls and stuck spears of fox-tail down their necks. Some of them rolled down the bank. Carl, when he was tired of this, came and lay down by Rose, and put his head in her lap. Other bridegrooms did the same with their brides. Some of the boys matched violets, by seeing which would hook the other's head off.

Silence fell on them. Some passion thrilled Rose as she looked down into Carl's sunny blue eyes. She brushed his hair as he looked up at the clouds sailing above the trees like wonderful mountains of snow.

She was thirteen years of age, but prophecy of womanhood, of change, of sorrow, was in her voice as she said, slowly, a look not childish upon her face :

"I'd like to live here forever, wouldn't you, Carl?"

"I guess we'd have to build a house," said Carl, the practical one.

She felt a terrible hunger, a desire to take his head in her arms and kiss it. Her muscles ached and quivered with something she could not fathom. As she resisted she grew calm, but mysteriously sad, as if something were passing from her forever. The leaves whispered a message to her, and the stream repeated an occult note of joy, which was mixed with sorrow.

The struggle of wild fear and bitter-sweet hunger of desire — this vague, mystical perception of her sex, did not last with Rose. It was lost when she came out of the wood into the road on the way homeward. It was a formless impulse and throbbing stir far down below definite thought. It was sweet and wild and innocent as the first coquettish love-note of the thrush, and yet it was the beginning of her love-life. It was the second great epoch of her life.

CHAPTER V

HER FIRST PERIL

SHE came in contact during her school-life with a variety of teachers. Most of the women she did not like, but one sweet and thoughtful girl had her unbounded love and confidence. She was from Madison, that was in itself a great distinction, for the capital of the State had come to mean something great and beautiful and heroic to Rose.

There it was the Governor lived. There the soldiers went to enter the army, she remembered hearing the neighbors say, and her father's weekly paper was printed there. It was a great thing to have come from so far away and from Madison, and Rose hung about the door of the school-house at the close of the first day, hoping the teacher would permit her to walk home by her side.

The young woman, worried almost to despair over the arrangement of her classes, did not rise from her desk until the sun was low, rolling upon the tree-fringed ridge of the western bluff.

She was deeply touched to find this dusky-complexioned, bare-legged girl waiting for her.

"It was very nice of you, Rose," she said, and they walked off together. She talked about the flowers in the grass, and Rose ran to and fro, climbing fences to pick all sorts that she knew. She did not laugh when the teacher told her their botanical names. She wished she could remember them.

"When you grow up you can study botany too. But you must run home now, it's almost dark."

"I ain't afraid of the dark," said Rose, stoutly, and she went so far that Miss Lavalle was quite alarmed.

"Now you must go."

She kissed the child good-by, and Rose ran off with her heart big with emotion, like an accepted lover.

It was well Rose turned to her for help, for few of her teachers heretofore had the refinement of Miss Lavalle. They were generally farmers' daughters or girls from neighboring towns, who taught for a little extra money to buy dresses with — worthy girls indeed, but they expressed less of refining thought to the children.

One day this young teacher, with Rose and two or three other little ones, was sitting on a sunny southward sloping swell. Her hands were full of flowers and her great dark eyes were opened wide as if to mirror the whole scene, a valley flooded with light and warm with the radiant grass of spring. She was small and dark and dainty, and still carried the emotional characteristics of her French ancestry. She saw nature definitely, and did not scruple to say so.

"Oh, it is beautiful!" she said, as her eyes swept along the high broken line of the Western coolly ridge,

down to the vast blue cliffs ; where the river broke its way
into the larger valley. " Children, see how beautiful it
is !" The children stared away at it, but Rose looked
into the teacher's eager face. Then her flowers dropped
to the ground, the sunlight fell upon her with a richer
glow, the dandelions shone like stars in a heaven of
green, the birds and the wind sang a sweet new song in
the doors of her ears, and her heart swelled with unutterable emotion. She was overpowered by the beauty of
the world, as she had been by its immensity that day on
the hill-top with her father.

She saw the purple mists, the smooth, green, warm
slopes dotted with dandelions, and the woodlands with
their amber and purple-gray and gray-green foliage. The
big world had grown distinctly beautiful to her. It was
as if a thin gray veil had been withdrawn from the face
of created things — but this perception did not last. The
mist fell again before her eyes when the presence of the
teacher was withdrawn. She felt the beautiful and
splendid phases of nature, and absorbed and related them
to herself, but she did not consciously perceive, except at
rare moments.

The men, who taught her in winter, were blunt and
crude, but occasionally one of a high type came, some
young fellow studying law, or taking a course at some
school, teaching to keep his place or to go higher.
These men studied nights and mornings out of great
Latin books which were the wonder of the children.
Such teachers appealed to the better class of pupils with
great power, but excited rebellion in others.

It seemed a wonderful and important day to Rose, the first time she entered the scarred and greasy room in winter, because it was swarming with big girls and boys. She took her seat at one of the little benches on the north side of the room, where all the girls sat. At some far time the girls had been put on that, the coldest side of the house, and they still sat there; change was impossible.

Rose was a little bit awed by the scene. The big boys never seemed so rough, and the big girls never seemed so tall. They were all talking loudly, hanging about the old square stove which sat in the middle of a puddle of bricks.

She was an unimportant factor in the winter school, however, for the big boys and girls ignored the little ones, or ordered them out of their games. " I hate to be little," she said once, " I want to be grown up."

In winter also her physical superiority to the other girls was less apparent, for she wore thick shoes and shapeless dresses, and muffled her head and neck like the boys.

She plodded to school along the deep sleigh-tracks, facing a bitter wind, with the heart of a man. It made her cry sometimes, but there was more of rage than fear in her sobbing. She coughed and wheezed like the rest, but through it all her perfect lungs and powerful little heart carried her triumphantly.

The winter she was fourteen years of age she had for a teacher a girl whose beautiful presence brought a curse with it. She was small and graceful, with a face full of sudden tears and laughter and dreams of desire. She fascinated the children, and the larger boys woke to a sudden savagery of rivalry over her, which no one seemed to understand. The older boys fought over her smiles and low-voiced words of praise. The girls grew vaguely jealous or were abject slaves to her whims. The school became farcical in session, with ever-increasing play hours and ever-shortening recitations, and yet such was the teacher's power over the students they did not report her. She gathered the larger girls around her as she flirted with the young men, until children like Carl and Rose became involved in its ever-hastening whirlpool of passion.

At night the young men of the neighborhood flocked about the teacher's boarding-place, actually fighting in her very presence for the promise which she withheld, out of coquettish perversity. She went out to parties and dances every night and came languidly to school each morning. Most of the men of the district laughed at the words of the women who began to talk excitedly about the stories they had heard.

At school the most dangerous practices were winked at. The older boys did not scruple to put their arms about the teacher's waist as they stood by her side. All the reserve and purity which is organic in the intercourse of most country girls and boys seemed lost, and parties and sleigh-rides left a feeling of remorse and guilt behind. There was something feverish and unwholesome in the air.

The teacher's fame mysteriously extended to Tyre, and when evil-minded men began to hitch their horses

at the fence before her boarding-house and to enter into
rivalry with the young men of the neighborhood, then
the fathers of the coolly suddenly awoke to their children's danger, and turning the teacher away (tearful and
looking harmless as a kitten), they closed and locked
the school-house door.

Instantly the young people grew aware of their out-
break of premature passion. Some of them, like Rose,
went to their parents and told all they knew about it.
John Dutcher received his daughter's answers to his
questions with deep sorrow, but he reflected long before
he spoke. She was only a child, not yet fifteen; she
would outgrow the touch of thoughtless hands.

He sent for Carl, and as they stood before him, with
drooping heads, he talked to them in his low, mild voice,
which had the power of bringing tears to the sturdy boy's
eyes.

"Carl, I thought I could trust you. You've done
wrong — don't you know it? You've made my old
heart ache. When you get old and have a little girl
you may know how I feel, but you can't now. I don't
know what I can say to you. I don't know what I
am going to do about it, but I want you to know what
you've done to me — both of you. Look into my face
now — you too, Rose — look into your old father's
face!"

The scarred children looked into his face with its
streaming tears, then broke out into sobbing that shook
them to their heart's centre. They could not bear to
see him cry. "That's what you do to your parents

when you do wrong. I haven't felt so bad since your mother died, Rose."

The children sobbed out their contrition and desire to do better, and John ended it all at last by saying, "Now, Carl, you may go, but I shall keep watch of you and see that you grow up a good, true man. When I see you're real sorry I'll let you come to see Rose again."

After Carl went out, Rose pressed into his ready arms. "I didn't mean to be bad, pappa."

"I know you didn't, Rosie, but I want you to know how you can make me suffer by doing wrong — but there, there! don't cry any more. Just be good and kind and true, like your mother was. Now run away and help get supper."

The buoyancy of a healthy child's nature enabled her to throw off the oppression of that dark day, the most terrible day of her life, and she was soon cheerful again — not the child she had been, but still a happy child. After a few weeks John sent for Carl to come over, and they popped corn and played dominoes all the evening, and the innocency of their former childish companionship seemed restored.

D

CHAPTER VI

HER FIRST IDEAL

ONE June day a man came riding swiftly up the lanes, in a buggy with a guilded box. As he passed the school-house he flung a handful of fluttering yellow and red bills into the air.

"A circus! a circus!" was the cry as the boys rushed for the blowing sheets of paper. It was a circus, the annual "monstrous aggregation of Gregorian games and colossal cataracts of gilded chariots," and it was coming to Tyre.

The children read every word of those high-sounding posters, standing in knots by the roadside. It was the mightiest event of their lives. Most of them had never been to a circus. Many had never been so far as Tyre. The few who had, however, straightway became fountains of wisdom, and declaimed upon the splendors of other "aggregations of world-wide wonders."

Rose looked at the lines of knights and ladies winding down the yellow broad-side of the sheet, and wondered if she would ever have the joy of seeing them.

The courier rode on. He flung a handful of the bills over into the corn-field where Carl was ploughing

corn with the hired man, and Carl straightway began to
plan.

He flung a handful of the alluring yellow leaves into
the bed of the wagon which poor old John Rapp was
driving, and he sighed and wondered how he could raise
the money to take the children down, and he also longed
to see it himself. The whole county awoke to the significance of the event and began preparation and plans,
though it was nearly three weeks away. An enormous
distance it seemed to the boys and girls.

At school and at church it was talked of. The boys
selected their girls, and parties of four or six were made
up to go to Tyre, ten miles away, in the larger valley
below. In some way, without words, Rose agreed to go
with Carl. John Nixon and Ella Pierce made up the
other couple. They were to go in a " bowery wagon."

The whole population awoke to pathetic, absorbing
interest in the quality of the posters and the probable
truth of the foreword. The circus was the mightiest
contrast to their slow and lonely lives that could be imagined. It came in trailing clouds of glorified dust and
grouped itself under vast tents, whose lift and fall had
more majesty than summer clouds, and its streamers had
more significance than the lightning.

It brought the throb of drum and scream of fife, and
roar of wild beast. For one day each humdrum town
was filled with romance like the " Arabian Nights ";
with helmeted horsemen, glittering war maidens on
weirdly spotted horses; elephants with howdahs and
head-plates of armor; with lions dreadful, sorrowful,

sedate, and savage; with tigers and hyenas in unmanageable ferocity pacing up and down their gilded dens while their impassive keepers, dressed in red, sat in awful silence amidst them.

There was something remote and splendid in the ladies who rode haughtily through the streets on prancing horses, covered with red and gold trappings. There was something heroic, something of splendid art in the pose of the athletes in the ring.

From the dust and drudgery of their farms the farm boys dreamed and dreamed of the power and splendor of the pageantry. They talked of it each Sunday night as they sat up with their sweethearts. The girls planned their dresses and hats, and the lunch they were to take. Everything was arranged weeks ahead. Carl was to furnish one team, John the other; Ella was to bring cake and jelly and biscuit; Rose to take a chicken and a shortcake.

They were to start early and drive a certain route and arrive at the ground at a certain hour to see the parade. After the parade they were to take dinner at the hotel, and then the circus! No court ball ever thrilled a young girl's heart like this event.

It was trebly important to Rose. It was her first really long dress. It was her first going out into the world with an escort, and it was her first circus. She trembled with excitement whenever she thought of it, and sometimes burst into tears at the uncertainty of it. It might rain, she might be sick, or something might happen!

She worked away with feverish haste, trimming her hat and helping on her dress, which was to be white, trimmed with real lace from the store. Some dim perception of what it all meant to his girl penetrated John Dutcher's head, and he gave Rose a dollar to buy some extra ribbon with, and told Mrs. Diehl to give the child a good outfit.

On the night before the circus Carl could not work in the corn. He drove furiously about the neighborhood on inconsequential errands. He called twice on Rose, and they looked into each other's face with transports of fear and joy.

" Oh, if it should rain ! "

" It won't. I just know it's going to be fine. Don't you worry. I am the son of a prophet. I know it can't rain."

There was no real sleep for Rose that night. Twice she woke from an uneasy doze, thinking she heard the patter of rain, but listening close she found it to be only the rustle of the cotton-wood trees about the house.

Her room was a little rough-plastered garret room, with an eastern window, and at last she saw the yellow light interfiltrate the dark-blue of the eastern sky, and she rose and pattered about in her bare feet, while she put up her hair like a woman and slipped on her underskirt, stiff with starch, and then her dress, with its open-work sleeves and ruche of lace, threaded with blue ribbon. She moved about on her bare feet, rejoicing in the crisp rustle of her new clothing, and put on her wide hat with its hectic rose-buds and paris-green thick leaves. Her undistorted feet were the most beautiful of all, but she did not know that.

She sat on the bed completely dressed, but hardly daring to move for fear of waking her aunt. She watched the yellow glow deepen to a saffron dome of ever-spreading light. She knew the weather signs herself, and she was sure the day was to be hot but clear. She did not fear the heat.

As she sat so, a feeling of joy, of realization of the abounding goodness and sweetness of living, made her want to thank something — to give praise. She moved her lips in a little prayer of thanks to the sun, as his first glittering rim of light came above the low hills.

" Rosie ! " called Mrs. Diehl.

" I'm up," she replied, and hastily drew on her shoes and stockings. She took her hat in her hand and went down the stairs and through the little sitting-room out to the doorstep. She heard someone whistling. Then a shout of laughter — they are coming !

She had packed her basket the night before, and she stood ready at the gate when Carl and his companions drove up. They had four horses hitched to a large wagon, which was set about with branches of oak and willow. Carl was driving and Rose mounted to the front seat with him. He cracked his whip and they whirled away, leaving the old folks calling warnings after them.

The sun was just rising, the dew was still globed on the wild roses. The wagon rumbled, the bower over their heads shook with the jar of the wheels. The horses were fresh and strong and the day was before them. Rose felt something vague and sweet, something that laved the whole world like sunlight.

She was too happy to sing. She only sat and dreamed. She felt her clothes, but she was no longer acutely conscious of them.

Carl was moved too, but his emotion vented itself in shouts and cheery calls to the horses, and to the pistol-like cracking of his whip.

He looked at her with clear-eyed admiration. She abashed him a little by her silence. She seemed so unwontedly womanly in that pose, and the glow of her firm arms through her sleeve was alien, somehow.

The way led around hill-sides, under young oak-trees, across dappled sands, and over little streams where the horses stopped to drink. It was like some world-old idyl, this ride in a heavy rumbling wagon; it led to glory and light, this road among the hills.

Rounding a long, low line of bluffs they caught the flutter of flags in Tyre, and saw the valley spotted with other teams, crawling like beetles down the sandy river roads. The whole land seemed to be moving in gala dress toward Tyre. Everywhere appeared the same expectancy, the same exultation between lovers.

Carl pulled up with a flourish at the wooden porch of the Farmers' Hotel, and the girls alighted and went into the parlor, while the boys took the horses into a back alley and gave them their oats and hay in the end of the box.

As Rose walked into the parlor, filled with other girls

and young men, the proud consciousness of her clothes came back to her, and she carried herself with a lift of the head, which made her dark gypsy-like face look haughty as a young queen's. She knew her dress was as good as any other there, and she had no need to be ashamed, and besides it was her first long dress and she wore low shoes.

The boys came bustling back and hurried the girls out on the sidewalk. "They're coming!" they cried breathlessly, as a far-off burst of music came in on a warm puff of wind.

On they came, a band leading the way. Just behind, with glitter of lance and shine of helmet, came a dozen knights and fair ladies riding spirited chargers. They all looked strange and haughty and sneeringly indifferent to the cheers of the people. The women seemed small and firm and scornful, and the men rode with lances uplifted, looking down at the crowd with a haughty droop in their eyelids.

Rose shuddered with a new emotion as they swept past. She had never looked into eyes like those. They had wearied of all splendor and triumph, those eyes. They cared nothing for flaunt of flag or blast of bugle. They rode straight out of the wonder and mystery of the morning to her. They came from the unknown spaces of song and story beyond the hills.

The chariots rumbled on almost unheeded by Rose. She did not laugh at the clown jiggling along in a pony-cart, for there was a face between her and all that followed. The face of a bare-armed knight, with brown hair and a curling mustache, whose proud neck had a curve in it as he bent his head to speak to his rearing horse.   He turned his face toward where Rose stood, and her soul fluttered, and her flesh shrank as if from fire, but he rode on.   His face was fine, like pictures she had seen.   It was a pleasant face, too, proud, but not coarse and stern like the others.

The calliope (a musical monster, hideous as the hippopotamus) and the dens of beasts went past without arousing her interest; then an open cage of lions rolled by with the trainer carelessly seated on a camp-stool amid his dun-colored monsters.   His gaudy red-and-gold coat was like Washington's and his impassive face was stern and sad.   At last the procession ended, carrying with it swarms of detached boys and girls, whose parents fearfully called after them and unavailingly pleaded with them to come back as they broke away.

"Oh, I wish it would all come by again!" sighed Ella.

"So do I," said Carl.

Rose remained silent.   Somehow those knights and ladies dwarfed all else.   She did not look forward to eating a hotel dinner with the same pleasure now, but was eager to get to the tent, whose pennants streamed above the roofs of the houses.

The Farmers' House swarmed with country folks, whose loud voices could be heard uttering shouts of satisfaction over the promise of the parade.   It was the best ever seen in the town.

"Right this way, ladies and gentlemen," said the landlord, as he ushered Carl's party down to a table at the end of the dining-room.

Rose lifted her head with joy and pride; she was a grown-up person at last. This landlord recognized her assumption and it made the dinner almost enjoyable. She saw no one better dressed than herself, and she had a feeling that she was good to look at. She was indeed more beautiful than she knew. A city drummer sitting at another table eyed her all through the meal with breathless admiration. Her health and color, and the firm lines of her nose and chin were especially attractive.

They all ate with unusual formality, using their forks instead of knives for their pie, and otherwise trying to seem citified. Ella laughed at the antics John cut up over his fork, and the sly digs that he gave Carl, who chased the crust of his pie around his plate with a fork and at last gave up hope and seized it with his fingers.

No one noticed these pranks, because everyone else was carrying on in much the same way. At length they rose and returned to the parlor, where they sat about on the cheap red plush chairs and waited for one o'clock.

" Well, it's about time to go," said Carl, on returning from one of his many visits to the street. " Gee-Whittaker! but it's hot out there! "

" It'll be cool under the tent."

" Well, come on."

Out on the street they joined the stream of lovers like themselves, moving hand in hand down the walk, assaulted by cries of lemonade, candy and fruit hucksters.

The sun beat upon their heads; a dust rose from the feet of the passing teams and settled on the white dresses of the girls, and sank through the meshes of their sleeves and gathered in the moist folds of their ruches. They moved on rapidly toward the clanging band, the flutter of the pennants and the brazen outcries of the ticket-takers. On to the square before the tents, thronged with innumerable people; there an avenue of sideshows faced them like a gauntlet to be run. Before each flapping sign of fat woman, or snake-charmer, stood a man who cried in strange, clanging, monotonous, and rhythmical voice :

"You have still a half an hour, ladies and gentlemen, before the great show opens. Come in and see the wonders of the world."

Before the ticket-wagon a straggling, excited crowd wrestled, suspicious, determined, hurried. Leaving their girls in the more open space, the boys gripping their dollars with sweaty fingers drew deep breaths of resolution and plunged into the press with set, determined faces.

They returned soon, hot, disarranged but triumphant. "Come on, girls."

They moved upon the main entrance, where a man stood snatching at the tickets which were handed to him. He was humorous, and talked as he pushed the people in.

"Hurry up, old man; trot close after your mother. Have your tickets ready, everybody. Yes, right this way, uncle. Bless your dear little face — right ahead. H'y'ere, bub, this ticket's no good! — Oh, so it is, I didn't see the right side — get on quick."

As Rose passed him he said, "You go in free, my dear, " and resumed his bawling cry, " Have your tickets ready. "

Under the tent ! Rose looked up at the lifting, tremulous, translucent canvas with such awe as the traveller feels in St. Peter's dome. Her feet stumbled on, while she clung to Carl's hand without knowing it. Oh, the enormous crowds of people, the glitter and change of it all ! They followed in the stream which flowed around the circle of animal dens, and Rose silently looked at all she saw. The others laughed and exclaimed, but she did not. Everything seem inexplicable and mysterious, and roused confusing trains of thought.

She saw the great tigers, and caught the yellow-green sheen of their eyes. She saw the lions rise like clouds of dust in their corners, silent as mist and terrible as lightning. She looked at the elephant and wondered how he could live and still be so like the toy elephants she had at home. On past shrieking tropical birds and grunting, wallowing beasts, and chattering crowds of people she moved, without a word, till they came around to the circus entrance, and then she lifted her eyes again around the great amphitheatre.

" Peanuts, peanuts here, five a bag ! "

" Here's your lemonade, cool and fresh ! "

On all sides brazen-voiced young men were selling, at appalling prices, sticks of candy, glasses of lemonade, palm-leaf fans, and popcorn balls. There was something about them that frightened her, and she walked a little closer to Carl. " Let's get a seat, Carl, " she said.

They heard familiar voices call, and looking up saw some young people from their coolly, and so clambered up to join them. The boards were narrow and the seats low, but nobody minded that, for that was part of the circus.

They were settled at last and ready to enjoy all that came. Two or three volunteered to say: "This is great! the best place to see 'em come in." Then they passed the peanut-bag in reckless liberality.

Rose sat in a dream of delight as the band began to play. It was an ambitious band and played operatic selections with variations, and it seemed to Rose to be the most splendid music in the world. All other bands she had heard played right along tum-tummy, tum-tummy tummy, tummy-tum. This band sang and talked and whispered and dreamed. It was her first conception of the power of music.

She heard nothing that was said about her, and she did not know she was squeezing Carl's arm during the opening piece.

People streamed by in enormous crowds. Ladies in elegant dresses, and hats such as she had never seen before. Handsome young men went by, but she gave them no second look. They were like figures in a dream.

At last the band blared an announcing note, and the uniformed attendants filing into the ring took positions at set points like sentries. Then the music struck into a splendid galop, and out from the curtained mysteries beyond, the knights and ladies darted, two and two,

in glory of crimson and gold, and green and silver.   At
their head rode the man with the brown mustache.

They swirled rapidly into position, and then began a
series of bewildering changes, directed by her knight,
whose shout dominated the noise of the horses and the
blare of the band, with wild, echoing sound.

They vanished as they entered; then came the clowns,
and tricks, and feats of strength.   The iron-jawed woman
lifted incredible weights; the Japanese jugglers tossed
cannon-balls, knives, and feathers; the baby elephant
stood on his head — and then suddenly six men, dressed
in tights of blue and white and orange, ran into the ring,
and her hero led them!

He wore blue and silver, and on his breast was a gay
rosette.   He looked a god to her.   His naked limbs,
his proud neck, the lofty carriage of his head, made her
shiver with emotion.   They all came to her lit by the
white radiance; they were not naked, they were beautiful, but *he* was something more.

She had seen nude boys, and her own companions
occasionally showed themselves nude and cowering before her, but these men stood there proud and splendid.
They invested their nakedness with something which
exalted them.   They became objects of luminous
beauty to her, though she knew nothing of art.

As she grew clearer-eyed, she saw that one was a
little too short, another too lean, but he of the rosette
was perfect.   The others leaped, with him, doing the
same feats, but as distances were increased, and the
number of camels and horses grew, the others stood by

to see him make his renowned double somersault over a herd of animals. When the applause broke out she joined in it, while her temples throbbed with emotion. To see him bow and kiss his fingers to the audience was a revelation of manly grace and courtesy. He moved under the curtain, bowing still to the cheering crowd.

Once more he came into the ring, leading a woman by the hand. She, too, was in tights throughout, and like him she walked with a calm and powerful movement, but she seemed petty beside him.

Something new seized upon Rose's heart, a cold contraction that she had never felt, and her teeth pressed together. She wondered if the woman were his wife.

The acrobat seized a rope with her right arm and was drawn to the tent roof. Her companion took a strap in his mouth and was drawn to his trapeze opposite. There, in mid-air, they performed their dangerous evolutions. It was all marvellous and incredible to the country girl.

She heard him clap his hands, then his glorious voice rang above the music, and the slim figure of his companion launched itself through the air, was caught by the shoulders in his great hands. Thence with a twist he tossed her, and hooked her by the hands.

Each time, the blood surged into Rose's throat as if to suffocate her. A horrible fear that was also a pleasure, rose and fell in her. She could not turn away her head.

She was a powerful girl, and the idea of fainting had

never come to her, but when, at the conclusion, her
hero dropped in a revolving ball into the net far beneath,
she turned sick and her eyes seemed to whirl in their
sockets. Then as he leaped to the ground, bowing and
smiling, the blood rushed back to her face, and the perspiration stood like rain on her brow.

Thereafter, riders came, and the clowns capered, and
the ring-master cracked his whip, and she enjoyed it,
but it was an after-climax. She saw it, but saw it
dimly. Nothing but the lions and their trainers aroused
her to applause. Her brain was full. It was a feast of
glories and her hunger had made her lay hold upon the
first that came, to the neglect of what followed.

At last the brazen, resounding voice of the ring-
master announced the end of the programme, and the
audience rising moved out in a sort of a hush, as if in
sorrow to think the glory was over, and the humdrum
world about to rush back upon them.

Rose moved along in perfect silence, clinging to
Carl's hand. Around her sounded the buzz of low
speech, the wailing of tired and hungry babies, and the
clamor of attendants selling tickets for the minstrel
show to follow.

Suddenly she perceived that her dress was wet with
perspiration and grimy with dust. All about her,
women with flushed faces and grimy hands, their hats
awry and their brows wrinkled with trouble, scolded
fretful children. The men walked along with their
coats over their arms, and their hats pushed back. The
dust arose under their feet with a strange smell. Out

in the animal tent the odor was stifling, and Rose hurried Carl out into the open air.

Somehow it seemed strange to find the same blue sky arching the earth; things seemed faded and dusty. Rose had grown older. She had developed immeasurably in those few hours. It took her some time to fully recover the use of her feet, and it took longer to get back a full realization of where she was.

The grass, crushed and trampled and littered with paper and orange-peel, gave out a fresh, farm-like odor, that helped her to recover herself. She would not talk, she could not listen yet. She but urged Carl to go home. She wanted to get home to think.

As they climbed the slope on the other side of the river, they looked back at the tents with their wilted streamers, at the swarming teams diminished to the size of beetles and the ant-like human beings, and it seemed to Rose as if she must weep, so poignant was her sense of personal loss.

She knew something sweet and splendid and mystical was passing out of her life after a few hours' stay there. Her feeling of loss was none the less real because it was indefinable in words.

The others chattered about the show, and shouted admiration about this and that feat, but Rose was silent. When they stopped at sunset beside a spring to eat their lunch she merely said:

" I don't feel hungry."

The others fell silent after a time, and all rode dreamily forward, with the roll of wheels making them sleepy

E.

and the trample of the horses' feet telling them how
rapidly they were leaving their great day's pleasure
behind them.

When Rose huddled into her little attic bed, her eyes
were wide open, and her brain active as at noonday.
There was no sleep for her then. Lying there in the
darkness she lived it all over again; the flutter of flags,
the wild voices, the blare of music, the chariots, the
wild beasts, the knights and ladies, the surging crowds;
but the crowning glory, the pictures which lingered
longest in her mind were the splendid and beautiful
men, whose naked majesty appealed to her pure wholesome awakening womanhood, with the power of beauty
and strength and sex combined.

These glorious, glittering, graceful beings, with their
marvellous strength and bravery, filled her with a deep,
sad hunger, which she could not understand. They
came out of the unknown, led by her chosen one, like
knights in "Ivanhoe."

She fell asleep thinking of the one in blue and silver,
and in her sleep she grew braver and went closer to
him, and he turned and spoke to her, and his voice was
like waters running, and his eyes shone into her eyes
like a light.

When she rose the next day she was changed. She
moved about the house dull and languid. Never before
had she failed to sleep when her head touched the pillow. She managed to be alone most of the time, and
at last her mind cleared. She began to live for him,

her ideal. She set him on high as a being to be worshipped, as a man fit to be her judge.

In the days and weeks which followed she asked herself, "Would he like me to do this?" or she thought, "I must not do that. What would he think of me if he saw me now?" And every night when she went to sleep it was with the radiant figure in blue and silver before her eyes.

When the sunset was very beautiful, she thought of him. When the stars seemed larger in the blue sky, she could see the star upon his grand breast. She knew his name; she had the bill in her little box of trinkets, and she could take it out and read, "William De Lisle, the world-famous leader in ground and lofty tumbling, in his stupendous leap over two elephants, six camels and two horses."

In all the talk of the circus which followed among her companions, she took no part because she feared she might be obliged to mention his name. When others spoke his name she could feel a hot flush surge up over her bosom, and she trembled for fear some one might discover her adoration of him.

She went about with Carl and Rob as before, only she no longer yearned for them; they seemed good, familiar comrades, but nothing more. To them she seemed stranger every day. Her eyes lost their clear, brave look; and became dreamy black, and her lids drooped.

Vast ambitions began in her. She determined to be a great scholar. She would be something great for his sake.   She could not determine what, but she, too, would be great.   At first she thought of being a circus woman.

She dreamed often of being his companion and coming on hand in hand with him, bowing to the multitude, but when she was drawn to the tent-roof, she awoke in a cold sweat of fear, and so she determined to be a writer.   She would write books like "Ivanhoe." Those were great days!   Her mind expanded like the wings of a young eagle.   She read everything; the *Ledger*, the *Weekly*, and all the dog-eared novels, of impassioned and unreal type in the neighborhood.

In short, she consecrated herself to him as to a king, and seized upon every chance to educate herself to be worthy of him.   Every effort was deeply pathetic, no matter how absurd to others.   She took no counsel, allowed no confidants.   She lived alone among her play-mates.

This ideal came in her romantic and perfervid period, and it did her immeasurable good.   It enabled her to escape the clutch of mere brute passion which seizes so many girls at that age.   It lifted her and developed her.

She did not refuse the pleasures of the autumn and the winter, only she did not seem so hearty in her enjoyment of the rides and parties.   She rode with the young fellows on moon-lit nights, lying side by side with them on the straw-filled bottom of the sleigh, and her heart leaped with the songs they sang, but her love went out toward her ideal; he filled the circle of her mind. The thought of him made the night magical with meaning. As she danced with Carl it was her hero's arm she felt. At night, when Carl left her on the door-step, she looked up at the stars and the sinking moon, and lifted her face in a vague, almost inarticulate vow, "I will be worthy of him!" That was the passionate resolution, but it did not reach to the definiteness of words.

As she worked about the house she took graceful attitudes, and wished he might see her; he would be pleased with her. The grace and power of her arm acquired new meaning to her. Her body, she recognized, was beautiful. In the secrecy of her room she walked up and down, feeling the splendid action of her limbs, muscled almost like his. And all this was fine and pure physical joy. Her idea remained indefinite, wordless.

These were days of formless imaginings and ambitions. "I will do! I will do!" was her ceaseless cry to herself, but what could she do? What should she do?

She would be wise, so she read. She got little out of her reading that she could make a showing of, but still it developed her. It made her dream great things, impossible things, but she had moments when she tried to live these things.

Meanwhile her manners changed. She became absent-minded, and at times seemed sullen and haughty to her companions. She did not giggle like the rest of the girls,

and though she had fine teeth, her smile was infrequent.
She laughed when occasion demanded, and laughed heartily, but was not easily stirred to laughter.

Just in proportion as she ignored the young beaux,
so they thronged about her. She took refuge in Carl's
company, and so escaped much persecution, for Carl
was growing to be a powerful young man, with fists
like mauls, and was respected among the athletes of the
neighborhood.

She did not realize how soon it would be necessary
to settle with Carl. She accepted his company as a
matter of course. He filled social requirements for the
time being.

Her teacher that winter was a plaintive sort of a middle-aged man, a man of considerable refinement, but with
little force. Rose liked him, but did not respect him
as she had two or three of the men who had filled the
teacher's chair. She could not go to him for advice.

As the winter wore on the figure of "William De
Lisle" grew dimmer, but not less beautiful. Her love
for him lost its under-current of inarticulate expectancy;
it was raised into a sentiment so ethereal that it seemed
a breath of derision might scatter it like vapor, and
yet it was immovable as granite. Time alone could
change it. He still dominated her thought at quiet times,
at dark when the stars began to shine, but in the day-
time he was faint as a figure in a dream.

CHAPTER VII

ROSE MEETS DR. THATCHER

THE school-house in Dutcher's coolly, like most country school-houses, was a squalid little den. It was as gray as a rock and as devoid of beauty as a dry-goods box. It sat in the midst of the valley and had no trees, to speak of, about it, and in winter it was almost as snow-swept as the school-houses of the prairie.

Its gray clap-boarding was hacked and scarred with knife and stone, and covered with mud and foul marks. A visitor who had turned in from the sun-smit winter road paused before knocking, and looked at the walls and the door with a feeling of mirth and sadness. Was there no place to escape the obscene outcome of sexual passion?

Dr. Thatcher had been a pupil here in this same school-house more than twenty years before, and the droning, shuffling sound within had a marvellous re-awakening power. He was a physician in Madison now, and was in the coolly on a visit.

His knock on the door brought a timid-looking man to the door.

"I'd like to come in awhile," said the Doctor.

55

"Certainly, certainly," replied the teacher, much embarrassed by the honor.

He brought him the chair he had been sitting upon, and helped his visitor remove his coat and hat.

"Now don't mind me, I want to see everything go on just as if I were not here."

"Very well, that's the way we do," the teacher replied, and returned to his desk and attempted, at least, to carry out his visitor's request.

A feeling of sadness, mingled with something wordlessly vast, came over the Doctor as he sat looking about the familiar things of the room.

He was in another world, an old, familiar world. His eyes wandered lovingly from point to point of the room, filled with whispering lips and shuffling feet and shock-heads of hair, under which shone bright eyes, animal-like in their shifty stare. The curtains, of a characterless shade, the battered maps, the scarred and scratched blackboards, the patched, precarious plastering, the worn floor on which the nails and knots stood like miniature mountains, the lop-sided seats, the master's hacked, unpainted pine desk, dark with dirt and polished with dirty hands, all seemed as familiar as his own face.

He sat there listening to the recitations in dreamy impassivity. He was far in the land of his youth thinking of the days when to pass from his seat to the other side of the room was an event ; when a visitor was a calamity — for the teacher; when the master was a tyrant and his school-room a ceaselessly rebellious kingdom.

As his eyes fell at last more closely upon the scholars, he caught the eyes of a young girl looking curiously at him, and so deep was he in the past, his heart gave a sudden movement, just as it used to leap when in those far-off days Stella Baird looked at him. He smiled at himself for it. It was really ludicrous, he thought; " I'll tell my wife of it."

The girl looked away slowly and without embarrassment. She was thinking deeply, looking out of the window. His first thought was, " She has beautiful eyes." Then he noticed that she wore her hair neatly arranged, and that her dress, though plain, fitted tastefully about the neck. The line of her head was magnificent. Her color was rich and dark; her mouth looked sad for one so young. Her face had the effect of being veiled by some warm, dusky color.

Was she young? Sometimes as he studied her she seemed a woman, especially as she looked away out of the window, and her head was in profile. But she looked younger when she bent her head upon her books, and her long eyelashes fell upon her cheek.

His persistent stare brought a vivid flush into her face, but she did not nudge her companion and whisper as another would have done.

" That is no common girl," the Doctor concluded.

He sat there while the classes were called up one after the other. He heard again inflections, and tones, perpetuated for centuries in the school-room, " The-cat-saw-a-rat." Again the curfew failed to ring, in the same hard, monotonous, rapid, breathless singsong, every

other line with a falling inflection. The same failure
to make the proper pause caused it to appear that "Bes-
sie saw him on her brow."

Again the heavy boy read the story of the ants, and
the teacher asked insinuatingly sweet questions.

"What did they do?"

"Made a tunnel."

"Yes! Now what *is* a tunnel?"

"A hole that runs under ground."

"Very good! It says that the ant is a voracious
creature. What does that mean?"

"Dunno."

"You don't know what a voracious creature is?"

"No, sir."

And then came the writing exercise, when each grimy
fist gripped a pen, and each red tongue rolled around a
laboring mouth in the vain effort to guide the pen. *Cramp,
cramp ; scratch, scratch ; sputter !* What a task it was!

The December afternoon sun struck in at the windows, and fell across the heads of the busy scholars,
and as he looked, Dr. Thatcher was a boy again, and
Rose and her companions were the "big girls" of the
school. He was looking at Stella, the prettiest girl in
the district, the sunlight on her hair, a dream of nameless passion in her eyes.

The little room grew wide as romance, and across
the aisle seemed over vast spaces Girlish eyes met his
like torches in the night. The dusty air, the shuffle of
feet, the murmuring of lips only added to the mysterious
power of the scene.

There they sat, these girls, just as in the far-off days, trying to study, and succeeding in dreaming of love-songs, and sweet embraces on moonlight nights, beneath limitless star-shot skies, with sound of bells in their ears, and the unspeakable glory of youth and pure passion in their souls.

The Doctor sighed. He was hardly forty yet, but he was old in the history of disillusion and in contempt of human nature. His deep-set eyes glowed with an inward fire of remembrance.

" O pathetic little band of men and women," thought he, " my heart thrills and aches for you."

He was brought back to the present with a start by the voice of the teacher.

" Rose, you may recite now."

The girl he had been admiring came forward. As she did so he perceived her to be not more than sixteen, but she still had in her eyes the look of a dreaming woman.

" Rose Dutcher is our best scholar," smiled the teacher proudly as Rose took her seat. She looked away out of the window abstractedly as the teacher opened the huge geography and passed it to the Doctor.

" Ask her anything you like from the first fifty-six pages." The Doctor smiled and shook his head.

" Bound the Sea of Okhotsk," commanded the teacher.

Thatcher leaned forward eagerly — her voice would tell the story!

Without looking around, with her hands in her lap, an absent look in her eyes, the girl began, in a husky contralto voice : " Bounded on the north — " and went through the whole rigmarole in careless, easeful fashion.

" What rivers would you cross in going from Moscow to Paris ? "

And the child who had never been ten miles from her home, uttered with contemptuous serenity the names of rivers which formed the pathways of the prehistoric hairy men.

" Good heavens ! " thought the Doctor, "they still teach that useless stuff. But how well she does it ! "

After some words of praise, which the girl hardly seemed to listen to, she took her seat again.

Rose, on her part, saw another man of grace and power. She noted every detail of his dress, his dark, sensitive face, the splendid slope of his shoulders, and the exquisite neatness and grace of his collar and tie and coat. But in his eyes was something that moved her, drew her. She felt something subtile there, refinement and sorrow, and emotions she could only dimly feel.

She could not keep her eyes from studying his face. She compared him with " William De Lisle," not deliberately, always unconsciously. He had nothing of the bold beauty of her ideal, but he was a scholar, and he had come out of the world beyond the Big Ridge, and besides, there was mystery and allurement in his face.

The teacher called as if commanding a regiment of cavalry. " Books. *Ready !* " There was a riotous clatter, which ended as quickly as it begun.

"*Kling!*" They all rose. "*Kling!*" and the boys moved out with clumping of heavy boots and burst into the open air with wild whoopings. The girls gathered into little knots and talked, glancing furtively at the stranger. Some of them wondered if he were the County Superintendent of Schools.

Rose sat in her seat, with her chin on her clasped hands. It was a sign of her complex organization, that the effect of a new experience was rooted deep, and changes took place noiselessly, far below the surface.

"Rose, come here a moment," called the teacher, "bring your history."

"Don't keep her from her playmates," Thatcher remonstrated.

"Oh, she'd rather recite any time than play with the others."

Rose stood near, a lovely figure of wistful hesitation. She had been curiously unembarrassed before, now she feared to do that which was so easy and so proper. At last she saw her opportunity as the teacher turned away to ring the bell.

She touched Thatcher on the arm. "Do you live in Madison, sir?"

"Yes. I am a doctor there."

She looked embarrassed now and twisted her fingers.

"Is it so very hard to get into the university?"

"No. It is very easy — it would be for you," he said with a touch of unconscious gallantry of which he was ashamed the next moment, for the girl was looking away again. "Do you want to go to the university?"

" Yes, sir, I do."

" Why ? "

" Oh! because — I want to know all I can."

" Why ?   What do you want to do ? "

" You won't tell on me, will you ? "   She was blush-
ing red as a carnation.   " Strange mixture of child and
woman," thought Thatcher and replied :

" Why, certainly not."

They stood over by the blackboard but the other girls
were pointing and snickering.

" I guess I won't tell, " she stammered ; " you'd laugh
at me like everybody else — I know you would."

He took her arm and turned her face toward his ; her
eyes were full of tears.

" Tell me.   I'll help you."

His eyes glowed with a kindly smile, and she warmed
under it.

" I want to write — stories — and books," she half
whispered, guiltily.   The secret was out and she wanted
to run away.   The Doctor's crucial time had come.   If
he laughed ! — but he did not laugh.   He looked
thoughful, almost sad.

" You are starting on a long, long road, Rose," he
said at last.   " Where it will lead to I cannot tell —
nobody can.   What put that into your head ? "

Rose handed him a newspaper clipping containing a
brief account of " how a Wisconsin poetess achieved
fame and fortune."

" Why, my dear girl," he began, " don't you know
that out of ten thousand — " He stopped.   She was

looking up at him in expectation, her great luminous gray-brown eyes burning with an inward hungry fire which thrilled him.

"You may be the one in ten thousand, and I'll help you," he said.

The ringing of the bell brought the pupils clattering back into their seats, puffing, gasping, as if at their last extremity. For a couple of minutes nothing could be done, so great was the noise. While they were getting settled Thatcher said to her:

"If you want to go to the university you will have to go to a preparatory school. Here is my card — write to me when you get through here and I'll see what can be done for you."

Rose went back to her seat, her eyes filled with a burning light, her hands strained together. This great man from Madison had believed in her. Oh, if he would only come home and see her father!

She painfully penciled a note and handed it to him as she came past the blackboard. He was putting on his coat to go, but he looked down at the crumpled note, with its painfully ornate Spencerian handwriting.

"Please, sir, won't you come down and see pappa and ask him if I can't go to Madison?"

He looked at the girl whose eyes, big and sombre and full of wistful timidity, were fixed upon him. Obeying a sudden impulse, he stepped to her side and said, "Yes, I'll help you; don't be troubled."

He stayed until school was out and the winter sun was setting behind the hills. Rose studied his face with more than admiration. She trusted him. He had said he would help her, and his position was one of power in her fancy, and something in his manner impressed her more deeply than that of any man she had ever seen save "William De Lisle," her dim and shadowy, yet kingly figure.

On his part he was surprised at himself. He was waiting a final hour in this school-room out of interest and curiosity in a country school-girl. His was a childless marriage, and this girl stirred the parental tenderness native to him. He wished he had such a child to educate, to develop.

The school was out at last, and, as she put on her things and came timidly toward him, he turned from the teacher to her.

"So you are John Dutcher's daughter? I knew your father when I was a lad here. I am stopping at the Wallace farm, but I'll come over a little later and see your father."

Rose rushed away homeward, full of deep excitement. She burst into the barn where John was rubbing the wet fetlocks of the horses he had been driving. Her eyes were shining and her cheeks were a beautiful pink.

"Oh, pappa, he said I ought to go to Madison to school. He said he'd help me go."

John looked up in astonishment at her excitement. "Who said so?"

"Dr. Thatcher, the man who visited our school to-day. He said I'd ought to go, and he said he'd help me."

Her exultation passed suddenly. Somehow there was not so much to tell as she had fancied, indeed she suddenly found herself unable to explain the basis of her enthusiasm. The perceived, but untranslatable expression of the Doctor's face was the real foundation of her hope, and that she had not definitely and consciously noted. If her father could only have seen him!

"I guess you'd better wait awhile," her father said, with a smile, which Rose resented.

"He's coming to-night."

"Who's he?"

"Dr. Thatcher. He used to live here. He knows you."

John grew a little more intent on her news.

"Does! I wonder if he is old Stuart Thatcher's son? He had a boy who went East to school somewheres."

Rose went into the house and set to work with the graceful celerity which Mrs. Diehl called "knack."

"Rose, you can turn off work when you really want to, to beat anything I ever see."

Rose smiled and hummed a little song. Mrs. Diehl was made curious.

"You're wonderful good-natured, it seems to me. What's the reason, already?"

"We're going to have company."

"Who, for Peter's sake?"

"Dr. Thatcher."

"What's he come here for?"

" To see pappa," said Rose, as she rushed upstairs into her attic-room. It was cold up there, warmed only by the stove-pipe from the sitting-room, but she sat down and fell into a dream in which she recalled every look and word he had given her.

She came suddenly to herself, and began putting on her red dress, which was her company dress. When she came downstairs in her creaking new shoes Mrs. Diehl was properly indignant.

" Well ! I declare. Couldn't you get along in your calico ? "

" No, I couldn't ! " Rose replied, with easy sharpness, which showed the frequent passages at arms between them.

When Thatcher came in with the teacher he was quite startled by the change in her. She looked taller and older and more womanly in every way.

She took his hat and coat and made him at home in much better fashion than he had reason to think she knew. She on her part watched him closely. His manner at the table was a source of enlightenment to her. She felt him to be a strong man, therefore his delicacy and consideration meant a great deal to her. It suggested related things dimly. It made her appreciate vaguely the charm of the world from whence he came.

Dr Thatcher was not young, and his experience as a physician had added to his natural insight. He studied Rose keenly while he talked with John concerning the changes in the neighborhood.

He saw in the girl great energy and resolution, and a

mental organization not simple. She had reason and reserve force not apprehended by her father. The problem was, should he continue to encourage her. Education of a girl like that might be glorious — or tragic! After supper John Dutcher took him into the corner, and, while Rose helped clear away the dishes, the two men talked.

" You see, " John explained, " she's been talkin' about going on studyin', for the last six months. I don't know what's got into the girl, but she wants to go to Madison. I suppose her learnin' of that Bluff-Sidin' girl goin' has kind o' spurred her on. I want her to go to the high school at the Sidin', but she wants to go away " — he choked a little on that phrase — " but if you an' her teacher think the girl'd ought to go, why, I'll send her."

The younger man looked grave — very grave. He foresaw lonely hours for John Dutcher.

"Well—the girl interests me very much, Mr. Dutcher. It's a strong point in her favor that she wants to go. Most girls of her age have little ambition beyond candy and new dresses. I guess it's your duty to send her. What she wants is the larger life that will come to her in Madison. The preparatory work can be done here at the Siding. I believe it is one of the accredited schools. Of course she will come home often, and when she comes to Madison, I will see that she has a home until she gets ' wunted,' as you farmers say."

The teacher came in at this point full of wild praise of Rose's ability. " She's great on history and geography.

She knows about every city and river and mountain on the maps."

"She's always been great for geography," confirmed John. "Used to sit and follow out lines on the maps when she wasn't knee-high to a 'tater." A tender tone came into his voice, almost as if he were speaking of a dead child. He too had a quick imagination, and he felt already the loss of his girl, his daily companion.

The matter was decided there. "You send her to me, when she gets ready, and I'll have Mrs. Thatcher look after her for a week or so, till we find her a place to stay."

Rose was in a fever of excitement though she caught only disconnected words as she came and went about the table. At last she saw Dr. Thatcher rise to go and approached him timorously. With a smile he said:

"Well, Rose, when you come to Madison you must come to our house. Mrs. Thatcher will be glad to see you." She could not utter a word in thanks. After he had gone Rose turned to her father with a swift appeal.

"Oh, pappa, am I going?"

He smiled a little. "We'll see when the time comes, Rosie."

She knew what that meant, and she leaped with a joy swift as a flame. John sat silently looking at the wall, his arm flung over the back of his chair wondering why she should feel so happy at the thought of leaving home, when to think of losing her for a single day out of his life, was bitter as death to him.

Thenceforward the world began to open to Rose.

Every sign of spring was doubly significant ; the warm sun, the passing of wild fowl, the first robin, the green grass, the fall of the frost, all appealed to her with a power which transcended words. All she did during these days was preparation for her great career beyond the Ridge.

She pictured the world outside in colors of such splendor that the romance of her story papers seemed weak and pale.

Out there in the world was William De Lisle. Out there were ladies with white faces and heavy-lidded, haughty eyes, in carriages and in ball-rooms. Out there was battle for her, and from her dull little valley battle seemed somehow alluring.

CHAPTER VIII

LEAVING HOME

As the time for leaving came on Rose had hours of depression, wherein she wondered if it were worth her while. Sometimes it began when she noticed a fugitive look of sorrow on her father's face, and sometimes it was at parting with some of her girl friends, and sometimes it was at thought of Carl. She had spent a year in the Siding in preparation for the work in Madison, and the time of her adventure with the world was near.

Carl came to be a disturbing force during those last few weeks. He had been a factor in all the days of her life. Almost without thought on her part she had relied upon him. She had run to him for any sort of material help, precisely as to a brother, and now he was a man and would not be easily set aside.

He usually drove her to meeting on Sunday, and they loitered on the shady stretches of the coolly roads. He frequently put his arm around her, and she permitted it, because it was the way all young lovers, but she really never considered him in the light of a possible husband.

Most of the girls were precocious in the direction of marriage, and brought all their little allurements to bear with the same purpose which directs the coquetry of a city belle. At sixteen they had beaux, at seventeen many of them actually married, and at eighteen they might often be seen with their husbands, covered with dust, clasping wailing babes in their arms; at twenty they were not infrequently thin and bent in the shoulders, and flat and stiff in the hips, having degenerated into sallow and querulous wives of slovenly, careless husbands.

Rose was not ready to acknowledge that Carl had any claim upon her.

But Carl was grown to be a stalwart young fellow, with the blood and sinew of a man, and the passions of a man were developing in his rather thick head. The arm which he laid along the buggy-seat was less passive and respectful of late. It clutched in upon her at times; though she shook herself angrily free, he merely laughed.

So matters stood when she told him that the time had nearly come for going away to school in Madison.

"That's so?" he said, and not much else till the next Sunday. With all the week to think about it in, he began to ask himself, in current slang, "Where do I come in?"

So the next time they drove together he tried again to tighten his arm about her while he said:

"I'll miss you, Rosie."

"So'll pap," she said.

There was a long pause, then he said: "What's the use o' going away anyhow? I thought you an' me was goin' to be married when we grew up."

She drew away from him. "We ain't grown up yet."

"I guess we won't neither of us ever get our growth, then," he said, with a chuckle; "you don't need that extra schoolin' any more'n I do."

They rode in silence down the beautiful valley, with the gold and purple light of early autumn lying over it.

"You mustn't go and forget me off there in Madison," he said, giving her a squeeze.

"Carl, you stop that! You mustn't do that! I'll jump out o' the buggy if you do that again!"

There was genuine anger in her voice.

"Why, it's all right, Rosie; ain't we engaged?"

"No, we're not, and we never will be, either."

There was a note in her voice that struck through even Carl's thick thought. He did not reply, but continued to dwell upon that reply until its entire meaning came to him. Then his face became pitiful to see. It was usually round and red, but now it looked long and heavy and bitter. He was so infertile of phrases he could only say:

"Then we might as well drive right back home."

"Well, you made me say it," she replied in a softer tone, being much moved by the change in his face. "I like you, Carl, but I'm not a-goin' to promise anything. I'll see when I come back, after I graduate."

They drove on. She was not much more of a talker than he, and so they rode in a silence that was sullen on Carl's part. At the gate she relented a little. "Won't you come in, Carl?"

"No, I guess not," he said, shortly, and drove off.

Rose went into the house feeling more and more the injustice of her anger. "If he hadn't pinched me like that," she said to herself in apology.

She went to work at her packing again, putting in things she would not possibly have any use for. As she worked the ache and weariness at her heart increased, and when they called her to supper the tears were falling again like a shower. It was a silent and miserable meal, though the doors and windows were open and the pleasant sounds of the farm-yard came in, and the red light of the setting sun shone in, magically warm and mellow.

John ate slowly, his eyes fixed on his plate. Rose ate not at all and looked out of the window, with big tears rolling childishly down her cheeks. She didn't want to go at all now. Her home seemed all at once so comfortable and happy and *safe!*

John looked up and saw her tears, and immediately he, too, was choked and could not eat.

"There, there! Rosie, don't cry. We'll be all right, and you'll be back almost 'fore you know it. June comes early in the summer, you know." They were both so childlike they did not consider it possible to come home before the year was up. She came around and knelt down by his side and buried her face on his knees.

"I wish I hadn't promised to go," she wailed; "I don't want to go one bit. I want to stay with you."

He understood her feeling and soothed her and diverted her, though tears would have been a relief to him.

She went with him out to the barn, and she cried over the bossies and the horses, and said good-by to them under her breath, so that her father might not hear.

When she went to bed she lay down disconsolate and miserable. Oh, it was so hard to go, and it was hard not to go. Life was not so simple as it had seemed before. Why did this great fear rise up in her heart? Why should she have this terrible revulsion at the last moment? So she thought and thought. Her only stay in the midst of chaos was Dr. Thatcher. William De Lisle was very far away, like a cold white star.

Just as she made up her mind that she could not sleep, she heard her father call her.

" Rose, time to get up! "

Her heart contracted with a painful spasm that made her cry out. The time had come for action — momentous, irrevocable action, like Napoleon's embarking from Elba for France.

It was very chill and dark. She rose and groped about for a light. Her teeth chattered with cold and it seemed to her that a chill was upon her as she dressed hurriedly and went down.

John and her aunt were already at the table and Rose slipped into her seat, white and silent. It was still dark and the lighted lamps made it seem like a midnight meal.

John was strenuously cheerful. " We have to get up early if we get that seven o'clock train," he said.

" Better take some coffee anyhow," urged Mrs. Diehl.

" Oh, I can't eat a thing," Rose insisted,

"Don't worry her, sis," interposed John. "She'll feel like it later."

While John went to get the team Rose got on her things and walked about, uttering a little moaning sound, like a babe in delirium, which was terrible to hear, and Mrs. Diehl lost patience at last.

"Stop that fuss! Good land! anybody'd think you was goin' to die dead as a hammer, the way you take on, and after all the time we've had gettin' you ready. I declare to goodness I never see such a young 'un in all my born days. I will be glad to get rid of you already!"

This was pungent medicine to Rose, and thereafter she uttered no word of grief, and punished her aunt by refusing to say good-by at the door, which grieved John very much. "You folks had a tiff this morning a'ready?"

Rose did not reply.

It was cold and damp. The wind pushed against their faces with a touch as if of wet palms. The horses splashed along in pools of water, and out of the dim light the hills rose against the sky full of soft sprawling rain-clouds.

They rode in silence. Rose's eyes reflected no more her splendid visions of the world. All was dark and rainy now. Home and peace and comfort were all behind her. She was so miserable it seemed as if she must cry out, but her aunt's contemptuous words helped her to maintain her silence.

John talked a little about the trains on the road, and

the weather, but talk was an effort to him also. As he rode he thought the days all over again. He felt as if he were losing his heart, but he did not waver.

He helped Rose into the car and then stooped and hugged her hard without kissing her, and so stumbled out again, while she sat white and rigid, moaning piteously. And so the familiar things passed away.

The sun came out after a while, and covered the earth with a glory that found its way into the girl's heart. She ceased to sob, and the ache passed out of her throat, although the shadow still hung about her eyes.

The car interested her. It seemed a palatial carriage to her, and of enormous size. She figured out the number of people it would hold, and wondered how the seats which were turned the other way came to be so. The car was mainly occupied by men in careless clothing. Everybody seemed sleepy and unkempt, and she wondered where they all came from, and where they were going, and so speculating, lost something of her poignant sorrow.

At last came a moment of quiet elation. She was going out into the world! the enormous, the incredible had happened! She was going to Madison, the State capital. The speed of the train, which seemed to her very great, aided her to realize how swiftly she was getting into the world. The fields and farms whirled by in dizzying fashion, and the whistle of the engine was like the furious, defiant neigh of a rushing horse. It was all on a scale more splendid than her dreams.

In the midst of her exultant moment the brakeman

came through and eyed her with an insolent glare. She started as if a hot iron had touched her flesh, and shrank back into herself, like a scared mollusk. The man passed on, but her exultation was gone.

She noticed that the hills grew lower as they sped southward, and queer rocks rose squarely up from the flat lands, which were covered with wild swamps of small trees, out of which long skeletons of dead pines lifted with a desolate effect.

There were several tunnels, and every time they went through one Rose clung to the seat in terror. Some impudent young men in the rear of the car smacked their lips to represent kisses, and laughed boisterously afterward, as if that were a very good joke indeed.

The conductor, when he came through the next time, eyed her closely and smiled broadly. She did not understand why he should smile at her. After he had been through the car several times he came and sat down by her.

" Nice day, ain't it ? Live in Madison ? "

" No, sir," she replied, looking away. She did not want to say more, but some power made her add, " I am going to school there."

He seemed pleased.

" Ah, hah ! Going to the university ? "

" Yes, sir."

" Oh, I see." He put his knee against the back of the seat in front of her and took an easy position.

" It's a nice town. Wish I could stop off and help you find a boarding-place."

The brakeman, coming through, winked at the conductor as if to say: "I like your 'mash,'" and the terror and shame of her position flashed over Rose, flushing her from head to foot. Her eyes filled with angry tears, and she looked out of the window, not knowing what to do. She was so helpless here, for she was out in the world alone.

The conductor went on serenely, knowing well how scared and angry she was.

"Yes, sir; it's a fine little town. Great place for boating, summer or winter. You'll see a hundred ice-boats out on Monona there all at once. I've got a cousin there who has a boat. He'd be glad to take you out if I'd tell him about you."

"I don't want to know him," she said, in what she intended to be a fierce tone, but which was a pitifully scared tone.

The conductor knew that the brakeman was observing him, and in order to convey the impression that he was getting on nicely he bent forward and looked around into the girl's face.

"Oh, you'd like him first rate."

Rose would have screamed, or broken out into some wild action had not the engine whistled. This gave the conductor an excuse to give the talk up for the moment.

"She's a daisy and as green as grass," he said to the brakeman. Her innocence seemed to place her in his hand.

For the next hour they persecuted the girl with their

attentions. First one and then the other came along the aisle and sat down beside her. And when she put her valise there, blocking the seat, the brakeman sat on the arm-rest and tormented her with questions to which she gave no answer.

Just after Pine City a cool, firm woman's voice sounded in her ear: " May I sit with you ? "

She looked up and made room for a handsome, middle-aged woman, in a neat travelling dress.

"It's a shame!" she said. " I've just got in, but I saw at once how those men were torturing you. Strange no one in the car could see it and take your part."

Rose turned gratefully, and laid her head on the lady's stalwart shoulder and cried.

" There, there, no harm done! You must learn to expect such things from some men. It would be libellous on the brutes to call them beasts." She said a great many things which Rose hardly understood, but her presence was strong and helpful and Rose liked her very much.

" How far are you going ? "

Rose told her in a few words.

" Ah, are you ? You could not have made a better choice. Who sends you there — pardon me ? "

" Dr. Thatcher."

" Dr. Thatcher! Well, well, how things come about. I know the Doctor very well."

" Do you ? I'm going to live there for a while."

Rose was almost smiling now.

"Well, you couldn't be more fortunate. You'll get into the most progressive home in the city."

From this on they had a royal good time. Rose grew happier than she had been for weeks. There was something very assuring about this woman, and her sweet smile and soft gray eyes seemed very beautiful to the lonely child.

When the conductor came down the aisle again Rose's protector met his eye with a keen, stern glance.

"Young man, I shall have you discharged from this road."

The astonished cur took her card, and when he read the name of a famous woman lawyer of Milwaukee his face fell.

"I didn't mean any harm."

"I know better. I shall see Mr. Millet, and see that he makes an example of you."

Rose was awed by her calm and commanding voice.

"It has been our boast that American girls could travel from east to west in our broad land, and be safe from insult, and I'm not going to let such a thing pass."

She returned to her gentle mood presently, and began to talk of other things.

As they neared the town where they were to part company, the elder woman said:

"Now, my dear, I am to get off here. I may never see you again, but I think I shall. You interest me very much. I am likely to be in Madison during the year, and if I do I will look you up. I am getting old though, and things of this life are uncertain to us who

wear gray hair. I like that forehead on you, it tells me
you are not to be a victim to the first man who lays his
hand on you. Let me give one last word of advice.
Don't marry till you are thirty. Choose a profession
and work for it. Marry only when you want to be a
mother."

She rose. "You don't understand what I mean now,
but keep my words in your mind. Some day you will
comprehend all I mean — good-by. " Rose was tearful
as Mrs. Spencer kissed her and moved away.

Rose saw her on the steps and waved her hand back at
her as the train drew away. Her presence had been
oppressive in spite of her kindness, and her last words
filled the girl's mind with vague doubts of life and of men.
Everything seemed forcing her thoughts of marriage to
definiteness. Her sex was so emphasized, so insisted upon
by this first day's experience in the world, that she leaned
her head against the window and cried out : " Oh, I wish
I was dead."

But the train shot round the low green hills fringed with
the glorious foliage of the maples, the lake sparkled in the
afternoon's sun, the dome of the capitol building loomed
against the sky, and the romance and terror of her entry
into the world came back to her, driving out her more
morbid emotions. She became again the healthy country
girl to whom Madison was a centre of art and society
and literature.

G

CHAPTER IX

ROSE ENTERS MADISON

THE train drew up to a long platform swarming with people, moving anxiously about with valises in hand, broad-hatted and kindly ; many of them were like the people of " the Coolly. " But the young hackmen terrified her with their hard, bold eyes and cruel, tobacco-stained mouths.

She alighted from the car, white and tremulous with fear, and her eyes moved about anxiously. When they fell upon Thatcher the blood rushed up over her face, and her eyes filled with tears of relief.

" Ah, here you are ! " he said, with a smile, as he shook her hand and took her valise. " I began to fear you'd been delayed. "

She followed him to the carriage with downcast eyes. Her regard for him would not permit her to say a word, even when they were seated together in the carriage and driving up the street. Her breath came so quick and strange the Doctor noticed it.

" A little bit excited about it, aren't you ? " he smilingly said. " I remember how I felt when I went to Chicago the first time. I suppose this seems like Chicago to you. How did you leave the people in the coolly, all well?"

"Yes, sir," she replied, without looking up.

"Well, now you are about to begin work. I've got everything all arranged. You are to stay with us for the present at least. My niece is with us and you will get along famously, I know. How do you like my horse?" he asked, in his effort to relieve the tension.

She studied the horse critically.

"First rate!" she said at last.

He laughed. "Well, I am glad you like him, for I know you are a judge. He is a pretty good stepper, too, though he hasn't quite enough fling in his knees, you notice. I'll let you drive him some time."

He drew up before a pretty cottage, set in the midst of a neat lawn. It was discouragingly fine and handsome to the girl. She was afraid it was too good for her to enter.

A very blond young girl came dancing out to the block.

"Oh, Uncle Ed, did Rose —" Rose suddenly appeared.

"This is Rose. Rose, this is our little chatterbox."

"Now, Uncle Ed! Come right in, Rose. I'm going to call you Rose, mayn't I?"

Mrs. Thatcher, a tall thin woman, welcomed Rose in sober fashion, and led the way into the little parlor, which seemed incredibly elegant to the shy girl.

She sat silently while the rest moved about her. There was a certain dignity in this reserve, and both

Mrs. Thatcher and Josie were impressed by it. She was larger and handsomer than either of them, and that gave her an advantage, though she did not realize it. She was comparing, in swift, disparaging fashion, her own heavy boots with their dainty soft shoes, and wondering in what way she could escape from them.

"Josie, take her right up to her room," said Mrs. Thatcher, "and let her get ready for dinner."

"Yes, come up, you must feel like having a good scrub."

Rose flushed again, wondering if her face had grown grimy enough to be noticeable.

The young girl led Rose into a pretty room with light green walls, and lovely curtains at the windows. There were two dainty little beds occupying opposite corners.

"We're to occupy this room together," said Josie. "This is my dressing-case and that's yours."

She bustled about helping Rose to lay off her things, pouring water for her, talking on and on with gleeful flow.

"I'm awful glad you've come. I know we'll be just as thick! I wish you were in my classes though, but you won't be, so Doctor says. Don't you think this is a nice room?"

Rose washed her hands as quickly as possible because they looked so big and dingy beside the supple whiteness of Josephine's. She felt dusty and coarse and hopeless in the midst of this exquisite room, the most beautiful chamber she had ever seen.

Her eyes, moving about, fell upon a picture which had the gleam of white limbs in it. Josephine followed her look. " Oh, that's young Sampson choking the lion. I just love that; isn't he lovely ? "

Rose blushed and tried to answer, but could not. The beautiful splendid limbs of the young man flamed upon her with marvellous appeal. It was beautiful, and yet her training made her think it somehow not to be talked about.

Josephine led the way downstairs into the little parlor, which was quite as uncomfortably beautiful as the bed-room. The vases and flowers, and simple pictures, and the piano, all seemed like the furnishings of the homes she had read about in stories.

But dazed as she was she kept her self-command, at least she kept silence and sat in sombre, almost sullen dejection amid it all. Mrs. Thatcher hardly knew what to think of her, but the Doctor comprehended her mood fairly well for he had passed through similar experiences himself. He talked to her for a few minutes about her plans, and then they went out to dinner.

Rose entered the dining-room with a still greater fear in her heart. She longed to run away and hide.

" Oh, I don't know anything ! " was the bitter cry welling up in her throat again and again, and she nearly cried out upon the impulse.

The Doctor liked to have his dinner at one, and so Rose found two knives and two forks at her plate, and two spoons also. She had read in stories of " formal dinners," and this seemed likely to be her greatest trial. She sat very stiff and silent as the soup was brought on by the Norwegian girl.

She took the plate as it was handed to her, and handed back the one which was turned down with the napkin on top of it. The Norwegian girl smiled broadly and handed them both back. Then Rose saw her mistake and the hot blood swept over her brown face in a purple wave.

The Doctor and his wife passed it in silence. Josie fortunately was talking to the cat and did not see it.

Rose could hardly touch her soup, which was delicious, and her rebellious soul was filled with a desire to escape as soon as possible.

Which of the knives should she use first, and what was the extra little plate for, were the disturbing questions. She could use a fork, but she was afraid of betraying herself in the minutiæ of the service. As a matter of fact she got along very well, but of that she had no knowledge.

Some way she lived through the dainty dinner, scarcely tasting anything of it. At the close of it Mrs. Thatcher said :

" Wouldn't you like to lie down for a little while? Aren't you tired ? " Rose hardly knew what weariness was, but she assented because she wished to be alone.

" I 'll call you at three, may I ? " asked Josie, who was wildly in love with Rose already.

" Oh, isn't she big and splendid, but she's queer," she said when she came down.

" That'll wear off," said the Doctor. " She feels a little strange now. I know all about it. I went from a farm to the city myself."

Rose hardly dared lie down on the spotless bed. A latent good taste enabled her to perceive in every detail harmony of effect, and that she was the one discordant note in the house. " Oh, how dirty and rough and awkward I am ! " was her inward cry.

Looking out of the window she saw a couple of ladies come out of a large house opposite and walk down toward a carriage which waited at the gate. The ladies held their dresses with a dainty action of their gloved hands as they stood for a moment in consuita-tion. (How graceful their hats were !) Then they entered the carriage.

As they gathered their soft robes about their limbs and stooped to enter the door, the flexile, beautiful line of waist and hip and thigh came out modestly. Their gaiters were of the same color as their dresses. This was most wonderful of all.

The ladies were a revelation of elegance and grace to the farmer's daughter. Such unity and completeness of attire was unknown to her before and she looked down at her red dress which Mattie Teel had cut out for her, and she realized all its deformity. The sleeves didn't fit as Josie's did. It never did hang right; it just wrinkled all around the waist, and hung in bunches and she knew it. And her hat, made over from her last winter's hat was awful — just awful !

She might just as well die or go back home, and never go out of the coolly again. She was nothing but a great country gawk, anyway.

In this bitter fashion she raged on, lying face downward on the sofa until she heard dancing steps, and Josie crying out : " May I come in ? "

" Yes," Rose coldly answered.

" Oh, you've been having a good cry, I know! I just like to go off and have a good cry that way. It makes your eyes red, but you can fix that. Just sit still now and let me see what I can do."

She bustled about and Rose let her bathe her face with cool water and cologne, and fuss about. Her little fingers were like a baby's and she murmured and gurgled in the goodness of her heart like a kitten. Rose actually fell asleep under her touch.

Josie stopped astonished and startled for a moment, and then tip-toed out of the room like a burglar, and told Mrs. Thatcher all about it.

" And oh, auntie, she's very poor, isn't she ? Her clothes —— "

" Tut," warned Mrs. Thatcher, " you must be careful not to notice that. Edward, is she so very poor ? "

The Doctor, seated at his desk in the little office, looked up a moment.

"No, I don't think so. It is lack of judgment partially. A little tact and taste will fix her all right. Dutcher is fairly well-to-do, and she is all he has. He wrote me to get her what she needed, but I'll leave that to you girls."

Josie danced with delight. Buying things for yourself was fun, but buying for another was ecstasy!

" The poor child hasn't a dress that she can wear without alteration, and she is such a splendid creature, too. I can't conceive how they failed to fit her."

" It seems to me that putting her beside Josie is pretty hard on her. I am afraid you are not conversant with the wardrobe of farmers' girls."

" Well, I didn't suppose — and the other room is so small."

" Oh, well, it all depends upon Josie. Josie, come here."

The girl rose up, and he put his arm around her.

" Now, my kitten, you must be very careful not to allude to any little mistakes Rose makes."

" Oh, Uncle Ed — you know —— "

"Yes, I know chatterboxes mean all right but they forget. Now, Rose is going to be a great scholar, and she is going to be a lady, very soon, too; but she is awkward, now, and my little girl mustn't make it hard for her."

After Josie went out, Thatcher said:

" I know just how Rose feels. I went through it myself. It's hard, but it won't hurt her, only don't try to talk it over with her. If she's the girl I think she is, she'll work the whole matter out in a week or two, herself. If she's rested, ask her to come down."

Rose came into the Doctor's office in a numb sort of timidity, for there was a great change in the Doctor. He did not seem the same as when he sat in the school-room. She couldn't describe it, but there was something in his voice which awed her. He was now surrounded by his professional books and tools, which gave him dignity in her eyes.

" Sit down, Rose," he said, " I want to talk with you.

I've had a letter from your father about you and your expenses."

And then, in some way, she never knew exactly how, he talked away her bitterness and gave her hope and comfort. He advised about books, and said: "And you'll need some little things which Bluff Siding doesn't keep. Mrs. Thatcher will drive you up town to-morrow and you can get what you need. Your father has deposited some money here to pay your expenses. I am going over to University Hill to make a call; perhaps you'd like to go."

She assented, and went to get her hat.

It was the largest town she had ever seen and the capitol was wonderful to her, set in its shaded park, where squirrels ran about on the velvet green of the grass. The building towered up in the sky, just as she had seen it in pictures. Swarms of people came and went along the hard, blue-black paths, and round it the teams moved before the stores of the square. It was all mightily impressive to her.

They passed the Public Library, and the Doctor said: "You'll make great use of that, I imagine."

She could not make herself believe that. She saw students coming and going on the street, and they all seemed very gay and well dressed.

"All this will trouble you for a little while," the Doctor said. "When I came to the University the first time I was as uneasy as a cat in a bathtub. I thought everybody was laughing at me, but, as a matter of fact, nobody paid any attention to me at all. Then

I got mad, and I said, ' Well, I'll *make* you pay attention to me before I'm done.'" The Doctor smiled at her and she had the courage to smile back. It was wonderful how well he understood her.

He drove her around the Lake shore. It was beautiful, but in her weakness the more beautiful anything was the more it depressed her. The Doctor did not demand speech of her, well knowing she did not care to talk.

" I'm not mistaken in the girl," he said to his wife when they were alone. " She has immense reserve force — I feel it. Wait until she straightens up and broadens out a little, you'll see! There's some half-savage power in her, magnetism, impelling quality. I predict a great future for her if —— "

" If what ? "

" If she don't marry. She is passionate, wilful as a colt. It seems impossible she has come thus far without entanglement. She's going to be very handsome when she gets a little more at ease. I thought her a wonderful creature as she sat in that school-room, with the yellow sun striking across her head. She appeared to me to have destiny in her favor."

" She's fine, but I think you're over-enthusiastic, Edward. "

" Wait and see. She isn't a chatterbox like Josie, that is evident. "

" In fact, my dear, " he went on to say after a silence, " I should like to adopt her — I mean, of course, take a paternal interest in her. She has appealed to me very

strongly from the first.   You can be a mother to Josie
and I'll be a father to Rose. "

There was something sombre under his smiling utter-
ance of these words.   Mrs. Thatcher's eyes did not meet
his, and there was a silence.   At last the Doctor said :

" The girl's physical perfection is wonderful.   Most
farmers' girls are round in the shoulders, and flat in the
hips, but Rose has grown up like a young colt.   Add
culture and ease to her and she'll mow a wide swath,
largely without knowing it, for the girl is incapable of
vanity. "

The wife listened with a brooding face.   Rose's
splendid prophecy of maternity oppressed her in some
way.

When the girls went up to bed, terror and homesickness
and depression all came back upon Rose again.   She sat
down desolately upon the little cream-and-gold chair and
watched Josie as she pattered about taking down her hair
and arranging it for the night.   She could not help noting
the multitude of bottles and little combs and powder-puffs
and boxes and brushes which Josie gloated over, seeing
that her visitor was interested.

They were presents, she said, and named the giver of
each.   It was a revelation to Rose of the elegancies of a
dainty, finicky girl's toilet, and when she thought of the
ragged wash-brush and wooden-backed hair-brush and the
horn comb which made up her own toilet set, she grew
hot and cold with shame.

Josephine was delighted to have someone sit in
admiration of her, and displayed all her paces.   She

brushed her hair out with her ivory-backed brush, and laid out all her beautiful underwear, trimmed with lace and embroidered in silk. She did it without malice, but Rose thought of her worn cotton things, shapeless and ugly. She never could undress before Josephine in the world!

She delayed and delayed until Josie had cuddled down into her bed with her little pink nose sticking out, and her merry eyes blinking like the gaze of a sleepy kitten. Rose waited, hoping those bright eyes would close, but they would not. At last a desperate idea came to her. She sprang up and went to the gaslight.

" How do you put this out ? " she asked.

Josie gurgled with laughter. " Just turn that thing-umbob underneath. Yes, *that* — turn it quick — that's right. Oh, isn't it dark! But you aren't undressed yet, and the matches are out in the bath-room."

Rose was more at her ease in the dark.

" Never mind, I can get along in the dark. I'm used to it." She loosened the collar of her dress, slipped off her shoes, and lay down on the bed, bitter and rebellious.

When Josie awoke in the morning the country girl was awake and fully dressed, and reading a book by the window.

The wrinkly red dress could not utterly break up the fine lines of her firm bust and powerful waist, and the admiring little creature hopped out of bed and stole across the room, and threw her arms about Rose.

" How big and beautiful you are ! "

These wonderful words ran into the country girl's blood like some wonderful elixir. To be beautiful made some amends for being coarse and uncultured. As she had never felt abasement before, so she had never felt the need of being beautiful until now.

She turned a radiant, tearful face to Josie, and seized her hands.

" I — I like you — oh, so much! "

" I knew we'd be friends," cried the little one, dancing about. " And you'll let me go and help you buy your things, won't you ? "

" I'll be *glad* to have you — I'm such a gawk. I don't know anything at all that I ought to know."

" You're just splendid. I'm the one who don't know anything."

Then they entered upon a day of shopping. They toiled like ants and buzzed like bees.

Rose came home at night all worn out, discouraged, and dumb as an Indian. She had submitted to her fate, but she was mentally sore, lame, and confused. She no longer cared whether Josie saw her poor wardrobe or not, and she went to sleep out of utter fatigue, her eyes wet with tears of homesickness. All she hoped for seemed impossible and of no account, and to sleep once more in her own attic-bed, appeared to be the most desired thing in the world.

Her good, vigorous blood built up her courage during the night, but she was hardly a sweet and lovable companion in the days which followed. She (temporarily) hated Josie and feared Mrs. Thatcher. Thatcher himself, however, was her refuge and stay, she would surely have gone home had it not been for him.

She had a notable set-to with the dressmaker.

"I won't come here again," she said, sullenly. "I don't want any dresses; I'm going home. I'm tired of being pulled and hauled."

The dressmaker was a brisk little Alsatian, with something of the French adroitness in her manner.

"Oh, my dear young friend! If you only knew! I am in despair! You have such a beautiful figure. You would give me such pleasure if I might but finish this lovely gown."

Rose looked at her from under a scowling, prominent forehead. She had never been called beautiful before — at least not by one who was disinterested or a stranger, and she did not believe the woman.

The dressmaker passed her hands caressingly over the girl's splendid bust and side.

"Ah! I can make myself famous if I may but fit those lines."

Rose softened and put on the gown once more and silently permitted herself to be turned and turned about like a tin sign, while the little artist (which she was) went on with a mouth full of pins, gurgling, murmuring, and patting. This was the worst of the worry, and the end of all the shopping was in sight.

The touch of soft flannels upon her flesh, the flow of ample and graceful gowns, helped her at once. Her shoulders lifted and her bust expanded under properly cut and fitted garments. Quickly, unconsciously, she became herself again, moving with large, unfettered movements. She dominated her clothing, and yet her clothing helped her. Being fit to be seen, she was not so much troubled by the faces of people who scrutinized her.

It was wonderful to see how she took on (in the first few weeks) the graces and refinements of her new life. She met her schoolmates each day with added ease, and came at last to be a leader among them, just as in the home coolly. Her strength and grace and mastery they felt at once.

Her heart beat very hard and fast on the first day as she joined the stream of students moving toward the Central Hall. The maple-trees were still in full leaf and blazing color. The sunlight was a magical cataract of etherealized gold, and the clouds were too beautiful to look at without a choking in the throat.

As she stepped over the deeply worn stone sill, she thought of the thousands of other country girls whose feet had helped to wear that hollow, and her heart ached with unaccountable emotion.

Above her on the winding stairway hundreds of noisy feet clattered and bounded, and careless voices echoed. She mounted in silence. In such wise she entered upon the way of knowledge, the way which has no returning footsteps, and which becomes ever more lonely as the climber rises.

CHAPTER X

QUIET YEARS OF GROWTH

OUTWARDLY her days were uneventful. She came and went quietly, and answered her teachers with certainty and precision. She was not communicative to her companions, and came to know but few of them during the first term. She watched the trees go sere and bare, and calculated on the progress of the farmwork. She wondered if the men were in the corn yet, or whether the morning was too cold to plough. She studied the sky to see if there were signs of snow. She could not at once throw off her daily supervision of the weather and of farmwork.

Her father wrote only at long intervals. His chapped and stiffened hands managed the pen-stock but painfully. He treated of the farm affairs, the yield of corn, the weight of the steers or hogs he had sold, and asked her how many turkeys he had best keep over.

Carl was a still more dilatory correspondent, and he meant little to her now anyhow. The Doctor's dominion was absolute, and yet there was a subtle change in her relation toward him. She no longer blushed in his presence, and he seemed older and nearer to her, more like an uncle and adviser. The figure he had been, took its place beside that of William De Lisle. More substantial, and therefore less sweet and mythical.

Her school life was not her entire intellectual life by any means. She had the power of absorbing and making use of every sight and sound about her. She saw a graceful action at table or in the drawing-room, and her alert mind seized upon it and incorporated it. She did not imitate; she took something from everyone, but from no one too much.

Her eyes lost their round, nervous stare, but they searched, searched constantly, as was natural for a girl of her years and fine animal nature; but there was brain back of it all. The young men knew nothing of her searching eyes; indeed, they thought her cold, and a little contemptuous of them.

Meanwhile their elegance often alienated them from her. There were many types not far removed from Carl and Henry; farmers' boys with some touch of refinement and grace, but others there were who had a subtle quality, which told of homes of refinement and luxury.

Two wonderful things had come to her. One was the knowledge that she was beautiful, which she came to understand was the burning desire of all women; and again that she was master of things which had once scared her. She discovered that she could wear lovely dresses gracefully, and sit at table with ease, and walk before her classmates without tremor. She had a feeling of power in her heart, as well as in her fist.

Her winter was a quiet one. She came and went between her classes and her home at Dr. Thatcher's. She studied in her own room or recited to the Doctor when he was at leisure. He liked to have the girls come into his study when he was not too busy, and while he sat pondering the probable effect of cocaine or atropine in a certain case, the women folks read or talked.

Those were wonderful hours to the country girl. She was a long way from the little cottage on the home farm at such times, but Thatcher felt the same beauty and power in the face which had attracted him first in the old school-house, but enriched by nobler colorings now.

They went sleighing together, with shouting and laughter, as if the Doctor were a girl, too. They went skating, and once in a while to some entertainment at the church. They were not theatre-going people, and the lectures and socials of the town and college made up their outings. It was the Doctor's merry interest in their doings which made young men almost unnecessary to Rose as well as to Josephine.

Then came spring again; the southwest wind awoke, the snow began to go, the grass showed green in the lawns, and Rose's thoughts turned back toward the coolly. There were days when every drop of her blood called out for the hills and the country roads, the bleat of lambs, the odor of fields, and the hum of bees, but she kept on at work.

Something elemental stirred in her blood as the leaves came out. The young men took on added grace and power in her eyes. When they came before her in their athletic suits, strong and joyous, her eyes dreamed and her heart beat till the blood choked her breathing.

Oh, the beautiful sky! Oh, the shine and shade of leaves! Oh, the splendor of young manhood! She fought down the dizziness which came to her. She smiled mechanically as they stood before her with frank, clear eyes and laughing lips, and so, slowly, brain reasserted itself over flesh, and she, too, grew frank and gay.

Then came the vacation. The partings, the bitter pain of leaving the young people she had learned to love, and, too, came the thought of home. The dear old coolly with its peaks and camel humps, and pappa John! He was waiting to see her there!

So the pain of leaving her mates was mingled with the joy of home-coming. She romped on the grass with the young lambs. She followed pappa John about as of old, in the fields, while he wondered and marvelled at her. She had grown so fine and white and ladylike.

She was fain to know all the news of the farm, and the neighborhood. She felt like kissing all the dear old ladies in the coolly. Oh, the old friends were the best after all! You could rest on them. They didn't care how you ate soup. They didn't keep you keyed up to company manners all the time.

She went back to her old dresses and cotton underwear, and went dirty as she liked, and got brown and iron-muscled again.

Carl met her on the road one day and nodded and

drove on, with hurried action of the lines. He still bore her rejection of him fresh in mind. It was to his credit that he never made use of his youthful intimacy with her. He was a man, with all the honesty and sincerity and chivalry of a race of gentlemen in his head, slow-witted as he was.

CHAPTER XI

STUDY OF THE STARS

SHE came back each September with delight and exultation. It was not so much like going to the world's
end now, and besides, her father seemed resigned to it.
Back to the gleam of the lakes, the flaming sunsets, the
moonlit nights filled with the twang of guitars and the
floating harmony of fresh boyish voices, back to her girl
lovers and her books, back to the chalky odor of the rec-
itation room.

Ah, but it was so sweet to climb the circular stairway
again! The booming roar of the students' feet did not
disturb her now. The greetings of the professors, as
they passed, made her eyes sparkle with pleasure. The
spirit of the university had established dominion over
her.

These were days without care; days of silent, pleasant
growth and years of sweet gravity over books and
wholesome laughter over games. She studied hard, but
it was a quiet pleasure to study, for she had the power of
concentration which gives mastery.

She was never behind, never fagged out with study.
She had time for the splendor of nature and for the world

of books. She read more and more each year because she felt lacking in literary knowledge. She read the books she ought to know — read them religiously. Occasionally it chanced that the books were those she loved to read, but not often. Generally she had to bend to them as if they were lessons.

She read also Scott, Dickens, and Thackeray, a volume or two each. Then one day in midwinter it chanced she fell upon " Mosses from an Old Manse," and thereafter all other books waited. She read this wondrous book while she walked home from the library.

She read it after dinner and put it in her satchel as she went to recite. She finished it and secured the second volume; after that she seized upon " Twice-Told Tales," then the " Scarlet Letter," and the world of woman's sin and man's injustice opened to her!

She read that terrible book, rebelling against the dark picture, raging against the insatiable vengeance of the populace who condemned Hester as if she had opened the gates of hell in the path of every daughter of New England.

Rose could not understand, then nor thereafter, the ferocity of hate which went out against the poor defenceless woman. What had Hester done? The girl struggled over the problem, feeling in herself that terrible ceaseless urging. Her thoughts were not clear, they were still only slightly raised figures in the web of organic thought, but she was achieving fundamental conceptions.

She knew it was wrong, but why it was wrong troubled her. The law — yes, but what lay behind the law? The

Mormon had one law, the Turk another. Why was this English law better than any other? Why were the animals freer than men? Their lives were good and healthy, they lived in the sunshine and were untroubled. Such were a few of the questions she grappled with.

God only knows the temptations which came to her. She had days when all the (so-called) unclean things she had ever seen, all the overheard words of men's coarse jests, came back like vultures to trouble her. Sometimes, when she walked forth of a morning, the sun flamed across the grass with ineffable beauty. The whole earth was radiant; every sound was a song; every lithe youth moved like a god before her, and it was then that something deep in her, something drawn from generations of virtuous wives and mothers, saved her from the whirlpool of passion.

At such times she felt dimly the enormous difference between her own nature and that of Josephine. Josephine's passion was that of a child — while hers was that of an imaginative and complex woman.

She was not a chatterer at any time, but after these moods of abnormal gayety she became almost sullen and fell upon her lessons with renewed zeal, as a monk flagellates his rebellious flesh.

After days of searching with eager eyes, she refused to look at any of the young men, answering them but crustily or turned quickly away from them, but this did not serve to cure her nor to keep the young men away.

Always at such times William De Lisle's glorious

presence drew near in the dusk, insubstantial and luminous as a cloud, and she set her teeth in fresh resolve to be wise and famous; to be worthy his look and his word of praise.

She had suitors constantly. Her dark haughty face, warm with blood, her erect and powerful figure excited admiration among her young classmates, and they courted her with the wholesome frankness of sane and vigorous manhood. The free and natural intercourse of the college kept the young people as wholesome morally as in the home circle.

As the Doctor came to take a different place in her love, Rose became open to the attentions of other men. Twice during the winter she felt the hand of love upon her. In the first instance her eyes sought and found among her classmates a young man's physical beauty, and her imagination clothed him with power and mystery, and she looked for him each day, and life was less interesting and purposeful when he was not present.

She made no open advances, she scarcely needed to, for he also saw, and when he came to her and she flushed and trembled with weakness, it seemed as if her life had at last taken a fixed direction. For a few weeks the man was her ideal. She saw him before her constantly. She knew his smile, the lift of his eyebrows, the shape of his ears, the slope of his shoulders, the sound of his voice. She looked at him stealthily from her book. She contrived to sit where she could watch every motion. She walked down the street with him each day, half numb with her emotion.

But this ecstasy did not last. She felt eventually his shallowness and narrowness. He was vain and ungenerous. He grew sere and bare of grace and charm like the autumn elms, and at last he stood empty and characterless before her, and her eyes looked over and beyond him, into the blue sky again, and throughout it all she kept her place in her classes and no one was aware of her passion or her disappointment.

When she turned away from him he did not grow pale and lean. He grew a little vicious and said: "She is too cold and proud for my taste."

Her next suitor was a worthy young man who was studying law in the town. A fine, manly young fellow, who paid court to her with masterly address. He was older than she, and a better scholar, and brought to her less of the clothes-horse and more of the man than her freshly outgrown lover. Before spring began he had won great intimacy with her — almost an engagement.

He was adroit. He did not see her too much, and he came always at his best. He appealed to the most imaginative side of her nature. She glorified his calling as well as his person. He was less handsome than his predecessor, but he brought an ample and flowing phraseology, and a critical knowledge of farm-life as well as of town-life. Once he took her to the court-room to hear him plead.

He took her to the socials and once to the theatre. There was his mistake! The play made a most powerful impression upon her, more powerful than anything since the circus at Tyre.

It raised new and wordless ambitions. For the first time in her life she saw society dress on the stage. The play was one which pretended, at least, to show New York and London life. Therefore men in claw-hammer coats came and went, with strange accents and with cabalistic motions of hats and gloves, and women moved about with mystic swagger.

The heroine glowed like a precious stone in each act, now sapphire, now pearl, now ruby. She spoke in a thick, throaty murmur, and her white shoulders shone like silver, and her wide childish eyes were like wells of light-diffusing liquid.

Rose gazed at her with unwearying eyes. Her bosom rose and fell as if she had been running, and she said in her heart: "*I* can do that! I could stand there and do that!"

Then the theme of the play filled her with strange new thoughts. These people lived out before her a condition which she had read about but which had never been discussed in her presence. A husband discovers his wife to have been a lover and mother in her girlhood, and in a tempest of self-righteous passion flings her to the ground in scorn and horror.

She clung to his feet pleading for mercy: " I was so young ! "

He would not listen. " Go ! — or no, stay — *I* will go. I make the home over to you, but never look upon my face again."

While Rose burned with shame and indignation, the outraged woman on the stage grew white and stern.

"Who are you to condemn me so?" she asked in icy calm. "Are you the saint you profess to be? Will one offence contain your crime against me?"

"What do you mean?" thundered the man and husband.

"You know what I mean. In my weakness I was stained, ineffaceably; I admit it — but you, in your strength, have you not preyed upon weak women? The law allows you to escape disgrace — nature and law force me to suffer with mine."

Rose thought of Carl and his courtship with such a shudder as one feels in remembering a rescue from an abyss. A hundred great confusing questions floated by in her mind, like clouds in a mist of rain — formless, vast, trailing black shadows beneath them as the curtain fell. The self-sufficient young lawyer beside her said :

"There was nothing else for her husband to do but just fire her out."

Rose heard him but did not reply. She hated him for his coarse hard tone and when he laid his hand on her arm she shook it off. When he asked her to explain she did not reply. He was annoyed also, and so they waited in silence for the curtain to rise on the final act.

The wife was sick and dying. The dramatist had not the courage to work out his theme. He killed the woman in order that the husband should not appear to condone and take her to wife again. She died while he, magnanimously, forgave her.

As they walked home, her lover, with fatuous insistence, talked with Rose about the case. He took the man's side. He hinted at the reason — presuming upon their intimacy. Men outgrow such experiences, he said; women do not. They are either one thing or the other — either pure as angels or black as devils.

Rose closed her lips tight, and her eyes flamed with indignant protest, but she uttered no word in reply. In her heart she knew it to be a lie. A woman can set her foot above her dead self as well as a man.

When he tried to kiss her good-by she pushed him aside and left him without a word. He, too, was a bare and broken ideal. Her heart went back again to William De Lisle, as the young eagle goes back to the sun-warmed cliff to rest and dream with eyes to the sun.

That night put her girlhood far away from her. She grew years older in the weeks which followed. Her mind took up irresistibly one insoluble problem after another and wrestled with it in silence. Josie's chatter went on around her like the sound of the swallows in the eaves of the old barn at home.

Her mind was like a piece of inconceivably intricate machinery, full of latent and complicated motion. A word, a touch, and it set to work, and out of its working some fine inner heat and glow developed which changed the whole mental and physical equilibrium of her nature and she became something else, finer, more mysterious, and more alluring — though this she did not realize.

Thereafter the young men of her acquaintance did

not attract her. Her eyes had been raised to higher altitudes. She fell upon her books with terrible industry, in the hope that they would throw some light on her problems and ambitions.

There was nothing she did not think of during these character-forming days. The beauty and peace of love, the physical joy of it; the problem of marriage, the terror of birth — all the things girls are supposed not to think of, and which such girls as Rose must irresistibly think of, came to her, tormenting her, shaking her to the inmost centre of her nature, and through it all she seemed quite the hearty young school-girl she was, for this thought was wholesome and natural, not morbid in any degree.

She was a child in the presence of the Doctor, but a woman with her suitors. The Doctor helped her very much, but in the most trying moments of her life (and no man can realize these moments) some hidden force rose up to dominate the merely animal forces within. Some magnificent inheritance of organic moral purity.

She was saved by forces within, not by laws without. Opportunities to sin always offer in every hour of every life. Virtue is not negative, it is positive; it is a decoration won by fighting, resisting. This sweet and terrible attraction of men and women toward each other is as natural and as moral as the law of gravity, and as inexorable. Its perversion produces trouble. Love must be good and fine and according to nature, else why did it give such joy and beauty?

Natural as was this thought, she hid it from her

associates. Most women die with it unacknowledged, even to their own spoken thought. She would have been helped by talk with the Doctor, or at least with his wife. But there was a growing barrier between Mrs. Thatcher and herself, and the Doctor did not seem the same good friend. A change was impending in the Doctor's household and Rose felt it as one forecasts a storm.

When she went home at the close of her second year, she had a feeling that she would never again return to the old sweet companionship with Dr. Thatcher. He was too busy now, apparently, to give her the time he once seemed so glad to give. He never asked her to ride with him now. She was troubled by it, but concluded they were tired of her, and so she, too, grew cold and reserved.

*　*　*　*　*　*　*

The day she left, the Doctor, after he had driven Rose to the train, called his wife into the office.

"Sit down a moment, wife, I want to talk with you." He faced her bravely. "I guess we'd better arrange for Rose to go to one of the chapter-houses next year. There's no use beating around the bush — she takes up too much of my thought, and you know it and I know it."

It drew blood to say that. It took manhood to look his wife in the eyes then, but he did it.

"It isn't her fault, and it isn't yours — it isn't mine, as a matter of justice. Rose is just what she's always been, a good, sweet girl — I wouldn't have her see anything but friendly interest in my eyes for half my heart — I'm afraid she will, so — I guess ——— "

He was talking through set teeth. "I wish you'd tell her we can't offer her a home; I can't do it."

He rose and went to his wife. "My dear, don't cry — you've watched this thing come on in brave silence — not every wife would have kept silence so long. It won't break up our comradeship, will it, dear? We've jogged along so peacefully these fifteen years — we ought to overlook a little thing like this!" He smiled a little, then he stooped and put his arm about her.

"Come, give me a kiss, and let's adopt no more handsome girls till I'm sixty-five."

She rose and lifted her sad face to his. "It's my fault, if I ——— "

He kissed her and said: "No more of that! You're my faithful wife. What helps the matter materially is this — Rose thinks of me as a sober old settler now."

This ended a delicate matter so far as any outward showing ever defined his feeling, but the presence of the girl never left him. At night, as he sat at his desk at the hour which almost always used to bring Rose down from her room to discuss her lessons with him, he grew sad and lonely. "If I had a child," he said to himself, "I could bear it more easily."

When Rose returned, she went into one of the coöperative boarding-houses, and slowly drifted away from the Doctor and his family, never quite knowing why. It puzzled her for a time, and then she forgot it — in the fashion of youth.

CHAPTER XII

THE GATES OPEN WIDE

OF what avail the attempt to chronicle those days? They were all happy, and all busy, yet never alike. When the sun shone it was beautiful, and when the wind roared in the trees and the rain slashed like falling sails, it was equally glorious. On clear, crisp, bright winter days the air grew magical with bells, and the grating snarl of the ice-boat's rudder was thrilling as a lion's cry. It was apart from the world of care and politics and revolution.

There was fun, whirlwinds of it, at the chapter-house when studies were over, and there was fun at the professedly formal girl-banquets, where the chairman arose to say, " Gentlemen, the honor — " and everybody shrieked to see her pull an imaginary chin-whisker. There was more fun on winter nights, when loads of people packed into the bobtail mule-cars which tinkled up the snowy street with wonderful persistency, while the passengers trod on each other's toes and chaffed the driver. And O the wonderful nights under the stars, walking home with arm fast anchored in a fellow's grip! And strolls in summer beside the Lake, or dreamy hours floating at sunset in a boat which lay like a lily's petal, where skies of orange and purple met water of russet-gold and steely-blue.

And there was the glory of mounting also. One by one the formidable mesas of calculations, conjugations, argumentations, fell below her feet, and Rose grew tall in intellectual grace. She had no mental timidities. Truth with her came first, or if not first, certainly she had little superstitious sentiment to stand in the way. She was still the same impatient soul as when she shook her little fist at the Almighty's lightning.

It was this calm, subconscious assumption of truth's ultimate harmony with nature's first cause which delighted her as she entered its realm of physics and astronomy. Her enthusiasm for the hopeless study of the stars developed into a passion. They both exalted and saddened her.

When she lifted her eyes to them, and the illimitable distances of their orbits swept upon her with overwhelming power, she felt again the ache in the heart which came to her as a child on the bluff-top, when the world seemed spread before her feet. When she turned her face upward now it was to think of the awful void spaces there, of the mysteries of each flaming planet, and of the helplessness and weakness of the strongest man.

For a year she plunged into astronomy which had the allurement and the sombre aloofness of unrequited love. It harmonized well with her restless, limitless inner desire.

These sudden passions for this or that art were signs of strength and not of weakness. They sprang out of her swift and ready imagination, which enabled her to take on the personality of the artist, and to feel his joy of power. It was quite normal that she should desire to be successively circus rider, poet, and astronomer, and yet, now that her graduation was near, she was as far from a real decision as ever.

"What are you going to do after graduation?" Josie asked one day.

Rose grew grave. "I don't know. Go on studying somewhere, I suppose."

"I'm going to have a good time!"

"You're always having a good time, you little oriole." Rose had come to patronize Josie in these later days. "I envy you so," she sighed. "The world is so simple for you."

"I don't understand you when you go on like that — you'll come to-morrow and see my new dress, won't you?"

Graduation meant for Josephine the chance to wear a fetching gown, and be looked at by an immense crowd — and one extra man. This was supposed to be a secret, but everybody who cared to give it a thought knew of it and smiled at her as they would at a child. Josie could be nothing else but a child.

To most of the students graduation-day came rushing with sorrowful speed. It meant passing from sunlit lanes of maple and lilac out into the bleak highways of trade and labor. It meant the beginning of struggle with the pitiless ferocity of man and nature. As students they were not in the race for subsistence, but as citizens and professional men they were to be competitors in trades and crafts already overflowing.

As the great day drew near, a tremulous ecstasy came into the intercourse of the outgoing students — a joy made more precious by its certainty of passing.

To Rose graduation-day came as the sweetest, saddest day of her life. It seemed to close a gate upon something in her history. The smiling, yet mournful, faces of her friends, the wistful eyes of the young men who loved her, the rustle of leaves, the gleam of the water, the dapple of light and shade on the campus, the exaltation of the public moment, all these wondrous things rushed upon her like a flood, overwhelming her ambitions and desires, powerful as they were.

At last the books were closed and packed away. Graduation was at hand.

The commencement exercises began with the reception in Science Hall. The night fell slowly, and the fine new building grew alight story after story, and crowds began to stream in. The students led the way, rakish, full of airs, except when piloting their parents about. The fun had been almost furious all day.

There were many of the relatives of the students present, and often they stood out in sharp contrast with the decorations and with the joy of the young people. Beautiful girls might be seen leading bent and wrinkled fathers and mothers, who had sacrificed all they had for them. Rose wished for her father, and passionately desired to do something for him. He had written that he couldn't leave the farm, and so she wandered about with others, like herself, free. Everywhere the young men met her. She never escaped them for a moment, their pursuit was relentless.

The crowd swarmed into each room, where the professors stood beside show-cases, polite and patient, exhibiting machines, specimens, drawings. Sherbet was being served to the guests in the reception room, and music could be heard in the lower halls. Everywhere was the lisp of feet, the ripple of talk.

This was considered a bore by many of the pupils, for the peace-pipe ceremonial was preparing on the campus. Mysteriously, in the deep dusk, a huge heap of combustibles had been piled up on the wet grass, and one by one the two classes began to gather. There was a mutter of voices, a command, then a red flame flashed out, and with it the college yell soaring up from a little bunch of dark forms:

" RAH-RAH-RAH-WISCONSIN ! "

The stragglers on the walks turned toward the fire, like insects. They came in crawling dark lines like ants, across the wet grass. They formed a blue-black mass, lighted on one side by the orange light of the bonfire. The stars overhead grew green and dim in the light of the fire, and the encircling trees of the campus came out like silhouettes of purple-green cardboard.

The class rolled out its carpet for the girls and opened its boxes of long clay pipes. It seemed so much more important to Rose now that she stood there

in the centre as one of the graduating class. There
was not much talk. The two classes lined up and sang
song after song. Then the boys moved about showing
the girls how to light their pipes.

"You want to suck, not blow, on it!" a voice called
out, and everybody laughed dutifully. For a few moments all was laughter. The girls tried to assume the
airs of smokers, and puffed their kinnikinick furiously.
As they sang " There is a Tavern in our Town " and
" The Bullfrog in the Pool," they swung their pipes
with rakish grace — and their voices floated out and up
into the wreathing smoke of the fire, as deliciously
sweet as though their songs were hymns of praise as
they were hymns of youth.

The pipes needed constant relighting. In every
silence some girl cried out: " Oh, my pipe's gone
out!" One cried: " Give me a bite!" as if the pipe-
stem were taffy.

To Rose the whole ceremony was glorious. It carried
her out of herself. It gave her a glimpse into the world
which men keep to themselves, and, besides, she had
written the speech handing the pipe down to the custo-
dian of the succeeding class, a really admirable ceremony.

Here on this spot the red men warred and loved.
Here, with the sheen of lakes about, and the wild grass
under their feet, it was beautiful and appropriate that
they should be remembered by these young Western
sons and daughters of the white man.

The mock antagonism between seniors and juniors
seemed to have great meaning when Tom Harris spoke

the lofty phrases she had written for him, standing outlined against the soaring fire like a silhouette of velvet, his voice rolling out with lofty suspensive power.

"Here on the spot where our fathers have dwelt for countless suns and moons we ask for peace. We call upon you to bury the hatchet. Forgive and forget; you who have scars forgive, and you who have wrongs forget. Let all evil spirits be exorcised by the pipe. Here we break the arrow. Here we tender the sacred calumet. Brothers — sisters, we have spoken!"

The fire burned low. As they sat in circles on the ground and chanted their songs, the sky grew blacker, the trees melted into the darkness, the last wailing cadence floated into silence, and then subdued, tender, they rose and vanished, in pairs and groups, into the darkness like the songs they sang. The class of 189– had entered upon its long, long trail, some to the plains of failure, some to the mountains of victory.

This quaint and suggestive custom received new strength from the oration which Rose contributed. All felt its power and beauty. To the girls the whole ceremony was a rare and delicious piece of audacity and did them good. It gave them something to look back upon with laughter, into which a sigh and a little catching of the breath might also come.

Something elemental and primitive came to Rose amid all the laughter and song. What was she more than the swart women who had lived here and been wooed of men? Was there not something magnificent in their frank following of the trail of pure passion? They loved, and bore children, and ground at the corn-mills, and died as the female bison died, and other women came after them to do like unto them, to what end?

Some such questions, vague, ever shadowy, formless, moved Rose, as she lay down to sleep that night. Outside a mandolin twanged — the boys were serenading her, but she had not the wish to see them. She did not go to the window, as the other girls did, deliciously excited, almost hysteric with the daring of being possibly seen in their nightgowns. She kept sombre silence, stirred by profounder emotions than they were capable of.

She thought of William De Lisle but seldom now. In open daylight she was a little ashamed of her idolatry, but on nights like these, when love-songs and moonlight fused together, his figure came before her, not so clear a personality now, but as a type of beauty, as a centre of dreams, of something wild and free and splendid — something she was to attain to some good day. She had no thought of attaining him, but someone like unto him. Someone who was grand as her dream of heroes and loyal as her father.

It was characteristic of her that while the lovers singing without, made her companions utter hysterical laughter, she was sad and wished to be alone. Their desires were on the surface, shifting, sparkling, seeking kisses. Hers was dark, and deep down, sorrowful, savage, prophetic. Love with her a thing not to be uttered at all. She silenced all jests about it, and all familiarity on the part of her suitors she had put away.

During her first year she had allowed her lover to take her hand, as Carl used to do, because it seemed the usual thing, but after breaking off that entanglement she resolutely set to work to study, and no man had since considered himself her lover. To permit a caress now meant all the world to her. It meant change, undoing of plans, throwing away ambitions. It meant flinging herself to the immemorial sacrifice men had always demanded of women.

There were times when she felt the impulse to do this. She felt it that night as the clear voices of the serenaders came floating in at her window. What did it matter? What could she do in the mighty world? What did the Indian girl, when her lover sang from his canoe among the water-lilies in the lake? Why not go to one of these good, merry young men and be a wife? What did it matter — her ambition — her hope? "I will," she said, and a wild rush of blood choked her breathing, "I'll end it all."

But the singing died away, the moonlight vanished out of the room, and the passionate longing and tumult of her blood grew slowly quiet, and she slept.

When the sun rose there was no man in her world who could have won her consent to marriage. Her ambitions rose like the sun, buoyant as young eagles, while the singers of the night before were hapless fireflies, tangled in the dewy grass, their love-light dim, their singing lost in silence.

She was not done with this problem, however. She saw in one man's eyes something to be answered. She had her answer ready, though she hoped to escape the ordeal. He hovered close about her all the morning, and came by the chapter-house for her, but she had gone to the chapel.

She felt a little guilty toward him. She had attended concerts with him. She had accepted his company now and again 'because she liked him and because — well, it was convenient, and by selecting him she escaped the attentions of others. She had seemed to acquiesce in his proprietorship of her, and yet always when alone she had tried to show him that they could be nothing more than friends. This he had persistently misunderstood.

Being almost the tallest of her classmates, she led the march into the chapel for the final ceremonies, a splendid and terrible moment, toward which they had looked for weeks, and for which they had elaborately planned dresses and procedure.

It was all so wistfully beautiful. The cool, spacious hall filled with hushed people; the vivid green trees looking in at the windows and the soft air burdened with bee songs and the smell of flowers. The June sunlight dappled the lawn with marvels of shade and shine. The music seemed to wail as they marched, and the rustling stir and murmur of comment helped to unnerve them all, even the men.

The speaker looked down upon them with comprehension. He was an Eastern man and an old man, also he was a poet. He was just, and he had seen how wholesome and fine this coeducational school was. The day was beautiful to him as to them, and he comprehended their feelings well and looking down into their pensive faces, was aware of the sorrowful arching of their brows, the sad droop of their lips.

His shaggy head drooped forward as he talked to them, till his kind old face lined with genial wrinkles, seemed to grow beautiful and tender and maternal. He had reared many children of his own, and he now took the young people into his heart. He told them much of his life and trials — how work was in the world for them; play, too — but work, hard work, glorious work! work for humanity as well as for themselves. He conveyed to them something of the spirit of altruism into which the world seemed about to enter on its orbit as it swings through clouds of star-dust.

They cheered him when he ended, and then the president, in brief words, presented their diplomas. Among them now were bitten lips, and tremulous chins and tearful eyes. The doors had closed behind them and they faced the whole world, it seemed. For years they had studied here, in storm and sun, but now they remembered only the sunlight, all fused and blended into one radiant vista.

At the moment when they rose for their final benediction, a splendid, snowy cloud sailed across the sun, and the room darkened mystically. A shudder of exquisite pleasure and pain thrilled Rose, and a little moan pushed from her throat; but the shadow lifted, the organ sounded out a fine brave strain, and the class of

189– was ended. It was now a group of men and women facing the open road.

With low words of greeting and congratulation the graduates and their friends lingered about the chapel. Slowly it emptied and the hill grew populous again with groups of leisurely moving figures.

There were scholars showing their parents about the grounds, there were groups of visiting towns-people, and there were the lovers, two and two, loitering, wandering (she in dainty white gown, he in cap and jacket), two and two in world-old, sex-old fashion. They lay on the banks and watched the boats on the gleaming lake where other lovers were. They threaded the hill-paths where the thrush moved with quick rustle, and the pale wood-flowers peered above the fragrant mosses. They stood on the beach skipping pebbles, he lithe and laughing, she tender, palpitating, wistful and sad, or fitfully gay. Everywhere laughter had a solemn sweet undertone; "Good-by!" trembled so close to "I love you!"

Rose saw young Harris approaching, and a faintness took hold upon her limbs. He was at his princeliest estate — never would he be handsomer. His summer suit set close to his agile and sinewy figure. His cap rested lightly on his curly hair. His frank blue eyes were laughing, but his lips were tremulous with feeling.

"Well, Rose, all the girls have deserted me so I'm glad to find you alone," he said, but she knew he was never deserted. "Let's take a walk. The whole school seems to be divided off into teams. Looks as if the whole crowd would trot in double harness, don't it ? "

She did not reply, he hardly expected her to do so.

" Going to the ball with me to-night, aren't you ? "

" No, I guess not."

" I was in hopes you'd change your mind."

" I can't dance those new-fangled figures."

" Oh, you'd catch on in a jiffy. You should have gone out more."

They moved down the hill to the beach road, and as they walked Harris talked, talked against time, he would have said. They strolled on past the small boys fishing, past other low-voiced couples, out into comparative solitude where the farms began. She knew what was coming, but she could not stop, could not then turn back.

They came at last to a grassy little knoll which looked out upon the lake, and there he laughingly spread out his handkerchief for her.

" Sit here, my liege lady ! "

It was red clover, and its powerful fragrance swept upon her with a vision of the hay-field at home.

Harris lay down below her so that he could see her face, and the look in his eyes made her shiver again. Nothing so beautiful and powerful and pagan-free had come to her since that day when she danced with Carl beneath the dappling leaves, when woman's passion first stirred within her. The sailing clouds, the clicking insects, the smell of leaves and flowers all strove on the side of the lover.   It was immemorial, this scene, this impulse.

"Well, Rose, this is our last day at school, and what I want to know is this, is it the last we shall see of each other ? "

She made an effort and answered :

"Why, no, I hope not."

"You hope not — then there is hope for me ?   Confound it, Rose, I'm not going to talk in riddles.   You're the only girl in the world for me."   He took her hand.   "And I can't live without you.   You are going to live with me, aren't you, Rose ? "

She shook her head, but tears dropped upon his hand. He allured her like the sunshine, this eager young lover.

His keen eyes perceived a lack of decision in this head shake.   He held her hand and his fingers caressed her wrist.   Unconsciously, with pure intent, he used all the wiles of men, which women love, yet dread. His voice grew vibrant, yet remained low, his eyes spake in subtler language than his tongue.   His wrist touched her knee, his hair moved in the soft wind.

"I can't bear to go home without you, Rose, darling. Come, tell me, don't you care for me at all, not the least bit ? "

She tried to draw her hand away, but he held it and continued :

"I've got everything all planned.   I'm going into law with my father.   I've got plans for a house, and we'll begin life together to-day —— "

His physical charm united itself some way with the

smell of clover, the movement of the wind and the warm flood of sunshine. She had never loved him, though she had always liked him, but now something sweet and powerful, something deep buried, rose in her heart and shortened her breath. Her face burned, her throat was swollen shut, her face was distorted, for one moment she was mastered.

Then the swift revulsion came, and she drew her hand away and sprang up.

"No!" she cried, harshly and bitterly, "I can't do it; it is impossible. Go away!"

Then the blood slowly fell away from her neck and face, and her heart ceased to pound, her eyes cleared and she grew gentle again, seeing his pained and frightened face.

"I didn't mean that — I didn't mean to be so rough, Tom, but it's no use. I don't want to marry you, nor anybody else. All I want is to be let alone. I'm going to Chicago. I want to see the world. I can't be shut up in a little town like Lodi. I want to see people — thousands of people. I want to see what the world is like. I may go to Europe before I get done with it. I'm going to study art. I'm going to be great. I can't marry anyone now."

She poured out her confidences in swift, almost furious protest. She had never confided to him so much before.

His pain was not so overpowering but he found strength to say:

"I thought you were going to be a writer."

She flushed again. "Well, I am. But I'm going to be a painter, too. I'm going home," she said, abruptly, and in such wise they walked along the returning way.

The glamour was gone from the young man's hair and eyes. She saw him as he was, light, boyish, shallow. His physical charm was lost, and a sort of disgust of his supple waist and rounded limbs came upon her, and disgust at herself for that one moment of yielding weakness; and also the keen fear of having been unjust, of having given him a claim which she was repudiating, troubled her.

He made one last attempt.

"Rose, I wish you'd reconsider. What can you do in the world?"

"I don't know. I can be my own master for one thing," she replied. "I can see the world for another thing — and besides, I don't want to marry anyone just yet." Her voice was abrupt, merciless, and the young fellow bowed his head to his sentence. She was too mysterious and powerful for him to understand.

"What could I do in Lodi? Gossip with old women and grow old. I know those towns. I had rather live in the country than in one of those flat little towns."

"But I'll go to the city with you if you want me to. I can get a place there. I know two men ———"

"No, no! I can't do it. I want to be free. I've got something to do, and — I don't care for you ———"

"Well, go to the ball with me to-night, won't you?" he pleaded.

"Yes, if you never speak about this to me again."

He promised; of course he promised.   Standing where he did he would have promised anything.

It was a singular and lovely ball.   The people came together simply and quietly, on foot, or on the tinkling mule-car.

There were no ultra-fashionable dresses, and very little jewelry.   The men came in various cuts of evening coats, and the girls wore simple white or blue or mauve dresses, beneath which their supple untrammelled waists, and firm rounded limbs moved with splendid grace.

It was plain they were not all practised dancers. Some of the young men danced with hands waggling at the wrist, and the girls did not know all the changes, but laughter was hearty and without stint.

Around the walls sat or stood the parents of the dancers, dignified business men and their wives, keen-eyed farmers and village merchants and lawyers. There were also the alumni from all over the West, returned to take part in the exercises, to catch a glimpse of the dear old campus.   It was all a renewal of youth to them. Many came from the prairies.   Some came from the bleak mountain towns, and the gleam of the lakes, the smell of grass, the dapple of sunlight on the hillside affected them almost to tears.   Now they danced with their wives and were without thought or care of business.

Professors waltzed with their pupils, and husbands with their wives.   Lovely, slim young girls dragged their

K

bearded old fathers out into the middle of the floor, amid much laughter, and the orchestra played "Money-Musk" and "Old Zip Coon" and "The Fireman's Dance" for their benefit.

Then the old fellows warmed up to it, and danced right manfully, so that the young people applauded with swift clapping of their hands. Plump mothers took part in the quaint old-fashioned figures, and swung and balanced and "sashayed" in a gale of fun.

It was a beautiful coming together of the university. It represented the unspoiled neighborliness and sex *camaraderie* of the West. Its refinement was not finicky, its dignity was not frigidity, and its fun was frank and hearty. May the inexorable march of wealth and fashion pass by afar off, and leave us some little of these dear old forms of social life.

It had a tender and pensive quality, also. The old were re-living the past, and all expressed an unconscious feeling of the transitoriness of these tender and careless hours. Smiles flashed forth on the faces of the girls like hidden roses disclosed in deep hedges by a passing wind-gust, to disappear again in pensive, thoughtful deeps.

Rose danced with Dr. Thatcher, who took occasion to say:

"Well, Rose, you leave us soon."

"Yes, to-morrow, Doctor."

"What are your plans?"

"I don't know; I shall go home this summer, but I want to go to Chicago next winter."

"Aha, you go from world to world. Rose, you will

do whatever you dream of — *provided* you don't marry."
He said this as lightly as he could, but she knew he
meant it.

" There isn't much danger of that," she said, trying
to laugh.

" Well, no, perhaps not." They fell into a walk,
and moved slowly away, just outside the throng of
dancers.

" Now, mark you, I don't advise you at all. I have
realized from the first a fatality in you. No one can
advise you. You must test all things for yourself.
You are alone; advice cannot reach you nor influence
you except as it appeals to your own reason. To most
women marriage is the end of ambition; to you it may
be an incentive. If you are big enough, you will succeed in spite of being wife and mother. I believe in
you. Can't you come and see me to-morrow ? I want
to give you letters to some Chicago people."

The company began to disperse, and the sadness impending fell upon them all. One by one good-bys
were said, and the dancers one and all slipped silently
away into the night.

CHAPTER XIII

THE WOMAN'S PART

IT was all over at last, the good-bys, the tearful embraces, the cheery waving of hands, and Rose was off for home. There were other students on the train, but they were freshmen whom she did not know. At the moment it seemed as if she were leaving all that was worth while — five years of the most beautiful time of her life lay behind her.

She had gone there a country girl, scared and awkward. She was now a woman (it seemed to her) and the time for action of some sort had come. She did not look to marriage as a safe harbor. Neither had she regarded it as an end of all individual effort, as many of her companions unequivocally had done.

After her experiences during those last three days, she had moods when sex seemed an abomination, and she wished for freedom from courtship. She already had a premonition that she was of those who are destined to know much persecution of men.

Her strong, forceful, full-blooded, magnetic beauty could not be hidden so deep under sober garments but that the ever-seeking male eye quickly discovered it.

As she entered the car she felt its penetrating, remorseless glare, and her face darkened, though she was no longer exposed to the open insults of brakemen and drummers. There was something in the droop of her eyelids and in the curve of her mouth which kept all men at a distance, even the most depraved. She was not a victim — a girl to be preyed upon. She was quite evidently a proud, strong woman, to be sued for by all flatteries and attentions.

The train whirled along over the familiar route, and the land was most beautiful. Fresh grass everywhere, seas of green flashing foliage, alternating with smooth slopes of meadow whereon cattle fed, yet she saw little of it. With sombre eyes turned to the pane she thought and thought.

What was to be done now? That was the question. For a year she had been secretly writing verse and sending it to the magazines — only to have it all returned to her. It made her flush with humiliation to think that they came back to her with scarcely a civil word of encouragement. Evidently she was wrong. She was not intended for a writer after all. She thought of the stage, but she did not know how to get upon the stage.

The train drew steadily forward, and familiar lines of hill-tops aroused her, and as she turned her face toward home, the bent and grizzled figure of her father came to her mind as another determining cause. He demanded something of her now after nearly five years' absence from home, for he had paid her way — made it possible for her to be what she was.

There he sat holding his rearing horses and watching, waiting for her.   She had a sudden, swift realization of his being a type as he sat there, and it made her throat fill, for it seemed to put him so far away, seemed to take away something of his sweet dignified personality.

There was a crowd of people on the platform.   Some of them she knew, some of them she did not.   She looked very fine and ladylike to John Dutcher as she came down the car-steps, the brakeman assisting her, with elaborate and very respectful courtesy.

The horses pranced about, so that John could not even take her hand, and so she climbed into the buggy alone.

" Carl will take care of your trunk," he said. " Give him the check."

She turned to Carl, whom she had not observed. He bowed awkwardly.

" How de do, Rosie," he said, as he took the check. He wore brown denims, and a broad hat, and looked strong and clumsy.

She had no time to talk with him, for the restive horses whirled away up the street.   The air was heavy with the scent of clover, and the bitter-sweet, pungent smells of Lombardy poplar-trees.

They rode in silence till the village lay behind them and the horses calmed down.

" Cap's a perfect fool about the cars," said John. " But I had to take him ; Jennie's getting too heavy, I darsent take her."

" How is the stock ? "

"Oh, all right. We had a big crop of lambs this spring. The bees are doing well, but the clover don't seem to attract 'em this year. The corn looks well, except down near the creek — it's always been wet there in rainy seasons, you remember." He gave other reports concerning stock.

Rose felt for the first time the unusualness of this talk. All her life she had discussed such things with him, but on previous vacations she had not been conscious of its startling plainness, but it came to her now with a sudden hot flush, that such talk being reported of her to the Doctor and Mrs. Thatcher would shock them.

There was something strange in her father's manner, an excitement very badly concealed, which puzzled her. He drove with almost reckless swiftness up the winding coolly road. He called her attention to the wayside crops and succeeded in making her ask:

"Father, what in the world is the matter with you? I never knew you to act like this."

John laughed. "I'm a little upset, getting you home again, that's all."

She caught a gleam of new shingles through the trees.

"What have you been building?"

"Oh, nothing much — new granary — patchin' up a little," he replied, evasively. When they whirled into the yard she was bewildered — the old cottage was gone and a new house stood in its place; a big white structure, still littered about with lumber.

John broke into a laugh.

"How's that for a new granary?"

"Oh, father, did you do that *for me?*"

"For you and me together, Rosie."

They sat in the carriage and looked at it. Rose peered through tear-blurred lids. He loved her so — this bent old father! He had torn down the old home and built this *for her.*

Her aunt came out on the side porch. "Hello, Rosie, just in time! The shortcake is about ready. Ain't you comin' in?"

John gave the team up to the hired hand (who stared at Rose with wondering eyes) and then they walked upon the front porch and in at the front door. It was new — so new it glistened everywhere and was full of the fragrance of new lumber and the odor of paint.

"I didn't get any new furniture," John said. "I thought I'd let you do that."

Rose turned and put her arms about his neck.

"You dear old daddy, what can I do for you, you're so good to me?"

"There now, don't mind, I'm paid for it right now. I just want you to enjoy it, that's all, and if any feller comes around and you like him, why you can bring him right here. It's big enough and I'm ready to let the farm any time."

Rose understood his purpose to the uttermost line. He had built this to keep her at home. How little he comprehended her, to think that she could marry and bring her husband home to this place!

She kissed him and then they peered into all the rooms.

"Come here — I've got something to show you," he said, mysteriously. "I just *determined* to have it, no matter what it cost." He pushed open a door at the head of the stairway, calling, triumphantly:

"There — how's that — a bath-room!"

For an instant she felt like laughing. Then she looked at his kind and simple face and broke down again and cried.

John understood now that this was only her way of being glad, so he just patted her shoulder, and got her a chair, and waited for her to dry her eyes.

"Yes, sir," he went on, "cost me a hundred dollars to put that in, say nothin' of the fixin's. I had to have special set of eave-spouts made to run the water into a cistern on top of the kitchen. I thought of bringing the water from the spring, but that's a little hard."

They went down to supper at last, he full of talk, she very quiet. His loquacity was painful to her, for it seemed to indicate growing age and loneliness.

The meagreness of the furniture and tableware never struck her so forcibly as now, lost in the big new house. Intellectual poverty was shown also in the absence of books and newspapers, for John Dutcher read little, even of political newspapers, and magazines were quite outside his experimental knowledge till Rose began to bring a few home with her in her later vacations.

There were no elegancies at their table — that too was borne in upon her along with the other disturbing things. It was as if her eyes had suddenly been opened to all the intolerable meagreness of her old-time life.

" I didn't buy any carpets or wall-paper, Rosie; I thought you'd like to do that yourself," John explained, as she looked around the bare room.

But outside all was beautiful, very beautiful. Under the trees the sinking sun could be seen hanging just above the purple-green hills to the northwest. Robins clucked, orioles whistled, a ring-dove uttered its never-changing, sorrowful, sweet love-note. A thrush, high on a poplar, sang to the setting sun a wonderful hymn, and the vividly green valley, with its white houses and red barns, was flooded with orange light, heaped and brimming full of radiance and fragrance.

And yet of what avail the beauty of sky and grain to a girl without love, to a brain which craved activity, not repose? Vain were sunset sky, flaming green slopes and rows of purple hills to eyes which dreamed of cities and the movement of masses of men. She was young, not old; ambitious, not vegetative. She was seeking, seeking, and to wait was not her will or wish.

The old man perceived no difficulties in the way. Rose was educated at last. He had patiently sent her to school and now it was over; she was to be his daily pride and comfort as of olden time. Without knowing it he had forged the chains round her with great skill. Every carpet she bought would bind her to stay. She was to select the wall-paper, and by so doing, proclaim her intention to conform and to content herself in the new home.

She rose the next morning feeling, in spite of all disturbing thought, the wonderful peace and beauty of the coolly, while her heart responded to the birds, rioting in song as never before — orioles, thrushes, bobolinks, robins, larks — their voices wonderful and brilliant as the sunlight which streamed in upon her new, uncarpeted floor.

As she looked around at the large, fine new room, she thought of the slant-roofed little attic in which she had slept so many years. Yes, decidedly there would be pleasure in furnishing the house, in making her room pretty with delicate drapery and cheerful furniture.

She began to plan, only to break off — it seemed in some way to be deceit. No, before she did anything to it she must tell him she could not stay here, and she went down to breakfast with that resolution tightly clutched in her teeth, but when she saw his dear old smiling face she could not speak the word. He was so pathetically happy. She had never seen him so demonstrative, and this mood showed her how deeply he had missed her.

Now that she was home for good, there was no need of concealing his exceeding great joy of her daily presence with him. She remembered all the brave words he had spoken to her in order to make her feel he did not suffer when she was happy at school. Fortunately at breakfast he was full of another subject.

" I s'pose you heard that Carl is to be married ? " he announced rather than asked her.

She looked up quickly — " No, is he ? To whom ? "

"Little Sary Wilson."

"Well, I'm very glad to hear it," she said, quietly.

Some way, at that moment she seemed more alien to him than ever before, and he looked across at her in wonder. How ladylike she was in her tasty dress. How white her hands were! And it was wonderful to think she could sit so quietly and hear of Carl's approaching marriage. He remembered the time when he called them to his knee, the two young rogues. She was thinking of that too. It was far in the past, yet, far as it was, it was still measurable, and a faint flush crept over her face.

The first day she spent in looking about the farm with John. Toward evening she climbed the hills alone, and spent an hour on the familiar slope. It helped her to look down on her plans and her daily life, and the next day she met the question direct.

"Well, Rosie, when will you go to Tyre and do our buyin'?"

"Oh, not yet. I want to look around a few days first."

"All right — you're the captain! Only we can't have any company till we get some furniture."

True enough! there was the excuse for buying the furniture; even if she were to go to the city she would be home during the summer, and it was necessary to entertain her friends. The fever seized her thereupon, and she plunged into planning and cataloguing. They had but little to spend, and she was put to her wit's end to passably furnish the house.

This work filled in the first week or two of her stay, and she suffered less from loneliness than she had anticipated; it came only at intervals, just before going to sleep, or in the morning, as she made her toilet for each new but almost eventless day.

As the home came to look pretty and complete, she thought of asking Josie to come on to visit her, and finally wrote her, and when she had promised to come, there was something to look forward to.

Meanwhile, she found something interposing between herself and her old friends. She meant to be just the same as ever, and at first she seemed to succeed, but soon found herself not listening to them, or looking at them with alien musing eyes. She heard their harsh, loud voices, not their words, and she saw their stiff, ungraceful gestures instead of the fancy-work and worked-over dresses which they were showing her. At such times they looked at each other with significant nods. Other young people had gone away to school without acquiring airs, why should she?

It was not her knowledge of books, but of manners, which made her alien. She was educated above them, too. Her thoughts were higher than theirs, and she could not play the hypocrite. She was not interested in them; for the most part they bored her and in a few cases the misunderstanding grew into anger and distrust.

Carl drove over once with his bride-elect, and they all sat stiffly in the front room for one distressing hour; then they left, never to come again.

Sarah counted the visit not all in vain, however, for

she quite closely reproduced Rose's shirt-waist the following week — that much she got out of the call.   Carl
was awed and troubled a little by the failure of his bride
to get on with Rose, and Rose was bitter over it in heart.
She could not see the fun of all this, as so many story-
writers had done.   It was all pitiful and bitter and bar-
ren, and to eat with the knife and drink coffee with a
loud, sipping sound were inexcusable misdemeanors to
her then overwrought temper.

Josie came in like a joyous bird.   She fluffed down
off the train like a bunch of lilac bloom one July day.

"Oh, what a funny little town," she said, after kissing
Rose how-de-do.   "Are we to ride in a carriage?   Oh,
I'm *so* disappointed!"

"Why so?"

"Oh, I wanted to ride on a hay-cart or dray or whatever it is.   Mr. Dutcher, I'm so glad to see you." She
sprang upon John and kissed him, "like a swaller lightin'
on me," he said afterward.   It astonished, but gratified
him.

"Do you live far out in the country — the real country?" she asked.

"Well, you'd think so if you had to haul corn over
it in the spring," he replied.

"I'd like to haul corn over it," she replied.   "May
I?"

"You can do anything you want to," John said.

Josie got at the picturesque qualities of the people.
They all interested her and amused her like the cattle
without horns, and the guinea-hens which clacked like

clocks, and the tadpoles in the marsh. She had no personal relations — no responsibilities toward them such as Rose felt were inescapably hers. Josie had no responsibilities at all, none under heaven!

She laughed at the ill-made dresses, and winked over the heads of the old wives when they talked in dialect, and made fun of the boys who came courting her, and she sang "Where did they Get those Hats?" after coming out of the church.

Rose laughed and yet suffered, as one might whose blood relatives were ridiculed. It was a new experience to John Dutcher to have one about who cried out at every familiar thing as if it were the seventh wonder. The summer visitor had never before penetrated to his farm, and all the women he had ever known could talk about cattle and drainage and wool-washing almost like men. In his interest and desire to do the part of entertainer, he pushed on into subjects which the girl listened to with wonder-wide eyes and a flushed face.

He talked to her as he would to Rose, about "farrer cows" and other commonplaces of stock-raising, to which Rose would have listened abstractedly or with a slight feeling of disgust. To Josie it was deeply fascinating, and just a little bit like reading a forbidden book. It affected her a little unwholesomely, just as it would have made Ed, the hand, spasmodically guffaw to stand before the Venus de Milo — use and custom do much.

She sometimes asked questions which she would not have dared ask to her uncle, for John Dutcher was beyond sex; indeed, he had always been a man of pure

heart and plain speech.   Even in his youth he had been
perfectly free from any sensuality, and now in his later
middle life sex was a fact, like the color of a horse or a
squash, and all that pertained to it he talked of, on the
same plane.   It did not occur to him that he was going
beyond the lines of propriety in explaining to this delicate little woman various vital facts of stock-raising.

Josie sometimes went back to Rose smilingly, and
told her what had taken place.

"Why didn't you ask me — you little goose?   I
never thought you didn't know those things.   We farm
girls know all that when we are toddlers.   We can't
help it."

All this should have been tonic, thoroughly wholesome
to the dainty, over-bred girl, and so it ultimately became, though it disturbed her at the time.

The two girls went out into the meadows and upon
the hills almost daily.   They sought wild strawberries
in the sunny spots amid the hazel brush.   They buried
themselves in the hay in the field and climbed on the
huge loads with John and rode to the barn.   They
drank water out of the spring, lying flat on the ground ;
Rose showed how it was done.   They went up on the hill-
sides under the edges of great ledges of water-washed
sandstone, where Rose had made her playhouse in her
childhood, and she drew forth from the crevices in the
rocks the queer little worn pieces of rock which she had
once called horses and cows and soldiers.

Rose had not been so girlish since her first vacation
from school in Madison.   She romped and laughed with

the ever-joyous Josie, and together they grew brown and strong. But there came into the lusty, splendid joy of these days hours of almost sorrowful silence and dreaming. It all ended in nothing, this attempt at amusement.

Here in the riant and overflowing opulence of July, time without love's companionship was time wasted. Of what avail these soft winds, the song of birds, the gleam and lift and shimmer of leaves, if love were not there to share it?

Josie frankly confessed the name of the one she wished to share it with, but Rose looked into the sky and remained silent. Her soul was still seeking, restless, avid, yet evermore discerning, evermore difficult to satisfy.

They fell into long talks on marriage, and Rose confided to her some of her deepest thoughts, though she well knew how incapable this little twittering sparrow was of understanding her.

" I want to know the men who think the great thoughts of the world," she said once as they lay under the beeches on the hillside, far above the haying field. " I don't want to marry — I only want to know men who can lift me up by their great plans. I want to forget myself in work of some kind — I don't know what kind — any kind that will make me big and grand in my life. I can't stand these little petty things here in this valley; these women drive me crazy with their talk of butter and eggs and made-over bonnets."

" I think they're funny," said Josie. " They talk so loud, and they get so interested in such queer things."

L

Rose fell silent again for Josie was of equally petty type, only her affairs happened to be of a different sort, not larger, only different, a chatter of dress and teas.

"Oh, for a nice man!" sighed Josie. "Why didn't you tell me there weren't any nice men up here?"

Meanwhile the lack of men was not apparent. Hardly a day but some young fellow from Tyre or the Siding made bold to hitch his horses to the fence before Dutcher's place. Rose was annoyed and gave most of them scant courtesy. Josie, however, always saw them and managed to have great amusement out of their embarrassment.

Like summer girls in general she thought any man better than no man at all. Rose, however, could not endure a love-glance from any of them. She found her household duties pressing when they called, and Josie entertained them, and afterward entertained Rose by mimicking their looks and tones. It was very funny to see her screw her little face into quaint grimaces to represent her suitors' bashful grins and side-glances.

They were not always bashful, it must be said. Sometimes they were distressingly bold, and they came to the point of offensive warfare with a readiness and assurance which scared the little coquette. She had never seen anything like it.

Rose found Josie entertaining in any mood.

CHAPTER XIV

AGAIN THE QUESTION OF HOME-LEAVING

BUT the day came at last when Josie must say good-by, and then Rose's essential loneliness swept back upon her in a bitter flood. That night she walked her room in her naked feet, with her handkerchief stifling her sobs, so that John might not hear. She fought it out there (she supposed) and ended at last by determining to sacrifice herself to her father.

He could not be deserted, he needed her so, now that he was growing old and a little weaker. She must put away her vague, ambitious dreams of work in the great world and apply herself to making him happy.

And yet to what end was all her study, she thought, during these later years? Could it be applied to doing him good? Her indifferent talent as a musician seemed the only talent which gave him joy. He cared nothing — knew nothing of the things she loved and thought about!

Was her life, like his, to come down to the raising of cattle and the breeding of sheep? Was not his office served in educating her? Should not the old be sacrificed to the young?

All these devilish questions came into her mind like flashes of lurid light, but they all paled and faded before this one unchangeable radiance: he was her father, tender, loving, simple, laborious, and old.

She fell asleep after hours of writhing agony, worn out, yet triumphant — she imagined.

But she was not. Day followed day, each one seemingly more hopeless than the other. This consideration beat like a kneil into her brain, love could never come to her. Marriage with these young men was no longer possible. Love was out there, somewhere in the great world, in the city, among artists and music-lovers, and men of great thought and great deeds. Her powerful physical, mental, and emotional womanhood rebelled at this thought of lovelessness; like the prisoner of old, bound in a sunless cavern where the drip-drop of icy water fell upon his brain, she writhed and seemed like to go mad.

This was the age of cities. The world's thought went on in the great cities. The life in these valleys was mere stagnant water, the great stream of life swept by far out and down there, where men and women met in millions. To live here was to be a cow, a tadpole! Grass grew here, yes — but she could not live on grass. The birds sang here, yes — but there were Patti and Duse and Bernhardt out there in the world.

Here you could arise at five o'clock to cook breakfast and wash dishes, and get dinner, and sweep and mend, and get supper, and so on and on till you rotted, like a post stuck in the mud. Her soul would wither in such a life. She was already slipping back into shiftlessness, into minute untidiness — into actual slovenliness. There was no stimulus in these surroundings, she told herself; everything was against her higher self.

Once she had read a sentence from Lowell which flamed upon her mind now each time she mused upon her lot.

" The wilderness is all right for a vacation, but all wrong for a lifetime."

She considered the coolly a wilderness. It had nothing for her but nature, and nature palls upon a girl of twenty, with red blood in her veins, and splendid dreams in her heart.

Out there was her ideal. " Out there is the man who is to fill out my life," she uttered to herself, softly, so that only her inner ear heard.

So she argued, fought, wept, surrendered, and went to battle again. While all about her, John and his sister moved tranquilly to their daily duties, calm as the cattle in the meadows. To the discerning eye it was a suggestive picture, this dark, gloomy, restless girl seated opposite those serene, almost stolid faces, to whom " the world " was a breeze blowing in the tree-tops. She had the bearing of a rebellious royal captive — a duchess in exile. Mrs. Diehl and the hired man were the peasants who waited upon her, but ate with her — and her father was the secure freeholder, to whom kings were obscure, world-distant diseases.

Then the equinoctial storms came on, and days of dull, cold, unremitting rain confined her to the house.

The birds fell silent, the landscape, blurred with gray mist, looked grim and threatening, and there was prophecy of winter in the air. The season seemed to have rushed into darkness, cold, and decay, in one enormous bound. The hills no longer lifted buoyant crests to heaven; they grew cheerless and dank as prison walls.

One night Rose spoke. She had always been chary of caresses; even when a child she sat erect upon her father's knee, with a sober little face, and when she grew sleepy she seldom put her hands to his neck, but merely laid her head on his breast and went to sleep. John understood her in all this, but was he not of the same feeling? Love that babbled spent itself; his had no expression.

His heart was big with pride and affection when his splendid girl came over and put her arms about his neck, and put her forehead down on his shoulder.

"O pappa John, you're so good to me — I'm ashamed — I don't deserve this new house!"

"Oh, yes y' do, daughter." His voice when he said "daughter" always made her cry, it was deep and tender like the music of water. It stood for him in the place of "dear" and "darling," and he very, very seldom spoke it. All this made it harder for her to go on.

"No, I don't, father — Oh, father, I can't stay here — I can't bear to stay here now!"

"Why not, Rosie?"

"Oh, because it's so lonesome for me. There is nobody for me to talk to" (she had to use phrases he could understand), "and I want to go on with my studies."

John considered a moment.

" But, Rosie, seems to me you've got enough ; you're graduated."

Rose saw the hopelessness of making him understand that, so she went back.

" It's so lonesome for me here, pappa John ! "

He considered again.   " I s'pose it is.   Well, you can go to the Siding every day if you want to.   Hitch up old Doll every day —— "

" I don't care for the Siding; it's just as lonesome there for me.   I want to go to Chicago."

John grew rigid.   " Chicago !   What you want to do there ? "

" I want to study, pappa.   I want to go on with my work.   I'll come home summers just the same.   I'll come home Christmas if you want me to.   It won't cost much, I'll live just as cheap as I can —— "

" 'Tain't that, 'tain't that, Rose," he said.   Then he lifted his head and looked around.

She read his thought, and the tears came to her eyes in blinding rush.

" I know, pappa.   It's terrible to go now, when you've built this nice home for me, but what can I do ?   It's so lonesome here !   I thought maybe I'd get used to it, but it gets worse.   I can't stay here this winter.   You *must* let me go.   I'll go crazy if I stay here all winter. I must go out into the world.   I want to be an artist. I want to see great people.   I can't stay here, pappa John ! "

The terrible earnestness of every sentence stabbed

John Dutcher's heart like a poniard thrust. He put her away and rose stiffly.

"Well, well, Rosie, if you want to go —— "

He did not finish, but turned tremblingly and walked out. She remained on the floor near his chair and watched him go, her soul sick with wretchedness.

Why was the world so ordered? Why must she torture that beautiful, simple soul? Why was it that all her high thoughts, her dreams, her ambitions, her longings, seemed to carry her farther away from him?

She could have beaten her head against the wall in her suffering. She rose at last and crawled slowly to her room, and abandoned herself to black, rayless hopelessness.

John Dutcher went out to the hedgerow and sat down on a stool. Around him bees were humming in the wet clover. The calves thrust their inquiring noses through the fence and called to him. The rain-clouds were breaking up, and the sun was striking under the flying canopy at the west.

It was the bitterest moment of his life, since his wife's death. His eyes were opened to his fate; he saw what he had done; he had educated his daughter out of his world. Never again would she be content in the coolly beside him. He saw how foolish he had been all these years, to suppose he could educate and keep her. For a moment he flamed with resentment and said to himself:

"I wish she had never seen a book."

Then he grew tender. He saw her again in her

little blue apron with its pockets full of wheat — he saw her blowing hair, her sunny face; he heard again the wind-tossed chatter of her cunning lips. He ran swiftly over her development — how tall she grew and how splendid she was now, the handsomest girl in the coolly, and he softened. She was right. Who was there of the neighborhood (or even in Tyre) good enough for her?

So he rose to a conception which had never come to him before, and even now it was formlessly vast; he felt the power of the outside world, and reached to a divination of the fatality of it all. It had to be, for it was a part of progress. He was old and bent and dull. She was young, gloriously young. The old must give way to the young, while she was the one to be bowed down to. She was a queen and he was her subject.

With these conceptions in his mind he went back and looked for her. He called her softly, but she did not hear, she was sobbing deep into her pillow. He came up the stairs and saw her lying face downward on her bed. His heart rose in his throat, because it was a terrible thing to see his imperious girl weep.

"Rosie, old pappa John surrenders. You're right and he's an old dummy."

She turned her face upon him.

"No, you're right. We won't be separated."

"But we ain't goin' to be." He came over and sat down on the edge of the bed.

"You'll come home summers, and maybe I'll go to Chicago winters."

Her face flashed into a smile. She flung her arms about him again.

"Oh, will you, pappa John?"

"Course I will. Wait till you see me in a spike-tail coat and a boiled shirt. I'll astonish them city dudes."

Rose laughed a little wildly, and tightened her clasp about his neck.

"You're my dear old pappa John."

She went at once to her desk and wrote a letter to Mary Compton, an old schoolmate who had gone to Chicago, and whose guidance to bed and board now seemed invaluable.

That night John Dutcher did not go to sleep at once, as he usually did on entering his room. He went to his bureau — the old bureau he had bought for his wife thirty years before. In it he kept his pictures. There were several tintypes of Rose, in awkward, scared poses, and there too was the last picture of his wife which had been taken with Rose as a babe in her arms.

Dutcher sat for a long time looking at it, and the tears ran down his face unheeded, pitiful to see.

When he got up at last he moved stiffly, as if he had suddenly grown ten years older, and in his sleep his sister heard him groan and mutter. In the morning he said he had a touch of rheumatism, but it would most probably pass off as the sun came out.

CHAPTER XV

CHICAGO

ALMOST 6 o'clock, and the train due in Chicago at 6.30! The city grew more formidable to Rose as she approached it. She wondered how it would first appear on the plain. There was little sign of it yet.

As she looked out of the car-window she saw men stacking grain, and ploughing. It was supper-time at home, and John was just rising from the table. The calves were bleating for their pails of milk; the guinea-hens were clacking, and the little turkeys crying in the grass, the bees were homing, heavy with honey, and here she sat, rushing toward that appalling and un-imaginable presence — Chicago.

Somewhere just ahead it sat, this mighty hive of a million and a half of people. The thought of it made her heart beat quick, and her throat filled. She was going there; the lake was there; art was there, and music and the drama — and love! Always under each motion, always behind every success, was the understanding that love was to be the woman's reward and recompense. It was not articulate nor feverish, this thought; it was a deep, pure emotion, streaming always toward the unknown.

She dreamed as the train rumbled on. She would succeed, she *must* succeed. She gripped the seat-rail with her broad, strong hands, and braced herself like one entering a flood.

It was this wonderful thing again, a fresh, young, and powerful soul rushing to a great city, a shining atom of steel obeying the magnet, a clear rivulet from the hills hurrying to the sea. On every train at that same hour, from every direction, others, like her, were entering on the same search, to the same end.

" See that cloud ? " someone said; " that's Chicago."

Rose looked — far to the southeast a gigantic smoke-cloud soared above the low horizon line, in shape like an eagle, whose hovering wings extended from south to east, trailing mysterious shadows upon the earth. The sun lighted its mighty crest with crimson light, and its gloom and glow became each moment more sharply contrasted. Toward this portentous presence the train rushed, uttering an occasional shrill neigh, like a stallion's defiance.

The brazen bell upon the engine began to clang and clang; small towns of scattered wooden houses came into view and were left behind. Huge, misshapen buildings appeared in flat spaces, amid hundreds of cars. Webs of railway tracks spread out dangerously in acres of marvellous intricacy, amid which men moved, sooty, grimy, sullen, and sickly.

Terrors thickened. Smells assaulted her sensitive nostrils, incomprehensible and horrible odors. Everywhere men delved in dirt and murk and all unloveliness.

Streets began to stretch away on either side, interminable, squalid, filled with scowling, squaw-like women and elfish children. The darkness grew, making the tangle and tumult a deadly struggle.

Was this the city of her dreams? This the magnificent, the home of education and art?

The engine's bell seemed to call back " *Good cheer! Good cheer!* " The buildings grew mightier but not less gloomy; the freight-cars grew fewer, and the coaches more numerous. It was an illimitable jungle filled with unrecognizable forms, over which night was falling.

A man with a hoop of clinking checks came through. He was a handsome, brisk, and manly fellow, and his calm, kindly voice helped Rose to choke down her dread.

" Baggage checked! — Baggage, baggage checked to any part of the city. Baggage! "

In him she saw the native denizen to whom all these horrors were commonplace sensations, and it helped her. It couldn't be so bad as it looked to her.

" Chicago, *She-caw-go!* " called the brakeman, and her heart for a moment stood still, and a smothering sensation came upon her. She was at the gate of the city, and life with all its terrors and triumphs seemed just before her.

At that moment the most beautiful thing in the world was the smooth pasture by the spring, where the sheep were feeding in the fading light, and if she could, she would have turned back, but she was afloat, and retreat was impossible. She pressed on with the rest, wondering what she could do if Mary did not meet her.

Mary had hardly been more than an acquaintance at school, but now she seemed a staff to lean upon. Rose looked to her as a guide to a refuge, a hiding-place from all these terrors.

Out under the prodigious arching roof she stepped, into the tumult of clanging bells, of screeching, hissing steam, and of grinding wheels. The shouts of men echoed here and there in the vaulted roof, mysteriously as in a cavern. Up the long walk, streams of people moved, each one laden, like herself, with a valise. Electric lamps sputtered overhead. She hurried on, with sensitive ears tortured by the appalling clamor, her eyes wide and apprehensive.

Her friend was not to be seen, and she moved on mechanically with the rest, keeping step beside an old man who seemed to be familiar with the station, and who kept off (without knowing it) the attentions of two human vultures in wait for such as Rose.

They moved up the steps into the waiting-room before Rose gave up hope of her friend. So far she had gone securely, but could she find the house which was to be her home, alone?

She sat down for an instant on the long seat by the wall, and listened to the obscure thunder of the street outside. It was terrifying, confusing. Shrill screams and hoarse shouts rose above a hissing, scraping sound, the clang of gongs and the click of shoe-heels.

Every voice was pitched to an unnatural key, like those of men in a mill. The clangor seemed hot, some way, like smitten iron and brass. No sound was familiar to her, nothing cool and reposeful. Her head throbbed and her tongue was dry. She had eaten little since early morning, and she felt weak.

She looked far more composed and self-reliant than she was, and when her friend came swinging up to her she cried out: "Oh, Mary!" and her friend realized a little of her relief and gratitude.

"Oh, here you are! I got delayed — forgive me. I'm all out o' breath." (Here she kissed her.) "How well you look! Your complexion is magnificent. Give me your valise. We'll send for your trunk. Save twenty-five cents by having it done up town. This way — I'm glad to see you. How is Wisconsin?"

Mary Compton was tall, red-haired, and strong. Her eyes were keen and laughing, and the tilt of her chip hat and the swing of her skirts let everybody know how able she was to take care of herself — thank you! She had been the smart girl of a small town near Madison, and had come to the city, precisely as her brother Dan had gone to Idaho, for the adventure of it. It was quite like hunting bears.

"Shall we take the grip?"

Rose didn't know what she meant, but she said:

"Just as you like."

"I like to take the grip; it gives a fellow a little fresh air, if there is any at all."

A train of cable-cars came nosing along like vicious boars, with snouts close to the ground. Mary helped Rose upon the open forward car, which had seats facing outward.   A young man lifted his hat and made room for them.

"Hello, John!" said Mary, "aren't you a little early to-night?   Rose, my friend Mr. Hardy.   Mr. Hardy, Miss Dutcher."

The young fellow raised his hat again and bowed. He was a pleasant-faced young man in round straw hat and short coat.   Mary paid no further attention to him.

"I've got you a room right next to mine," she said to Rose, who was holding to the seat with one hand and clinging to her hat with the other.   The car stopped and started with vicious suddenness.

"You'd better hang on; the gripman is mad to-night," Mary explained.   "We're most to our street, anyway."

To Rose it was all a wild ride.   The noise, the leaping motion of the cars and the perilous passage of drays made it as pleasant to her as a ride behind a running team on a "corduroy road."

They came at last to quieter spaces, and alighted finally at a cross street.

"I'm pretty far up," said Mary, "but I want it decently quiet where I live.   I have noise enough at the office."

Rose thought it indecently noisy.   Peddlers were uttering strange singsong cries; children romped, screaming in high-pitched furious treble; laundry wagons and vegetable wagons clattered about.   There was a curious pungent odor in the air.

On the steps of the houses groups of young people, like Mary and John, sat on strips of carpet, and laughed and commented on the passers-by. Mary turned upon one fool who called a smart word at her:

"Left your manners in Squashville, didn't you, little man?"

They came at last to an imposing block of houses, situated at the corner. They entered the door and climbed a gas-lit stairway, which went round and round a sort of square well. They came at last to a door which closed all passage, and Mary got out her key and opened it.

"Here we are!" she said cheerily.

The main hall was carpeted and ran past several doors, which were open. In one room a young man in his shirt-sleeves was shaving before a glass. In another a girl was reading.

"Hello!" called Mary.

"Hello!" said the girl, without looking up.

"Here's my room, and this's yours." Mary pushed open a door at the end of the hall. It was a small room, papered in light buff and blue. It had an oak dresser and mirror, a couple of chairs, and a mantle-bed. It looked cheerful and clean, but very small. Mary put down her valise.

"I guess you'll find everything all right, water and towels. Wash up right off—dinner'll be ready soon."

Rose removed her hat and sat down, her head throbbing with the heat and noise. She heard the man at the glass whistling, and Mary was thumping about in her vigorous way.

The dash of cold water cleared her brain, but did not

M

remove her headache.   Her face was still flushed and
her eyes expanded.

Mary, coming back, looked at her a moment and
then rushed upon her and hugged her.

"Oh, what a beauty you are! I wish I had half what
you've got."

Rose smiled faintly; she cared little at that moment
whether she looked well or ill.

"The boys will all be dead in love with you before
dinner is over.   Let me tell you about them."   She
softened her reed-like voice down and glanced at the
transom furtively: "Never forget the transom when
you're talking secrets," she explained.

"First, there's Mr. Taylor; he's from Colorado
somewhere.   He's a lawyer.   He's a fine fellow too —
you'll like him.   Then there's Mr. Simons; he's a Jew,
but he's not *too much* of a Jew.   There's Alice Fletcher;
she's queer and grumpy, but she reads a lot and she can
talk when she wants to, and there's you and myself."

"I don't feel like meeting them to-night," Rose said;
"if I had a cup of tea I'd stay in my room."

"All right! I'll bring it."

The bell rang and then the movement of feet and the
banging of doors told of the rush to dinner.

Mary came back with a cup of tea and a biscuit and
some pudding.

"Have more, if you wish," she said.

"This will do nicely.   You're very kind, Mary
Compton.   I don't deserve it."

"You deserve the world," cried the adoring girl.   "If

I had your figure and complexion, I'd make the universe wait on me."

In spite of all this fervor of praise Rose felt herself to be a very dejected and spiritless beauty. She was irritated and angry with the nagging of strange sights and sounds and smells. The air seemed laden with disease and filth. It was all so far from the coolly with its purple hills looming against the sapphire sunset sky.

But this she came for — to see the city; to plunge into its life. She roused herself therefore with a blush of shame at her weakness. She had appeared to be a child before this girl, who had always been her inferior at school.

It was a very dignified young woman therefore who rose to greet Mrs. Wilcox, the landlady, whom Mary brought back. This dignity was not needed. Mrs. Wilcox was a sweet-voiced, smiling woman of fifty — being of those toilers who smile when they are tired enough to drop. She was flushed with fatigue and moved languidly, but her kind, patient, pathetic smile touched Rose almost to tears.

" I'm glad to have you come here," the landlady said. " We're all nice people here, aren't we, Miss Compton?" Her eyes twinkled with humorous self-analysis.

" Every one of us," corroborated Mary.

" I hope you'll rest well. If there's anything we can do for you, my dear, let me know." Such was the spirit in which the overworked woman served her boarders. They all called her " mother." She had no children of her own, and her husband was " not at all well," yet nothing could sour her sweet kindliness, which included all the world. She was a familiar type, and Rose loved her at once.

Miss Fletcher came in and was introduced. She was a teacher in a school near by.

"What anybody should come to this town for I can't understand. I stay here because I'm obliged to. I'm just back from the country to my work."

"The country is all right for a vacation," quoted Rose.

Mary broke in, "That's what I say. I lived on a farm and I lived in Castle Rock. When I lived on the farm I wanted to get to Castle Rock. When I got to Castle Rock I wanted to get to Madison. Madison made me hone for Chicago, and when I had a chance to come, I just dropped my work at the university and put for the city, and here I am and glad of it."

"I can't understand such folly," murmured Miss Fletcher.

"You could if you'd stayed on the farm the year round, with nobody to talk to and mighty little to read. It's all right for you to go up for a couple of months and lie about in a hammock, but you take a place like Castle Rock all the year round! It's worse than a farm. Gossip! They talk every rag of news to smith-ereens, don't they, Rose?"

Rose nodded.

"And then the people! They're the cullin's. All the bright boys and girls go to Madison and Chicago or Dakota, and then the rest marry and intermarry and have idiot boys and freckle-faced girls!"

They all laughed. Mary was always extreme, no matter what her subject of conversation.

Miss Fletcher sighed resignedly.

"Well, it's fate. Here this big city sits and swallows you bright people like a great dragon, and the old folks are left alone in these dull places you talk about."

Rose felt her eyes filling with tears. The figure of her lonely old father came before her. She saw him sitting beside the kitchen-table, his head on his palm, and all the new house empty and dark.

Mary jumped up. "Here now, stop that talk, we must leave Rose alone and let her go to sleep."

They left her alone, but sleep was impossible. The tramp of feet, the sound of pianos, the slam of doors, the singing and laughing of the other boarders, made sleep impossible. The cars jangled by, the click-clack of the horses' hoofs and the swift rattle of wagons kept up long after the house was silent. Between midnight and four o'clock she got a little sleep, out of which she awoke while a booming, clattering wagon thundered by. Other wagons clattered viciously along up the alleys, and then some early riser below began to sing, and Rose wearily dressed and sat down by the window to listen.

Far to the south a low, intermittent, yet ever deepening, crescendo bass note began to sound. It was Chicago waking from the three hours' doze, which is its only sleep. It grew to a raucous, hot roar; and then to the north she heard the clear musical cry of a fruit vender — then another: "*Blackberries! Fine fresh blackberries!*"

The cars thickened, the sun grew hot and lay in squares of blinding light across her carpet. That curious pungent smell came in with the wind. Newsboys cried their morning papers. Children fought and played in the street. Distant whistles began to sound, and her first morning in Chicago came to Rose, hot, brazen, unnatural, and fell upon her fiercely, although she was already blinded, bruised, discouraged, abased, homesick.

CHAPTER XVI

HER FIRST CONQUEST

SHE was still sitting by the window wondering what to do next, when Mary tapped at her door.

" May I come in ? "

She looked fresh and strong, and her cheery smile made her seem almost beautiful to Rose.

" How did you sleep ? "

Rose shook her head. Mary laughed.

" I can tell by the looks of you. Look's if you'd been pulled through a knot-hole, as they say up in Molasses Gap. Heard everything that took place, didn't you ? I did too. You'll get over that. I sleep like a top now."

" What is that smell ? Pah ! " shuddered Rose.

Mary elevated her freckled nose. " What smell ? Oh, you mean that rotten, piney, turpentiney smell — that's the Chicago smell. It comes from the pavin' blocks, I guess. I never inquired. I'll ask Mr. Reed, he knows everything mean about Chicago. Well, you hadn't better go to breakfast looking like that. I want you to paralyze that Boston snipe. I'll bring in your breakfast."

Rose accepted this service passively; nothing else was to be done in Mary Compton's presence. She had the energy of a steam threshing-machine, and affection to correspond.

Rose wondered again what she could do next. She was here to study art and literature — there was the library! She would read. And there were lectures perhaps; what she was to do would come to her after a while.

Mary returned a little hot of color, bringing a tray. "That Boston clothespin says you're a myth or a country gawk. You must lay him out cold as a handspike. I've been bragging about you, and they were all on tiptoe to see you this morning. You sail in on 'em at dinner the way you used to do at our chapter-house spreads. Weren't they great! There now, I've got to vamoose. I'm not a lady of leisure. I'm a typewriter on trial, and looks won't carry *me* through. I've got to rustle and walk chalk, as they say in Molasses Gap. So good-by. Take it easy to-day. If you want to walk, go over to the lake front," and she banged out of the door and faced the city in her daily encounter.

Rose ate her breakfast and felt much better. Her trunk came, and she got out her dresses and hung them up, and made other preparations for staying, although it seemed impossible she should ever sleep another night in this terrible city.

She got out her portfolio and wrote a letter home and one also to Dr. Thatcher. Then she looked over the

little bunch of letters of introduction she had. One
was to Dr. Isabel Herrick, one to Professor H. Bevan
Fowler at Evanston, and one was to Orrin Thatcher;
that was the doctor's cousin, a young lawyer in the
Woman's building, whatever that was. With these and
ten dollars a week she faced Chicago. The contest was
unequal.

She felt this more keenly as she stood on the lake
front a little later on in the day. She went there as the
New Hampshire girl goes to the sea. This body of
water, majestic in its immense shoreless spread, is
wonderful to the young girl from Iowa or interior
Wisconsin.

A fresh, keen east wind had arisen, pure and exhila-
rating, and the smooth expanse of glittering green-and-
blue water stretched out under a vivid blue sky, in which
great clouds floated like snow mountains, trailing great
shadows like robes of state upon the lake.

The curving lake-wall was wet and glistening with the
up-flung spray. The slender elms were fronded at the
top like palms, and the vivid green grass set opposite
the pink-gray wall and the brilliant many-colored lake,
in magnificent, harmonious contrast. The girl felt her
soul grow larger as she faced this scene, so strange, so
Oriental, and she looked and looked, until it became a
part of her.

It was all so remote and so splendid. There the
great violet-shadowed sails of ships stood, as she had
seen them in pictures of the sea. There a gleaming
steamer ran, trailing great banners of smoke. There

glittered the white bodies and slant wings of gulls, dipping, upshooting, and whirling. To her eyes this was infinity, and the purple mist in which the ships drave was ultimate mystery.

At last she turned to look behind her. There on the left stood rows of immense houses, barred and grated like jails or fortresses; palaces where lived the mighty ones of Chicago commerce. Before their doors carriages stood, with attendants in livery, such as she had read about and had never seen. Up and down the curving ribbon of lavender sand other carriages were driving, with jingle of silver chains and soft roll of wheels. The horses flung foam from their bits; they were magnificent teams (she knew horses as well as any coachman), and their brass-trimmed harnesses glittered in the sun like burnished gold.

There was no noise here beyond the tread of these stately animals, the babble of a few soft-voiced children on the grass, and the crackling, infrequent splash of the leaping breakers. It was a wide contrast to the Chicago of her first glimpses the day before. That side of the city terrified her, this oppressed and awed her. The social splendor of this life appealed to her fresh girlish perception as it would not to any man. Her quick imagination peopled these mansions with beautiful women and lordly men, and she felt herself rightful claimant of a place among them.

She turned and faced them with set teeth and a singular look in her half-closed eyes, and in her heart she said: " Before I die I'll go where I please in this

city. I'll be counted as good as any of you — poor as
I am."

To the onlooker — to Mrs. Oliver Frost, she was a
girl in a picturesque attitude; to the coachmen on the
carriages she was a possible nurse-girl; to the policeman
she was a speck on the lake-front lawn.

*　　*　　*　　*　　*　　*　　*

Something of this mood was with her still when she
went in to dinner with Mary. Mary ushered the way,
beaming with joy. Rose never looked more beautiful
nor more imperious. The Boston man was properly
astonished; the Jew salesman smiled till his chubby face
seemed not able to contain his gladness. Mr. Taylor,
a gaunt young man, alone seemed unmoved; the morose
teacher gave a sigh of sad envy.

Rose said little during the meal. She cordially hated
Mr. Reed at once. His Boston accent annoyed her,
and his brutal sarcasm upon the West aroused a new
anger in her. She had never listened to such talk before.
It didn't seem possible anybody could so disparage the
West.

"Civilization stops," he said during the meal, "after
you leave the Hudson River."

"Some folks' manners stop after they leave the
Hudson River, if they ever had any," Mary replied,
and the Jew cackled joyously.

He defended Chicago. "It is the greatest place in
the world to do business. I'm a New Yorker by birth,
but Chicago suits me. I like its hustle."

"That's the point. It thinks of nothing but hustle,"

said the Boston man. "I was speaking of higheh things. It lacks the aht atmospheah of Boston and Cambridge."

"It has all the atmosphere I need," said the Jew.

To Rose all this was new. It had not occurred to her to differentiate the cities sharply from each other. Chicago, to her, was a great city, a splendid example of enterprise, and it was to be her city, the pride of the West. To the country mind a city is a great city when it acquires a million people. Like the young Jew, Rose had not missed any atmosphere. The tall young man voiced her opinion when he said:

"This finicky criticism don't count. You might just as well talk about the lack of gondolas and old palaces in Boston. Conditions here are unexampled. It's a new town, and I think a splendid place to live in. Of course you can find fault anywhere."

Rose looked at him with interest. Such precision and unhesitancy of speech she had not heard since leaving college.

Mary glowed with gratified admiration. The Jew was delighted, although he did not quite follow the implied rebuke. Miss Fletcher merely said:

"If Mr. Reed don't like Chicago, he is privileged to go back to Boston. I don't think Chicago would experience any shock if he did."

Mr. Reed wilted a little, but he was not crushed.

"The trouble with you people is you don't know anything about any otheh city. You come in heah from Oshkosh and Kalamazoo, and Okookono —— "

"Hit him on the back!" called Mary, "he's choking."

"O-con-o-mo-woc," calmly interpreted Miss Fletcher.

Reed recovered — "An some otheh outlandish place ____"

"How about Squantum and Skowhegan and Passamaquoddy?" laughed Mary.

Reed collapsed — "Oh, well, those ah old, familiah ____"

The others shouted with laughter.

"Oh, yes! Everything old and New England goes. You are too provincial, old boy. You want to broaden out. I've seen a lot of fellows like you come here, snapping and snarling at Chicago, and end up by being wild promoters." The Jew was at the bat, and the table applauded every hit.

Rose did not share in the talk — she had so little knowledge of cities — but it served to make Mr. Taylor a strong figure in her eyes. He was tall and big-boned and unsmiling. He studied her with absent-minded interest, and she felt no irritation or embarrassment, for his eyes were kind and thoughtful. He looked at her as if she called up memories of some one he had loved in another world, and she somehow grew a little sad under his gaze.

As they sat in her room after dinner, Mary asked:

"How do you like our crowd?"

"I can't tell yet. I don't like that Boston man. I never could bear the sound of 'ah.'"

"He's a chump; but they ain't all like that. I have

met two or three decent Boston fellows down in the office.   Don't think they are all muffs."

"Of course not."

"Now take my 'boss' for example. He's fine. He's big enough so you don't mind his airs; but what do you think of Mr. Taylor?"

Rose looked thoughtful, and Mary hastened to say,

"Isn't he fine?"   She hoped to forestall criticism.

"Yes, I think he's fine.   He makes me think of Professor Jenks."

"A-hagh! so he does me.   Say, Rose, I'm going to tell you something, don't you ever tell, will you?"

"Why, no — of course not."

"Hope to die?"

"Hope to die, hands crossed."

"Well!"

"Well?"

"I came here to board because *he* was here."

"Why, Mary Compton!"

"Isn't it awful?   Of course, no one knows it but you.   I'd just die if he knew it.   I used to be afraid that he'd find out, but he can't, because, you see, he never saw me till I came here, and he thinks it is just accident.   He's so simple about such things anyway, and he's always dreaming of something away off.   Oh, he's wonderful!   He's been all over the mountains. He adores John Muir — you know that man Professor Ellis told us about?   Well, he's lived just that way weeks and weeks in the wildest mountains, and it's just glorious to hear him tell about it."

Rose was astonished at Mary, generally so self-contained. She talked as if she had volumes to tell and but short minutes to tell them in. Her cheeks glowed and her eyes grew deep and dark.

"He's here reading law, but he don't need to work. He's got a share in a big mine out there somewhere, which he discovered himself. He just thought he'd try civilization for a while, he said, and so he came to Chicago. He kind o' pokes around the law school (it's in our building — that's where I saw him first, in the elevator), just as an excuse. He hates the law; he told me so. He comes in to see me sometimes. Of course I leave the door open." She smiled. "But it don't make any difference to him. He's just the same here as he is anywhere — I mean he knows how to treat a woman. The school-ma'am said she thought it was terrible to have a man come into your room — the same room you sleep in — but I told her it depended on the man. That settled her, for Owen — I mean Mr. Taylor — don't like her."

Rose listened in silence to this torrent of words from Mary. Her mind was naturally fictive, and she divined the immense world suggested by the girl's incoherent sentences. The mysterious had come to her friend — the "one man of all the world," apparently — a striking personality, quite suited to Mary, with her practical ways and love of fun. It confirmed her in her conviction that a girl must adventure into the city to win a place and a husband.

She rose and put her arms about her friend's neck:

"I'm so glad, Mary."

"Oh, goodness! don't congratulate me *yet!* He's never said a word — and maybe he won't. I can't understand him — anyway it's great fun."

A slow step crossed the hall, and a rap at the door nearly took away Mary's breath; for a moment she could not reply, then Mr. Taylor's voice was heard.

"I beg your pardon." He was turning away when Mary sprang up and opened the door.

"Oh, Mr. Taylor, is it you?"

"Yes — I didn't know but you and your friend would like to go out somewhere."

"Would you, Rose?"

"Not to-night, thank you. But you go. Don't keep in on my account."

Mary struggled a moment, then she smiled with tender archness.

"Very well, thank you, Mr. Taylor. I'll be ready soon." After he had gone she said:

"Perhaps he'll propose!"

Rose glowed sympathetically. "I hope he will."

*   *   *   *   *   *   *

The next day Rose went down town alone. The wind had veered to the south, the dust blew, and the whole terrifying panorama of life in the streets seemed some way blurred together, and forms of men and animals were like figures in tapestry. The grind and clang and clatter and hiss and howl of the traffic was all about her.

She came upon the river just as the bridge was being opened. Down toward the lake, which had to her all the wonder and expanse of the sea, boats lay thickly; steamers from deep water, long, narrow, and black, excursion boats, gleaming white, and trimmed with shining brass, lay beside the wharves, and low-lying tugs, sturdy, rowdyish little things, passed by, floating like ducks and pulling like bull-dogs, guiding great two-masted sailing boats and long, low grimy grain steamers, with high decks at the ends. The river ran below, gray-green, covered with floating refuse. Mountainous buildings stood on either side of the waterway.

The draw, as it began to move, made a noise precisely like an old-fashioned threshing machine — a rising howl, which went to Rose's heart like a familiar voice. Her eyes for a moment released hold upon the scene before her, and took a slant far over the town to the coolly farm, and the days when the threshing machine howled and rattled in the yard came back, and she was rushing to get dinner ready for the crew. When the bridge returned to its place she walked slowly across, studying each vista. To the west, other bridges, swarming with people, arched the stream — on each side was equal mystery. These wonderful great boats and their grim brave sailors she had read about, but had never seen. They came from far up the great tumultuous lake, and they were going to anchor somewhere in that wild tangle of masts and chimneys and towering big buildings to the west. They looked as if they might go to the ends of the earth. At the stern of an outgoing boat four sailors were pulling at a rope, the leader singing a wild, thrilling song in time to the action.

N

So it was that the wonderful and the terrifying appealed to her mind first.   In all the city she saw the
huge and the fierce.   She perceived only contrasts.   She
saw the ragged newsboy and the towering policeman.
She saw the rag-pickers, the street vermin, with a shudder of pity and horror, and she saw also the gorgeous
show windows of the great stores.   She saw the beautiful new gowns and hats, and she saw also the curious
dresses of swart Italian girls scavenging with baskets on
their arms.   Their faces were old and grimy, their voices
sounded like the chattered colloquies of the monkeys in
the circus.

The street seemed a battle-field.   There was no hint
of repose or home in such a city.   People were just
staying here like herself, trying to get work, trying to
make a living, trying to make a name.   They had left
their homes as she had, and though she conceived of
them as having a foothold, she could not imagine them
as having reached security.   The home-life of the city
had not revealed itself to her.

She made her way about the first few blocks below
Water Street, looking for Dr. Herrick's address.   It
was ten o'clock, and the streets were in a frenzy of exchange.   The sidewalks were brooks, the streets rivers
of life, which curled into doors and swirled around
mountainous buildings.

She was pathetically helpless in the midst of these
alien sounds.   It took away from her the calm, almost
scornful, self-reliance which characterized her in familiar
surroundings.   Her senses were as acute as a hare's, and

sluiced in upon her a bewildering flood of sights and
sounds.   She did not appear childish, but she seemed
slow and stupid, which of course she was not.   She
thought and thought till she grew sick with thought.
She struggled to digest all that came to her, but it was
like trampling sand; she apparently gained nothing by
her toil.

The streets led away into thunderous tunnels, beyond
which some other strange hell of sound and stir imaginatively lay.   The brutal voices of drivers of cabs and
drays assaulted her.   The clang of gongs drew her
attention, now here, now there, and her anxiety to understand each sound and to appear calm added to her
confusion.

She heard crashes and yells that were of murder and
sudden death.   It was the crash of a falling bundle of
sheet iron, but she knew not that.   She looked around
thinking to see some savage, bloody battle-scene.

She saw women with painted faces and bleached hair
whom she took to be those mysterious and appalling
women who sell themselves to men.   They were in
fact simple-minded shop girls or vulgar little housewives
with sad lack of taste.

Every street she crossed, she studied, looking both up
and down it, in the effort to come at the end of its
mystery — but they all vanished in lurid, desolate distance, save toward the lake.   Out there, she knew, the
water lay serene and blue.

This walk was to her like entrance into war.   It
thrilled and engaged her at every turn.   She was in the

centre of human life.   To win here was to win all she cared to have.

It was a relief to pass into the rotunda of the splendid building in which Dr. Herrick's office was.   Outside the war sounded, and around her men hastened as if to rescue.   She entered the elevator as one in a dream. The man hustled her through the door without ceremony and clanged the door as if it were a prison gate. They soared to the ninth floor like a balloon suddenly liberated, and the attendant fairly pushed her out.

" Here's your floor — Herrick, to the left."

Rose was humiliated and indignant, but submitted. The hallway along which she moved was marble and specklessly clean.   On each side doors of glass with letters in black set forth the occupations of the tenants.

She came at length to the half-open door of Dr. Herrick's office and timidly entered.   A young girl came forward courteously.

"Would you like to see the Doctor ? " she asked, in a soft voice.

" Yes, please.   I have a letter to her from Dr. Thatcher of Madison."

"Oh! well, I will take it right in.   Be seated, please."

This good treatment, and the soft voice of the girl, were very grateful after the hoarse war-cries of the street.   Rose looked around the little room with growing composure and delight.   It was such a dainty little waiting-room, and augured something attractive in Dr. Herrick.

" Come right in," the girl said on returning.   " The

Doctor is attending to her mail, but she will see you for a few moments."

Rose entered the second and larger room, and faced a small, graceful woman, of keen, alert glance. She appeared to be about thirty-five years of age. She shook hands briskly, but not warmly.

Her hand was small and firm and her tone quick and decisive. " How-d'-you-do? Sit down! I had a note from Dr. Thatcher the other day saying I might expect you."

Rose took a chair while the Doctor studied her, sitting meanwhile with small, graceful head leaning on one palm, her elbow on the corner of her desk. No woman's eyes ever searched Rose like those of this little woman, and she rebelled against it inwardly, as Dr. Herrick curtly asked:

" Well, now, what can I do for you? Dr. Thatcher thought I could do something for you."

Rose was too dazed to reply. This small, resolute, brusque woman was a world's wonder to her. She looked down and stammered.

" I don't know — I — thought maybe you could help me to find out what I *could* do."

The Doctor studied her for an instant longer. She saw a large, apparently inexperienced girl, a little sullen and a little embarrassed — probably stupid.

" Don't you know what you want to do?"

" No — that is, I want to write," confessed Rose.

" Write! My dear girl, every addle-pate wants to write. Have you friends in the city?"

" One; a classmate."

" Man ? "

" No, a girl."

" Why did you leave home ? "

Rose began to grow angry. " Because I couldn't live the life of a cow or a cabbage. I wanted to see the city."

The Doctor arose. " Come here a moment." Rose obeyed and stood beside her at the window, and they looked out across a stretch of roofs, heaped and humped into mountainous masses, blurred and blent and made appalling by smoke and plumes of steam. A scene as desolate as a burnt-out volcano — a jumble of hot bricks, jagged eave-spouts, gas-vomiting chimneys, spiked railings, glass skylights, and lofty spires, a hideous and horrible stretch of stone and mortar, cracked and seamed into streets. It had no limits and it palpitated under the hot September sun, boundless and savage. At the bottom of the crevasses men and women speckled the pavement like minute larvæ.

" Is *that* what you came here to see ? " asked the Doctor.

Rose drew a deep breath and faced her.

" Yes, and I'm not afraid of it. It's mighty ! It is grander than I expected it to be — grand and terrible, but it's where things are done."

Isabel Herrick studied her a little closer.

" You'd leave your country home for this ? "

Rose turned upon her and towered above her. Her eyes flashed and her abundant eyebrows drew down in a dark scowl.

" Would you be content to spend your life, day and night, summer and winter, in Dutcher's Coolly ? "

" Pardon me," said Dr. Herrick, cuttingly, " the problem is not the same. I have not the same ―― I ―― the question ―― "

"Yes, *you* who are born in the city and who come up to see us on the farms for a couple of weeks in June — *you* take it on yourselves to advise us to stay there ! *You* who succeed are always ready to discourage us when we come to try *our* fortunes. I can succeed just as well as you, and I'll make you bow your head to me before I am five years older."

She was magnificent, masterful, in the flaming heat of her wrath. This little woman had gone too far.

Dr. Herrick turned abruptly.

" I guess I've made a mistake ; sit down again," she said, in softer tones.

Rose was not yet done. She kept her lofty pose.

" Yes, you certainly have. I am not afraid of this city ; I can take care of myself. I wouldn't be under obligations to you now for the world. I want you to know I'm not a beggar asking a dollar from you ; I'm not a schoolgirl, either. I know what I can do and you don't. I wouldn't have troubled you, only for Dr. Thatcher." She moved toward the door, gloriously angry, too angry to say good-day.

The Doctor's cold little face lighted up. She smiled the most radiant smile, and it made her look all at once like a girl.

" My dear ― I am crushed. I am an ant at your

feet.   Come here now, you great splendid creature, and let me hug you this minute."

Rose kept on to the door, where she turned: " I don't think I ought to trouble you further," she said coldly.

The Doctor advanced. " Come now, I beg your pardon.   I'm knocked out.   I took you for one of those romantic country girls, who come to the city — helpless as babes.   Come back."

Rose came near going on.   If she had, it would have lost her a good friend.   She felt that, and so when the Doctor put an arm around her to lead her back to the desk she yielded, though she was still palpitating with the fervor of her wrath.

" My dear, you fairly scared me.   I never was so taken by surprise in my life ; tell me all about yourself ; tell me how you came to come, where you are — and all about it."

Rose told her — not all, of course — she told her of her college work, of her father, of the coolly, and of her parting from her father.

" Oh, yes," the Doctor interrupted, " that's the way we go on — we new men and women.   The ways of our fathers are not ours ; it's tragedy either way you put it.   Go on ! "

At last she had the story, told with marvellous unconscious power, direct, personal, full of appeal.   She looked at Rose with reflective eyes for a little space.

" Well, now we'll take time to consider.   Bring me something of yours ; I'll show it to a friend of mine, an

editor here, and if it pleases him we'll know what to
do. And come and see me. I'll introduce you to
some nice people. Chicago is full of nice people if you
only come at them. Come and see me to-morrow, can't
you? Oh, you great, splendid creature! I wish I had
your inches." She glowed with admiration.

"Come Sunday at six and dine with me," yielding to
a sudden impulse. "Come early and let me talk to
you."

Rose promised and they went out into the waiting-
room.

"Etta, dear, this is Miss Dutcher; this is my sister.
I want you to know each other." The little girl tiptoed
up and took Rose's hand with a little inarticulate murmur.

There was a patient in waiting, but Dr. Herrick
ignored her and conducted Rose to the door.

"Good-by, dear, I'm glad you came. You've given
me a good shaking up. Remember, six, sharp!"

She looked after Rose with a wonderful glow in her
heart.

"The girl is a genius — a jewel in the rough," she
thought. "She must be guided. Heavens! How she
towered."

When she stepped into the street Rose felt taller and
stronger, and the street was less appalling. She raised
her eyes to the faces of the men she met. Her eyes
had begun their new search. The men streamed by in
hundreds; impressive in mass, but comparatively unin-
teresting singly.

It was a sad comment upon her changing conceptions

of life that she did not look at the poorly dressed men, the workmen. She put them aside as out of the question; not consciously, for the search at this stage was still unconscious, involuntary, like that of a bird seeking a mate, moved by a law which knows neither individuals nor time.

She saw also the splendor of the shop windows. She had a distinct love for beautiful fabrics as works of art, but she cared less for dress than one would suppose to see her lingering before great luminous cataracts of drapery. She was quietly and gracefully dressed, beyond this she had never cared to go, but she constructed wonderful homes and owners out of the glimpses of these windows, and from the passing of graceful young girls, clothed like duchesses, and painted (some of them) like women of the under world.

It all grew oppressive and disheartening to her at last, and she boarded a State Street car (the only car she knew) and took her way up home. All the people in the car looked at her as if she had intruded into a private drawing-room.

She was evidently from the country, for, though it was in the day of quaintness, she wore her hair plain. It was also the middle period of the curious and inexplicable little swagger which all duly informed girls assumed; but Rose walked on her strong elastic feet with a powerful swing, which was worth going miles to see. It was due to her unconscious imitation of the proud carriage of William De Lisle. She loved that forward swing of the thigh, with the flex of the side which accompanied it. It was her ideal of motion, that free action of knee, waist, and neck, which she felt rather than saw in the great athlete.

She made a goodly figure to look at, and it was no especial wonder that the people in the car scrutinized her. Her forehead was prominent and her eyes were sombre. It was impossible for the casual observer to define why she made so marked an impression upon him. It was because she was so fresh and strong, and unaffected and unconscious.

At lunch she found no one but Mr. Taylor, who loomed up at the farther end of the table, with gaunt, grave face and broad shoulders like a farmer. She studied him closely, now that she knew more about him. He had a big, wide, plain face, with gentle gray eyes. His beard was trimmed round and made him look older than he was. He was a man into whose eyes women could look unafraid and unabashed. He greeted Rose with a smile.

" I'm very glad you've come. I was afraid I should eat lunch alone. With your permission I'll move down to your end of the table."

Rose was very glad to have him take a seat near, and they were friends at once. They naturally fell upon Mary as a topic. Mr. Taylor spoke of her quietly :

" Mary's a fine girl," he said. " I don't like to see her work. I don't like to see any woman do work like that. I don't claim any right to say what women shall do or not do, but I imagine they wouldn't go into shops if they were not, in a way, forced into it."

Rose defended the right of a girl to earn her own living.   He hastened to explain further :

" Of course a woman should be free and independent, but is she free when pressure forces her into typewriting or working in a sweat-shop ? "

Rose turned his thoughts at last by asking about the West.   He expanded like flame at the thought.

" Ah ! the old equatorial wind is blowing to-day, and my hair crackles with electricity."   He smiled as he ran his hands through his hair.   " On such days I long for my pony again.   Sometimes, when I can't stand it any longer, I take a train to some little station and go out and lie flat down on the grass on my back, so that I can't see anything but sky ; then I can almost imagine myself back again where the lone old peaks bulge against the sky.   Do you know John Muir and Joaquin Miller ? "

" I know a little of them," said Rose.   Taylor's eyes glowed with enthusiasm.

" There are two men who know the wilderness. Your Thoreau I've read, but he don't interest me the way these Rocky Mountain fellows do.   Your Eastern fellows don't really know a wilderness — they're sort o' back pasture explorers.   John isn't a bit theatrical, he's been there.   He doesn't take a train of guides to explore a glacier, he sticks a crust of bread in his belt along with a tin cup, and goes alone.   I've been with John in the Sierras, and once he came over into my range."

Rose defended Emerson and Thoreau as if she were

the Easterner this Colorado hunter considered her. As she talked he fixed great absent-minded eyes upon her, and absorbed every line of her face, every curve of her lips — every changing wave of color.

"I don't care for the wilderness as you do. What is a bird compared to a man, anyway? I like people. I want to be where dramas are being played. Men make the world, bears don't." She argued, hotly.

He slowly withdrew his gaze.

"I guess you're right." He smiled a wise smile. "If the wilderness had been everything in the world, I wouldn't be here. A woman is more than a flower. A woman would make my mountains a paradise."

"You have no right to ask a woman to go there with you — not to stay," she added, quickly.

His smile passed.

"You're right again. Unless I could find a woman who loves the wilderness as I do."

"That is out of the question," she replied. "No woman loves the wilderness — as a home. All women love cities and streets and children." She had a young person's readiness to generalize, and pitilessly flung these hopeless truisms at him. He arose, apparently made sadder by them. He sighed.

"But civilization carries such terrible suffering with it."

Rose went to her room and looked at her other letters of introduction. Should she present them? What would be the use. The scene with Dr. Herrick had not been pleasant; true, it had apparently brought her a friend, but it was a rigorous experience, and she hardly felt it worth while at the moment to go through another such scene to win another such friend.

She fell to looking over her manuscripts. They were on lined paper, stitched together at the top. They were imitative, of course, and leaned toward the Elizabethan drama, and toward Tennyson and Mrs. Browning, so far as verse-form went. There were also essays which she had written at college, which inquired mournfully, who will take the place of the fallen giants, Bryant, Longfellow, Emerson? She had eloquent studies of Hugo and valiant defences of Dickens. She reflected in her writing (naturally) all the conventional positions in literature. She stood upon the graves of the dead as if she feared they might be desecrated.

She was a pupil, and as a pupil she had considered literature as something necessarily afar off, in England or France, in Boston and Cambridge, though she had come to think Chicago might be a place suitable for a humble beginning, but that it might be the subject of literature had not occurred to her. She had never known a person who had written a book. Professor Ellis and the President had written scientific treatises, but, not being a fool, she knew there was a difference between getting an article into a country weekly and getting into a big daily, to say nothing of the great magazines. She wished for advice. Being out in the world now, something must be done with her writings.

These essays were good and thoughtful, they represented study and toil, but they did not represent her real self, her real emotions, any more than her reading represented her real liking. Her emotions, big, vital, contemporaneous, had no part in this formal and colorless pedantry. Of this she was still ignorant, however.

She was sorting her poems over and dreaming about them when Mary came home.

" Oh, you dear! I've been thinking about you all day. Did you see your woman doctor ? "

" Yes."

" Did you like her ? "

" Well, I don't know — yes, I think I do. I didn't at first."

" Where else did you go ? "

" Nowhere. I came home to lunch."

" Eat alone ? " Mary was taking off her things and was more than usually fragmentary.

" No. Mr. Taylor was there." Mary faced her.

" Now see here, Rose Dutcher, do you want to break my heart into smithereens ? If you do, you go on lunching with Owen Taylor."

Rose laughed at her tone of simulated sorrow and dismay.

" He moved down to my end of the table, too."

Mary plumped into a chair in pretended collapse.

" Well, that finishes me. I'm coming home to lunch after this. If you prove a *terrater*, I'll have your back hair, Rose Dutcher."

" I couldn't help it. He didn't want to shout at me across the table."

Mary's voice softened.

"What did you talk about?"

"He talked about you."

"Did he? What did he say?"

"He said you were a good girl, and you are."

"Is that all?"

"What more could you ask?"

"He might 'ave praised me beauty!" Then she laughed and rushed at Rose and hugged her for some reason not expressed. "Isn't he just grand?"

"I'm going out to dinner Sunday night!"

"Where? Woman doctor's?"

"Yes. I met her sister, too."

"Oh, you'll soon be getting so swell you won't notice us. Well, anyhow, you'll leave me Owen?"

In the mood in which she went to sleep that night there was no premonition of conquest. The tide of her life sank low. It was impossible for her to succeed — she, a little country girl, of five feet nine. She looked at her bulk as it showed under the quilts. How small a thing she was to be set over against the mighty city.

And yet Napoleon was less than she. And Patti and Edwin Booth were not so large. The life of a great actor, like Edwin Booth, a singer, like Patti, interested her deeply. She wondered that they could do things like other people. They were so public, so admired, so lifted into the white-hot glare of success.

She brought her mind back to the point. They succeeded, small beings though they were; they faced the

millions of the earth and became the masters, the kings
and queens of art.

By what necromancy did they do this? If it was
born in them, then there was hope for her; if they
reached it by toil, then, surely, there was hope for her.

o

CHAPTER XVII

HER FIRST DINNER OUT

Rose went to see the parts of the city which no true Chicagoan ever visits. That is to say she spent Sunday in the park, admiring, with pathetic fortitude, the sward, the curving drives, the bridges and the statues, in company with the lowly and nameless multitude — she even crowded in to see the animals.

She had intended to get back to church, conformable to Mary's programme, which was to start at St. James, and go in rotation to all the great churches and hear the choirs; but it happened that on this first Sunday there was a fine west wind, and the many ships were setting sail to the north, close inshore, and when Rose found she could sit on the park benches and see those mighty birds of commerce sail by she was content to do that and nothing more.

She had no cheap, easy, and damnable comparisons. The passage of each purple-sailed lumber freighter was a poem to her. They floated noiselessly, effortlessly, on a beautiful sea of color. They drave like butterflies in dreams, their motive power indiscernible.

She sat with her chin in her palm, her big eyes like

beautiful windows, letting in the sunshine and the grace of ships and clouds without effort, fixed in an ecstasy of reverie. Around her streamed floods of the city's newly acquired residents, clerks, bookkeepers, type-writers, shop-girls, butchers' boys, salesmen, all fresh from the small towns and from the farms of the West. As the ships passed, she gave her attention to these people—recognized in them many familiar types. There was the smart young man, son of the tavern-keeper in Cyene. There was a blundering big wag, who looked like Ed Smith of Molasses Gap. There were types like Mary, hearty, loud-voiced, cheery, wholesome, whom the city could never rob of their native twang. There were Tom and Grace and Elsa and Bert and all the rest of the bright, restless spirits of the country towns and wide-awake school districts come to try their fortunes in the great city like herself.

They wore bargains in ready-made clothing pretty generally, but it was up-to-date and each one was clean as a new dime. They laughed, shouted jokes, scuffled and pushed the girls, quite in the good country way. They made quaint and sometimes insolent remarks about the park and its adornments, assuming the *blasé* airs of old residents, in pointing out to the later arrivals the various attractions.

There came by other groups, as alien to Rose as the foregoing were familiar. Dark-skinned, queer, bow-legged, bewhiskered little men, followed by their wives and children, all sallow and crooked. Great droves, whole neighborhoods drifted along, chattering unintel-

ligible languages as incomprehensible to the country girl
as Chinese. Whether they were Italians or Jews or
Bohemians she could not tell, but she could see the marks
of hunger and hard work on their pallid faces. These
were, no doubt, the people who moved about under the
murk of that deadly region through which she had been
borne by her train that first night.

She went home from this first visit to the park oppressed and overborne with the multitude of her new
impressions. She felt quite as she did upon her return
from the Art Institute, to which she had hastened early
in the first week. So much that was artificially beautiful tired and irritated her, like eating a meal of honey
and sponge-cake. Her head ached with the formal
curves of the drives, with the unchanging fixedness of
the statues, just as the unnatural murky tones of the
landscapes in frames gave her vague discomfort.

In the few days between her meeting with Isabel and
her dinner she saw the Wheat Exchange (which interested her mightily, like battle), she went again to the
Art Institute, she visited other parks, she went to the top
of the Masonic Temple, and did many other things which
the native high-class Chicagoan prides himself on never
doing. Happily she apprehended not at all the enor-
mity of her offence; on the contrary, she was seeing
life, and this feeling compensated her when she did not
otherwise enjoy " a sight." It was a duty, and she felt
grateful to the unknown city officials for the chance to
see these things, even if it nearly broke her neck and tired
her out to see them. She looked forward to her dinner

with great interest. She had thought a great deal about Dr. Herrick, and had come to the conclusion that she was not much to blame. "I suppose she thought I was a poor helpless ninny come in to ask her for a job," she said to Mary.

"Well, she couldn't have had much gumption," Mary loyally replied.

Mary came home from a walk with Mr. Taylor on purpose to help Rose "fix up and get off," but found her quite dressed and watching the clock.

"Well, you are a prompt one! Stand up now, and let me see if you're all right."

Rose obediently stood up and was twirled about in various lights.

"That's fine! That gray dress is such a fit, and scarlet goes well with it. Oh, you sweet thing! How're you going to get home?"

"Walk, of course."

"Shall I send Owen over for you?"

They both laughed at her tone.

"Oh, what a self-sacrificing friend!" Rose exclaimed. "I guess I can walk home alone. I'm not afraid of the dark."

"Oh, it isn't that. It would be sweller to have some-one come after you."

"Well, you and Owen both come."

"Well, I'll see. If I feel safe by nine-thirty I'll send him. But if you're not back here by ten o'clock I'll be after ye." This made them both laugh again.

"Where is this address?"

Rose gave her the card.

" Why, this is away up in the swell part. My, but you are comin' on! " Mary clucked with her tongue. " You'll be calling on the Lake Drive soon."

Rose looked neat and altogether well composed in her simple gray dress and sober-hued bonnet and gloves. She wasn't in the very latest fall fashion, of course, but she was not noticeably out of vogue. She felt quite at ease as she walked up the street.

This ease began to desert her as the houses grew larger and the door-plates more ornate. What if Dr. Herrick lived in one of these houses! They were not, of course, palatial like those houses on the lake front, but they looked too grand for any of her friends to live in. Her fear of getting tangled in social intricacies grew keener as she walked up the steps to a large cream-colored brick building. The mystery of " flats " was to be faced. The entrance was tiled and flecklessly clean. On the right were three bells, one above the other. Over the second one she saw Dr. Herrick's name. She pulled the bell and waited for developments.

Suddenly a hollow voice, hoarse and breathy, from the wall.

" Kim roight up." She turned to the inner door which opened mysteriously, and a small boy in buttons motioned her to the elevator. She began to comprehend and felt grateful to the small boy for his considerate gravity.

At the landing the door was opened by Etta, the pretty little sister.

She said " How-do-you-do!" in her soft, timid little voice, and let Rose into an exquisite little bedroom off the hall and asked her to lay off her hat. She stood in awe of Rose, who seemed very large and stern to her.

Rose felt a little nervous about what was to come after, but contrived to keep outwardly calm while following her gentle guide along the hall and into a small reception-room. Isabel arose and greeted her with a smile of delight.

" Ah! here you are! Do you know I began to fear you were mythical — that I'd dreamed you. Warren, this is Miss Dutcher. Miss Dutcher, Mr. Mason." A slow, large man stepped forward and looked her in the face with penetrating eyes. He was a little taller than she was and his face had a weary look. He was blond as a Norwegian.

" I am very glad you're not a myth," he said, and his face lost its tired look for a moment, his voice was very beautiful.

" This is my nephew, Mr. Paul Herrick; " a slim young man came up to shake hands. He was plainly a college man, and Rose comprehended him at once.

Isabel's voice changed and a little flush came to her face as she put her hand on the shoulder of a tall, black-bearded man standing quietly in the shadow.

" This is Dr. Sanborn, my husband-who-is-to-be."

" If nothing happens." He smiled as he shook hands.

" If she doesn't conclude to take me instead," remarked Mason.

Rose had perception enough at command to apprehend

the powerful personalities grouped about her.   She sat
near Dr. Sanborn, with whom she was at ease at once,
he was so awkward and so kindly.   He took off his
glasses and polished them carefully as if anxious to see
her better.

"Isabel tells me you gave her a little lecture the other
day.   I'm glad of it.   We city folks need it once
in awhile.   We get to thinking that country folks are
necessarily fools and stupids by reason of our farce-
comedies and our so-called comic weeklies."

"We're not so bad as that," said Rose.

"Of course not; nobody could be so bad as that."

Isabel took a seat near Mason.   "I tell you, Warren,
that girl has a future before her."

"No doubt.   It couldn't well be behind her."

"Don't be flippant!   See that head!   But it isn't that
— she has power.   I feel it, she made me feel it.   I
want you to see some of her writing and see what can
be done for her."

Mason looked bored.   "Writes, does she?"

"Of course she writes.   See that head, I say."

"I see the head and it's a handsome head.   I'll con-
cede that.   So is Sanborn's, but he can't write a pre-
scription without a printed form."

"Oh, well, if you are in the mood to be irreverent!"

Mason's face lighted up.   "There, *you* can write!
Anyone who is capable of a touch like that — in the
presence of gods, men should be meek.   At the same
time I would hasten to warn you, the Doctor is becoming marvellously interested in this girl with a future.

He has faced her; he is actually touching her knee with his forefinger!"

Isabel laughed. "He always does that when he argues anything. It won't do any harm."

"It mightn't do him any harm, or you for that matter,—but that innocent country girl!"

"She can take care of herself. You should have heard her put me down in my chair. I want you to take her in to dinner."

"I—madam? Etta is my choice, after the hostess, of course. I'm a little shy of these girls who write."

"Well, you take me in and I'll let Paul take Rose, but I want her to sit by you. I invited you, of all the men of my vast acquaintance, because I hoped your trained and fictive eye would see and appreciate her."

"My trained and fictive eye is regarding her, but maybe she is like an impressionist painting, better seen at a little distance. I confess she is attractive at this focus, but oh, if her mind——"

"You need not worry about her mind. She's a genius. Well, I guess Professor Roberts is not coming. Suppose we go in!"

"Aren't we rather formal to-night?"

"Well, yes, but Dr. Sanborn had no dinner in the middle of the day, so I transferred ours."

"I'm glad you did, for I'm hungry too."

And so it happened Rose found herself seated beside the big blond man whose face seemed so weary and so old. Paul sat on her left, and they chatted easily on college affairs. He was from Ann Arbor, he told her.

Rose looked with wonder at Dr. Herrick. She was quite another woman, entirely unprofessional. Her face was warm with color, and she wore an exquisite dress, simple as a uniform, yet falling into graceful soft folds about her feet. Her brown hair was drawn about her pretty head in wavy masses. Her eyes sparkled with the pleasure and pride of being hostess to such company. Altogether she looked scarcely older than Rose. The table was set with tall candles with colored shades, and the simple little dinner was exquisitely served. At the same time it all seemed artificial and unhomelike to Rose. The home which had no cellar and no yard was to her false, transitory, and unwholesome, no matter how lovely the walls might be. Air seemed lacking and the free flow of electricity. It was like staying in an hotel.

Mason turned to her after a little talk with Etta.

" And so *you* have joined the stream of fortune-seekers setting always to the city. Do you feel yourself to be a part of a predestinated movement ? "

" I did not when I started — I do now."

" That's right. This is the Napoleon of cities. A city of colossal vices and colossal virtues. It is now devouring, one day it will begin to send back its best arterial blood into the nation. My metaphor is a bit questionable, but that is due to my two minds concerning this salad — I alternately curse and bow down in wonder before this city. Its future is appalling to think of. In 1920 it will be the mightiest centre of the English-speaking race — thank you, I'll not take any more dressing — I envy you young people who come now when the worst of the fight against material greed is nearly over. We who have given twenty years of our lives — I beg your pardon. I don't know why I should moralize for your benefit — I meant to say I hope you have not come to Chicago to make your living."

" Why, yes — I hope to — but my father gives me a little to live on till I find something to do."

" That's good. Then sit down and watch the city. It doesn't matter how humble your living place — sit above the city's tumult. Observe it, laugh at it, but don't fight it — don't mix in the grind. Keep it in your brain, don't let it get into your blood."

Rose looked at him in wonder, his voice was so quiet and his words so vibrant with meaning.

" I never felt so drawn to a woman in my life," Isabel said to her betrothed. " I don't pretend to understand it. I just love her this minute."

" With due qualifications I can agree with you, my dear. She is very promising indeed."

" She has the power that compels. I wish she'd get hold of Mason." Isabel smiled wisely. " You see Mason is really listening to her now, and poor Etta is left alone. I wish Professor Roberts were here. He's such good fun for her. Before the evening's out every man in the house will be hovering around that Wisconsin girl, and I don't blame 'em a bit."

A little later the maid announced Professor Roberts.

" Ah! bring him right in, Mary!"

A cheery voice was heard in the hallway.

"Don't rise, I'll find a place somewhere. I am delinquent I know; what's this — a roast?"

"Now don't you pretend to be starving just to please me; this Sunday evening dinner was given for me especially," said Sanborn.

"Hungry? Of course I'm hungry. I've come all the way from Fifty-second Street."

Professor Roberts was a middle-aged man, with a chin whisker. He had a small, elegant figure, and his eyes were humorous.

Everybody took on new life the moment he came in.

"The fact is I got bridged," he explained, after being introduced to Rose.

"All for living on the South Side," said Paul.

"I know — I know! However, *somebody* must live on the South Side, and so I stay to keep up the general average."

"How modest and kind of you!"

"Professor belongs to the University settlement — down near the Indiana line," explained Paul to Rose.

"Anybody'd think, to hear you North Siders talk, that Fifty-second Street was at the uttermost parts of the earth."

"It is."

"Well, we don't have weekly burglaries on our side."

"We no longer sing 'Lily Dale' and the Sankey hymns up here."

All this banter was amusing to Rose. It opened to

her the inner social landmarks of the city.   She didn't know before that there was a West Side and a North Side to the city.

Professor Roberts bubbled over with fun.   He was curiously like some of the men Rose had known at Bluff Siding.   His chin whiskers, his mirthful eyes, and his hearty laughter were familiar as a dandelion.   What could he be professor of, she thought — and asked her neighbor.

Paul told her.   " He's professor of geology and paleontology, and knows, besides, a tremendous lot about bugs and animals.   He made a trip up into the Yukon country a year or two ago.   He was gone eighteen months, with no one but a couple of Indian guides.   He's a big fellow, for all he's so jolly and everyday in his manners."

The talk that went on was a revelation of intellectual subtlety to the country girl.   The three men addressed themselves to Isabel, and every conceivable subject received some sort of mention.   Roberts joked incessantly, and Dr. Sanborn held him a good second, while Mason said the most enigmatical things in his smooth, melodious bass.   His face lost its heavy look under the eyes, and his smile became very attractive — though he did not laugh.

Rose sat with them, absorbed in the touch and go, brilliancy and fun, of the talk.   It was wonderful to her that Dr. Herrick could sit so entirely at ease before three such keen conversationalists as these men seemed to be.

After dinner the talk took on a quieter tone. Mason asked the privilege of ruminating over his coffee and cigar.

"Ruminate, yes; but don't make it an excuse for going to sleep," said Isabel. "You must wake up at any rate and tell us a story before the evening is over."

She got Roberts started on his recent trip to see the Indian snake-dance at Walpi, and they listened breathlessly till he rounded up safely half-an-hour later. Then Dr. Sanborn was called upon.

"Come, Doctor, we must have your song!"

"His song!" exclaimed Roberts.

"*One* song?" asked Mason.

"One song alone is all he knows, and the only way he acquired that was by damnable iteration. It was a cheerful lay sung by his nurse in the hospital during a spell of brain fever," explained Isabel.

"Is this thing unavoidable?" asked Mason, in illy concealed apprehension.

"Thus we earn our dinner," replied Roberts. "To what length this love of food will carry a man!"

"Well, let's have the agony over at once."

The Doctor lifted his tall frame to the perpendicular as if pulled by a string, and, marching to the piano, asked Etta to accompany him. His face was expressionless, but his eyes laughed.

His voice shook the floor with the doleful cadences of a distressing ballad about a man who murdered his wife because she was "untrew," and was afterwards haunted by a "figger in white with pityous eyes and cries." He eventually died of remorse and the ballad ended by warning all men to refrain from hasty judgments upon their wives.

"Amen! So say we all!" Professor Roberts heartily agreed. A lively discussion was precipitated by Mason, who said: "The man must be judged by the facts before him at the time the deed was done, not afterwards. I've no doubt there are wives whose murder would be justifiable homicide."

Isabel interrupted it at last by saying: "That will do, that is quite enough. You are on the road to vituperation."

"Miss Dutcher, you will sing for us, won't you?"

"Oh, I don't sing." Rose turned upon her in terror.

"Really and truly?"

"Really and truly."

"Then you play?"

"I have no accomplishments at all. All the music I can make is a whistle and a jews'-harp, I assure you."

This set Roberts off. "Ah! *La Belle Siffleuse!* we will hear you whistle. Dr. Sanborn, Miss Dutcher can whistle."

Rose shrank back. "Oh, I can't whistle before company; I learned on the farm, I was alone so much."

They fell upon her in entreaties, and at last she half promised.

"If you won't look at me ———"

"Turn down the gas!" shouted Roberts.

They made the room dim. There was a little silence, and then into the room crept a keen little sweet piping sound. It broadened out into a clear fluting and entered upon an old dance tune. As she went on she put more and more go into it, till Roberts burst out with a long-drawn nasal cry, " Sash-ay all ! " and Rose broke down promptly. Everybody shouted " Bravo ! "

Roberts exulted. " Oh, but I'd like to see an old-fashioned country dance again. Give us another old-fashioned tune."

" I don't know that I do them right," said Rose. " I learned from hearing the fiddlers play them."

" More ! more ! " cried Roberts. " I like those old things. Mason here pretends not to know them, but he's danced them many a time."

Rose whistled more of the old tunes. " Haste to the Wedding," " Honest John," " Polly Perkins," and at last reached some fantastic furious tunes, which she had caught from the Norwegians of the coolly.

Then she stopped and they turned up the light. She looked a little ashamed of her performance, and Isabel seemed to understand it, so she said:

" Now that is only fooling, and I'm going to ask Miss Dutcher to read some of her verses to us. Dr. Thatcher writes me that she does verses excellently well." This sobered the company at once, as it well might, and Rose was in despair.

" Oh, no, don't ask me to do that, please."

" This is your chance, rise to it," insisted Isabel.

" If you will, I'll sing my song again for you," Sanborn said.

At last Rose gave up resistance.   Her heart beat so terribly hard she seemed about to smother, but she recited a blank verse poem.   It was an echo of Tennyson, of course, not exactly " Enoch Arden," but reminiscent of it, and the not too critical taste of Dr. Sanborn and Professor Roberts accepted it with applause.

Mason stole a sly look at Isabel, who did not give up.   She asked for one more, and Rose read a second selection, a spasmodic, equally artificial graft, a supposedly deeply emotional lyric, an echo of Mrs. Browning, with a third line which went plumping to the deeps of passion after a rhyme.   It had power in it, and a sort of sincerity in the reading which carried even Isabel away. For the girl's magnificent figure was a poem in itself.

" What a voice you have ! " she said, as she seized her by the hands.   " You read beautifully — and you write well, too."

Rose noticed that Mr. Mason, · the large man, said nothing at all.   In the midst of the talk the maid approached Isabel.

" Someone has called for Miss Dutcher."   Rose sprang up to go with a feeling that she had stayed too long.   Every one said " Good-by.   I hope we'll see you again ; " and Isabel went with her to help her put on her things.

" My dear, you've pleased them all, and I've fallen in love with you.   I'm going to have you at the Woman's Club.   You must come and see me again.   Come often, won't you ? "

"I shall be glad to," Rose said, simply, but her face was flushed and her eyes were shining with joy.

Owen was outside in the hall alone.

"Didn't Mary come too?"

"No, she concluded it would look awkward if she came and stood outside the door."

They walked along side by side. Taylor considered it an affectation to offer a strong young woman his arm, except at critical passages of the street.

"Did you have a good time?"

"Oh splendid!" she said, the joy of her social success upon her. "It was lovely! I never met such fine people. Everything was so full of fun and they were intellectual, too. Dr. Herrick is wonderful! Mr. Mason, too."

"What Mr. Mason?"

"Warren Mason, I think they call him."

"Is that so? Warren Mason is considered one of the finest newspaper men in the city. All the fellows look up to him."

"I'm glad I met him. Oh, now I see! Dr. Herrick invited him there to hear me read. I made a failure, I'm afraid."

She thought so more and more as the rose-color of her little triumph grew gray. She ended by tossing to and fro on her bed, raging against her foolish action. The long poem was bad. It was involved and twisted and dull. She saw Mason's face darken again, and it seemed now it was a look of disgust.

And the whistling! Good heavens! was there no limit to her folly, her childishness?

So she writhed and groaned, her hopes all pathetically trampled and dust-covered now. Everybody would hear of her idiocy. She had been so determined to do something worth while, and she had read her worst lines, and whistled — whistled like a cow-boy. The houses of the Lake Shore Drive seemed like impenetrable castles in the depth of her despair, and Mason's words about the city grew each moment deeper in meaning.

*   ·*   *   *   *   *   *

After Rose left, Dr. Herrick came back into the room radiant.

"There, what do you think of her? Am I crazy or not? I claim to have discovered a genius."

"My dear, seems to me Thatcher has a prior claim."

"Well, anyhow she *is* a genius. Don't you think so, Warren?"

"She can whistle."

"Oh, don't be so enigmatical, it is out of place. She's got power. You can't deny that."

"Time enough to say what she can do when she finds out what polly-rot she is writing now. The whistling interested me," he added, malevolently.

Isabel's face darkened a little.

"I understand this is one of your frank nights. But I shall not allow it to affect me. You cannot sneer down that beautiful girl."

"I'm not sneering her down. I am merely indicating where she needs help. She is a glorious creature physically, and she's keen mentally — morally, no doubt, she's well instructed — after the manner of country girls — but æsthetically she's in a sorrowful way. Taste is our weak point in America, and in the rural regions — well there isn't any taste above that for short-cake, dollar chromos, and the New York *Repository*."

"He's started, he's off!" said Roberts. "Now, I like the girl's verses; they are full of dignity and fervor, it seems to me."

"Full of fever, you mean. You specialists in nerve diseases and spotted bugs wouldn't know a crass imitation of Tennyson if you had it in a glass vial. It's such poor creatures as you who keep these young writers imitating successes. The girl has a fine roll of voice and a splendid curve of bust, and that made the stuff she read, poetry — to impressionable persons."

"Oh! Oh! Oh!" chorused the young people.

"Roberts, you are a sensualist," Sanborn interposed, gravely.

Mason imperturbably proceeded.

"The girl has power of some sort. I rather suspect it to be dramatic, but that's mimetic and of a low order, anyway. Her primary distinction, with me, consists in something quite other than these. The girl has character, and that's saying a good deal about a woman, especially a girl. She has departed widely from the conventional type without losing essential womanliness."

"Ah, now we are coming at it!" they all exclaimed, as they drew around him, with exaggerated expressions of interest.

"The girl is darkly individual, and very attractive

because of it; but you make of her a social success, as
I can see Isabel is planning to do, and get her wearing
low-necked dresses and impoverishing her people, and
you'll take all the charm out of her."

" I don't believe it!" said Isabel.

" It hasn't hurt Dr. Herrick," put in Roberts. "I
must say I'd like to see the girl in a low-necked dress"
— he waved his hand to hold them in check. " Now,
hold on! I know that sounds bad, but I mean it all
right."

"Oh, no doubt!" They laughed at his embarrassment.

Mason interposed. " Roberts's long stay among the
Wallapi and Tlinkit wigwams has perverted his naturally
moral nature."

Roberts shook his hands in deprecation, but uttered no
further protest.

Sanborn said : " It's a serious thing to advise a girl like
that. What do you intend to do, Isabel? Is a social
success the thing the girl needs?"

" It won't do her any harm to meet nice people — of
course, she ought not to go out too much if she's going
to write."

" You amuse me," Mason began again, in his measured way. " First because you assume that the girl can
go where she pleases —— "

" She can, too, if she has the quality we think she has.
Chicago society isn't the New York Four Hundred.
We're all workers out here."

"Workers and thieves," Mason went on; "but if
the girl has the quality I think she has, she will map

out her own career and follow it irresistibly. The question that interests me is this — how did the girl get here? Why didn't she stay on the farm like Susan, and Sally, and Ed, and Joe? How did she get through college without marrying Harry or Tommy? These are the vital questions."

"I don't know," replied Isabel. "I thought of those things, but of course I couldn't ask her on first acquaintance."

Mason lifted his eyebrows. "Ah! You drew the line at love and marriage. Most women ——"

Isabel resented this.

"I'm not 'most women'—I'm not even a type. Don't lecture me, please."

"I beg your pardon, Isabel; you're quite right." His tone was sincere, and restored peace. "I always except you in any generalization."

"This is the most significant thing of all," Isabel said, finally. "The girl has set us talking of her as if she were a personage, instead of a girl from a Wisconsin valley ——"

"That's true," Mason admitted. "She's of the countless unknown hundreds of the brightest minds from the country, streaming into the city side by side with the most vicious and licentious loafers of the town.

"It leaves the country dull, but moral. The end is not yet. In the end the dull and moral people survey the ruined walls of the bright and vicious cities."

"And the dull and the moral are prolific," Sanborn put in.

"Precisely, and they can eat and sleep, which gives them vast stomachs and long life."

Roberts sprang up. "I propose to escape while I can. Mason is wound up for all night."

There was a little bustle of parting, and eventually Sanborn and Mason walked off together.

"It's no time to go to sleep. Come to my room and smoke a pipe," suggested Mason. "I'm in a mood to talk if you're in a mood to listen."

Sanborn was a modest fellow, who admired his friend. "I am always ready to listen to you," he said.

"Probably that is your amiable weakness." Mason dryly responded.

CHAPTER XVIII

MASON TALKS ON MARRIAGE

MEN are not easily intimate. They confide in each other rather seldom. Of love and marriage coarse men speak with sneers and obscene jests, while serious men express themselves in hints, with apologetic smiles, as if they were betraying a weakness, seldom going to any length of direct statement.

Sanborn had known Mason for some years. They were both from the country; Mason from a small interior town in Illinois, Sanborn from Indiana. Mason was an older man than Sanborn, and generally presumed upon it; also upon Sanborn's reticence.

They rode up the elevator in the Berkeley flats in silence, and in silence they removed their coats and filled their pipes, and took seats before the fire. Mason was accustomed to say he supported two rooms and an open grate fire, and he regretted it was not cold enough to have the grate lighted for that evening.

They sat some minutes in smoke. Mason, sitting low in his chair, with his face in repose, looked old and tired, and Sanborn was moved to say:

" Mason, I'm going to ask you a plump question: Why don't you get married? You're getting old."

" I've tried to."

" What ! tried to ? "

" Exactly."

" That is incredible ! "

" It is the fact," replied the older man, placidly.

Sanborn did not believe it. He knew Mason to be somewhat seclusive in his life, but he also knew the high place he held in the eyes of several women.

Mason went on, finally, in his best manner, as Sanborn called it.

" For ten years I've been trying to marry, and I've been conscientious and thorough in my search, too."

Sanborn was violently interested. He drew a long breath of smoke.

" What seems to be the matter ? "

" Don't hurry me. For one thing, I suppose, I've gone too far in my knowledge of women. I've gone beyond the capability of being bamboozled. I see too much of the ropes and props that do sustain the paste-board rose-tree."

" That is flat blasphemy," put in Sanborn. " I know more about women than you do, and —— "

" I don't mean to say that women deceive in a base way — often they are not intentionally deceptive ; but hereditarily transmitted, necessarily defensive wiles lead them to turn their best side toward men. Before I was thirty I could still call upon a young woman without observing that she received me in a room shadowed to

conceal her crows-feet. The pre-arranged position of
the chairs and color of the lamp-shade did not trouble
me."

He seemed to pause over some specific case. "And
once I believed a girl wore a patch on her chin to conceal a sore. Now I know she does it to locate a dimple. I know perfectly well what any young woman
would do if I called upon her to-morrow. She would
take a seat so that the softest shadows would fall over
her face. If she had good teeth she would smile often.
If her teeth were poor she would be grave. If her arms
were fair her sleeves would be loose, if they were thin
she'd wear ruffles. If she had a fine bosom her dress
would be open a little at the neck ———"

"Oh, look here, Mason!" Sanborn interrupted, "I
can't listen to such calumny without protest."

"I don't mean to say that all this would be conscious. As a matter of fact it is generally innocent and
unintentional. A woman does not deliberately say : 'I
have a dimple, therefore I will smile.' She inherited
the dimples and the smile from a long line of coquettes.
Women are painfully alike from generation to generation. It's all moonshine and misty sky about their infinite variety."

"Suppose I grant that — who's to blame? mind you
I don't grant it — but suppose I do, for argument."

"You are a lover and a fortunate man. You have
in Isabel a woman of character. Mark you! These
wiles and seductions on the part of women were forced
upon them. I admit that they have been forced to use

them in defence for a million years. Had they been our physical superiors unquestionably the lying graces would have been ours. At the same time it doesn't help me. I can't trust such past-masters in deceit, albeit they deceive me to my good."

"Are we not deceptive also? It seems to me the same indictment would hold regarding men."

"Undoubtedly — but we are not now under indictment. You asked me a question — I am answering it." This silenced Sanborn effectually. Mason refilled his pipe and then resumed:

"Again I can't seem to retain a vital interest in any given case — that is to say, an exclusive interest."

"That is a relic of polygamy," Sanborn said. "I imagine we all have moments when we feel that old instinct tumbling around in our blood."

"I meet a woman to-day who seems to possess that glamour which the romantic poets and high-falutin novelists tell us the woman of our choice must have. I go home exulting — at last I am to reach the mystic happiness marriage is supposed to bring. But to-morrow I meet her and the glamour is faded. I go again and again, every spark of electric aureole vanishes; we get to be good friends, maybe — nothing more."

"Perhaps a friendship like that is the best plane for a marriage. Isabel and I have never pretended to any school-boy or school-girl sentiment."

Mason replied in such wise Sanborn did not know whether to think him bitterly in earnest or only lightly derisive.

"That would overturn all the sentiment and love-lore of a thousand years. It would make every poet from Sappho down to Swinburne a pretender or a madman. Such ideas are supreme treason to all the inspired idiots of poetry. No! glamour we must have."

Sanborn smiled broadly, but Mason did not see him.

"So I say, marry young or marry on the impulse, or you'll come at last to my condition, when no head wears an aureole."

"I wonder what started you off on this trail, Mason?"

Mason pushed on resolutely:

"I have become interested and analytical in the matter. I follow up each case and catalogue it away. This failure due to a distressing giggle; that to an empty skull; this to a bad complexion; that to a too-ready sentiment. If I could marry while the glamour lasts! I admit I have met many women whose first appeal filled me with hope; if I might contrive to marry then it might be done once for all. That, of course, is impossible, because no woman, I am forced to admit, would discover any seductive glamour in a taffy-colored blonde like me. My glamour comes out upon intimate acquaintance."

"Perhaps the glamour needed could be developed on closer acquaintance with women who seem plain at first sight."

"Possibly! But I can't go about developing glamour in strange, plain women. They might not understand my motives."

Sanborn laughed, dismally.

" Then the case seems to me hopeless."

"Precisely. The case seems hopeless. After ten years' careful study of the matter I have come to the conclusion that I was born to something besides matrimony. Cases of glamour get less and less common now, and I foresee the time when the most beautiful creature in the world will possess no glamour."

Sanborn imaginatively entered into this gloomy mood.

" Nothing will then remain but death."

"Exactly! Peaceful old age and decay. But there are deeper deeps to this marriage question, as I warn you now on the eve of your venture. I find in myself a growing inability to conceive of one woman in the light of an exclusive ideal, an ideal of more interest than all the world of women. I am troubled by the ' possible woman.' "

" I don't quite conceive —— "

" I mean the woman who might, quite possibly, appeal to me in a more powerful and beautiful way than the one I have. I am not prepared as I approach the point to say I will love and cherish till death. In the unknown deeps of life there are other women, more alluring, more beautiful still. So I must refuse to make a promise which I am not sure I can keep."

" Isabel and I have agreed to leave that out of our ceremony," said Sanborn; " also the clause which demands obedience from her."

" I am watching you. If your experiment succeeds, and I can find a woman as fine and sensible and self-reliant — but there again my confounded altruism comes in. I think also of the woman. Ought I to break into the orderly progress of any woman's life? I can't afford to throw myself away, I can't afford to place a barrier between me and the 'possible woman,' and per contra, neither can the woman afford to make a mistake; it bears harder upon women than it does upon men. When the glorious 'possible woman' comes along I want to be free. So the woman might reasonably want to be free when the ideal man comes along."

"If you really love, these considerations would not count."

Mason waved a silencing palm.

"That will do. I've heard those wise words before. I am ready to be submerged in such excluding emotions."

"Mason," said Sanborn, "one of two things I must believe : Either that you have fallen in love with that superb country girl to-night or you've been giving me a chapter from your new novel."

Mason looked around with a mystic gleam in his eyes.

"Well, which is it?"

CHAPTER XIX

ROSE SITS IN THE BLAZE OF A THOUSAND EYES

LIFE quickened for the coolly girl. She accommodated herself to the pace of the daily papers with amazing facility. She studied the amusement columns, and read the book reviews, and frequented the beautiful reading-room of the Newberry Library. She went to all the matinees, taking gallery tickets, of course, ever mindful of her slender resources — studying as truly, as intently, as if she were still at college.

She had written her father to say that three hundred dollars would carry her through till June, and she was determined it should do so. She had not begun to think of any work to do beyond her writing. Her mind was still in unrest — life's problem was seemingly more difficult of solution than ever.

She took hold upon the city with the power of a fresh mind capable of enormous feeling and digesting. She seemed to be in the world at last, plunged in it, enveloped by it, and she came to delight in the roar and tumult of it all, as if it were the sound of winds and waters; and each day she entered upon a little wider circle of adventure. Once the first confusion was past, the movement and faces of the crowds were of endless interest to her. She walked down into the city every day, returning to her little nook in the noisy flat building, as the young eagle to its eerie above the lashing tree-tops. She was sitting above the tumult, as Mr. Mason had advised her to do.

She came soon to know that the west side of State Street was tabooed by wealthy shoppers, who bought only on the east side; that Wabash Avenue was yet more select, and that no one who owned a carriage ever traded in the bargain stores. She did all her shopping there because it was cheaper, but deep in her heart she felt no kinship with the cross, hurrying, pushing, perspiring crowds at the bargain counters. Her place was among the graceful, leisurely, beautifully attired groups of people on the east side of State Street. She was not troubled at this stage of her development by any idea of being faithful to the people of her own material condition and origin. She had always loved the graces of life, and her father was a man of innate refinement. The idea of caste, of arbitrary classes of people, had only come to her newly or obscurely through newspapers or novels. She did not like dirty people, nor surly people, nor boorish people. In fact, she did not class people at all; they were individuals with her yet. She was allured by the conditions of life on the Lake Shore Drive because the people lived such quiet, clean, and joyous lives apparently, with time to think and be kind.

She met few people outside of the circle at the boarding-house, and an occasional visiting friend of Miss Fletcher or Mr. Taylor.   Owen she saw much of, and he pleased her greatly.   He was a man she could have married under other circumstances.   He had means to live a scholarly unhurried life and was an unusual character, almost elemental in his simple sincerity, but she considered him committed to Mary, and, besides, Mason had become a deterring cause, though she hardly realized that.

Through all the days which followed that evening at Dr. Herrick's she saw Mason's face with growing distinctness.   It was not a genial face, but it was one to remember, a face of power.   The line of the lips, the half-averted chin, the eyes, expressed disgust or weariness.   He was the most powerful man she had ever known, a man of critical insight, and for that reason especially she had sought in her last reading to please him.   She had failed, and so she was afraid to see him again.   When Isabel said to her:

" Mason is a man you should know.   He can do a great deal for you in the city," Rose replied, in her blunt fashion:

" I don't want him to do anything for me."

" Oh, yes, you do!   He's really a kind-hearted man. He puts on a manner which scares people sometimes, but he's a man of the highest character.   He's the greatest thinker I ever met — Oh, I'm not disloyal to Dr. Sanborn, he's the *best* man I ever met."   There was a story in that tender inflection.   " So you must let me send in something to Warren, and let him advise you."

Rose finally consented, but it seemed to her like laying an only child upon the rack. She had come almost to fear, certainly to dread, that strange, imperturbable man. His abiding-place and his office were alike so far removed from any manner of living she had knowledge of, and he concealed his own likes and dislikes so effectually that not even Isabel (as she confessed) could learn them.

A few days after putting her packet of poems into Isabel's hands Rose received a note from her to come over and see her — that she had an invitation for her.

"We are invited, you and Dr. Sanborn and I, to sit in a box at the symphony concert Saturday night, with Mr. and Mrs. Harvey. Mrs. Harvey is one of my dearest friends, and I've talked about you so much she is eager to see you."

Rose took the matter very quietly. She was mightily pleased, but she was not accustomed to gushing her thanks; besides, she had recovered her equilibrium.

Isabel was a little surprised at her coolness, but was keen enough to see that Rose did not mean to be ungrateful.

"I thought perhaps you'd like to advise about dress," she said. "The boxes are very brilliant, but you'll look well in anything. You won't need a bonnet, your hair is so pretty, and that little gray dress will do, with a little change."

"You know I'm a farmer's daughter," Rose explained; "I can't afford new dresses in order to go to the opera."

"I understand, my dear. I have my own limitations in that way. I keep one or two nice gowns and the rest of the time I wear a uniform. I told Mrs. Harvey you were poor like myself, and that we'd need to be the background for her, and she said she'd trust me."

(What Mrs. Harvey had said was this: "My dear Isabel, you've got judgment, and if you say the girl's worth knowing I want to know her. And if you say the girl will be presentable I'd like to have her come. The boys are both in New York, anyway, and we've got three unoccupied seats.")

"Now you come over to dinner with me Saturday; come at five. I want you to help me dress. Doctor will be over, and we'll have a nice time before the carriage comes."

Rose was much more elated than she cared to show. Once as she sat in the gallery of the theatre and looked at the boxes she had shut her teeth in a vow: "I'll sit there where you do, one of these days!" and now it had come in a few weeks instead of years — like a fairy gift. She told Mary nothing about her invitation for several days. She dreaded her outcry, which was inescapable.

"Oh! isn't that fine! How you *do* get ahead — what will you wear?"

"I haven't a bewildering choice," Rose said. "I thought I'd wear my gray dress."

"Oh, this is a wonderful chance for you! Can't you afford a new dress?"

"No, I'm afraid not. There isn't time now, anyway. I'll keep close to the wall. Fortunately I have a new cloak that will do."

"Well, that gray dress is lovely — when it's on you."

Rose hated the bother about the dress.

"I wish I could wear a dress suit like a man," she said to Isabel when they were in the midst of the final stress of it.

"So do I, but we can't. There's a law against it, I believe. Now I'm going to dress your hair for you. That is, I'm going to superintend it, and Etta's deft little fingers shall do the work."

After dinner, Isabel ordered things cleared and said to Sanborn :

"Doctor, you go and smoke while we put on our frills."

Sanborn acquiesced readily enough.

"Very well — if you find me gone when you come forth, don't worry. I've gone ahead with my friend Yerkes. Your carriage will be full, anyhow."

"All right." She went over and gave him a hug. "You're a good, obedient boy — that's what you are!"

He spoke (with his chin over her wrist) addressing Rose :

"The study of chemicals and nerve-tissues has not left us utterly desolate, you perceive."

When they were in their dressing-room, Rose asked what the Doctor meant by that speech.

Isabel laughed and colored a little.

"Oh, he meant that a study of bones and muscles and diseased bodies had not made us prosaic and — and old. I think it has made me still more in love with healthy human flesh — but never mind that now; we must hurry."

Rose looked at Isabel in silent worship as she stood before her ready for the carriage. Her ordinarily cold little face glowed with color, and her eyes were full of mirthful gleams like a child's. It seemed impossible that she had written a treatise on " Nervous Diseases," and was ranked among the best alienists in the city.

Etta made no secret of her adoration. She fairly bowed down before her sister and before Rose also. She was so little and so commonplace before these beings of light.

Down at the carriage it was too dark to see anyone distinctly, but Rose liked the cordial, hearty voice of Mrs. Harvey. Mr. Harvey's hand was small and firm, Mrs. Harvey's plump and warm. Mr. Harvey spoke only once or twice during the ride.

As the carriage rumbled and rolled southward at a swift pace, Rose kept watch out of the window. The street had not lost a particle of its power over her.

As they plunged deeper into the city, and the roll of other carriages thickened around them, the importance of this event grew upon Rose. She was bewildered when they alighted, but concealed it by impassivity, as usual. The carriages stood in long rows waiting to unload. Others were rolling swiftly away; doors slammed; voices called, " All right!" A mighty stream of people was entering the vast arched entrance, with rustle of garments and low murmur of laughing comment. Rose caught the flash of beautiful eyes and the elusive gleam of jewels on every side, as the ladies bowed to their acquaintances.

Everything was massive, and spacious, and enduring. The entrance way was magnificent, and Rose followed Mr. Harvey as if in a dream. They took a mysterious short cut somewhere, and came out into a narrow balcony, which was divided into stalls. Through arched openings Rose caught glimpses of the mighty hall, immense as a mountain-cave, and radiant as a flower.

As they moved along, Mrs. Harvey turned to Isabel.

" She'll do ; don't worry ! "

At their box Mr. Harvey paused and said, with a pleasant smile :

" Here we are."

Dr. Sanborn met them, and there was the usual bustle in getting settled.

" You sit here, my dear," said Mrs. Harvey. She was a plump, plain, pleasant-voiced person, and put Rose at ease at once. She gave Rose the outside seat, and before she realized it the coolly girl was seated in plain view of a thousand people, under a soft but penetrating light.

She shrank like some nocturnal insect suddenly brought into sunlight. She turned white, and then the blood flamed to her face and neck. She sprang up.

" Oh, Mrs. Harvey, I can't sit here," she gasped out.

"You must!—that is the place for you," said Mrs. Harvey. "Do you suppose an old housewife like me would occupy a front seat with such a beauty in the background? Not a bit of it! The public welfare demands that you sit there." She smiled into the scared girl's face with kindly humor.

Isabel leaned over and whispered: "Sit there; you're magnificent."

Rose sank back into her seat, and stared straight ahead. She felt as if something hot and withering were blowing on that side of her face which was exposed to the audience. She wished she had not allowed the neck of her dress to be lowered an inch. She vowed never again to get into such a trap.

Mr. Harvey talked to her from behind her chair. He was very kind and thoughtful, and said just enough to let her feel his presence, and not enough to weary her.

Gradually the beauty and grandeur of the scene robbed her of her absurd self-consciousness. She did not need to be told that this was the heart and brain of Chicago. This was the Chicago she had dreamed about. A perfumed rustling rose from below her. Around her the boxes filled with girls in gowns of pink, and rose, and blue, and faint green. Human flowers they seemed, dewed with diamonds. All about was the movement of orderly, leisurely, happy-toned, and dignified men and women. All was health, pleasure, sanity, kindliness. Wealth here displayed its wondrous charm, its peace, its poetry.

Her romantic conception of these people did them an injustice. She clothed them with the attributes of the men and women of English society novels and they became mysterious and haughty to her. This Mr. Harvey did not know, but he helped her to rectify her mistaken estimate of the people around her by saying:

"We business men can't get out to the Friday rehearsals, but Saturday night finds us ready to enjoy an evening of art."

He looked very handsome in evening dress, and his face was very pleasant to see, yet Isabel had told her that not only was he a hard-working business man, but a man of wide interests, a great railway director, in fact.

"I suppose you know many of the people here," she said at last.

"Oh, yes," he replied, "I know most of them. Chicago is large, but some way we still keep track of each other."

As he talked, she gained courage to raise her eyes to the roof, soaring far up above, glowing with color. Balcony after balcony circled at the back, and she thought with a little flush that perhaps Owen and Mary were sitting up in one of those balconies and could see her in the box.

The hall was buff and light-blue to her eyes, and the procession of figures over the arch, the immense stage, the ceiling, the lights, all were of great beauty and interest.

But the people! the beautiful dresses! the dainty bonnets! the flow of perfumed drapery! the movement of strong, clean, supple limbs! — these were most glorious of all to her. She had no room for envy in her heart. She was very happy, for she seemed to have attained a share in the city's ultimate magnificence.

She longed for gowns and bonnets like these, but there was no bitterness in her longing.

She herself was a beautiful picture as she sat there. From her bust, proud and maternal, rose her strong smooth neck, and young, graceful, reflective head. If the head had been held high she would have seemed arrogant; with that reflective, forward droop, she produced upon the gazer an effect both sweet and sad. In the proud bust was prophecy of matronly beauty, and much of the freshness of youth.

Mason, seated below among a group of musical critics, looked at her with brooding eyes. At that moment she seemed to be the woman he had long sought. Certainly the glamour was around her then. She sat above him, and her brown hair and rich coloring stood out from the drapery like a painting. A chill came over him as he thought of the letter he had sent to her that very morning. It was brutal; he could see that now. He might have put the criticism in softer phrases.

Isabel leaned over and spoke to Rose and then Rose began searching for him. He was amazed to experience a thrill of excitement as he saw that strong, dark face turned toward him; and when his eyes met hers he started a little, as if a ray of light had fallen suddenly upon him. She colored a little, he thought, and bowed. Where did the girl acquire that regal, indifferent inclination of the head? It was like a princess dropping a favor to a faithful subject, but it pleased him.

" The girl has imagination ! " he said. " She claims her own."

Then he meditated : " What an absurdity ! Why should I fix upon that girl, when here, all about me, are other women more beautiful, and rich and accomplished besides ? That confounded farmer's girl has a raft of stupid and vulgar relatives, no doubt, and her refinement is a mere appearance."

He solaced himself with a general reflection.

" Furthermore, why should any man select any woman, when they are all dots and dashes in a web of human life, anyhow ? Their differences are about like the imperceptible differences of a flock of wrens. Why not go out and marry the first one that offers, and so end it all ? "

The mystery of human genius came also to Rose as Mr. Harvey pointed out to her the city's most noted men and women. They were mere dabs of color — sober color, for the most part — upon this flood of humankind. She was to Mason, probably, only a neutral spot in the glorious band of color, which swept, in a graceful curve, back from the footlights. It was wonderful to her, also, to think that these smiling men were the millionaire directors of vast interests — they seemed without a care in the world.

At last the stage chairs were completely filled by a crowd of twanging, booming, sawing, squeaking instrumentalists. At last the leader, a large man of military erectness, came down to the leader's desk and bowed, amidst thunderous applause. Then rapping sharply with his baton he brought orderly silence out of the tumult, and the concert began.

The music did not mean much to Rose during the first half hour, for the splendor of the whole spectacle dominated the appeal of the instruments. Such music and such audiences were possible only in the largest cities, and that consideration moved her deeply. It seemed too good to be true that she was sitting here securely, ready to enjoy all that came. It had come to her, too, almost without effort, almost without deserving, she humbly acknowledged that. But there came at last a number on the programme which dimmed the splendor of the spectacle. The voice of Wagner came to her for the first time, and shook her and thrilled her and lifted her into wonderful regions where the green trees dripped golden moss, and the grasses were jewelled in very truth. Wistful young voices rose above the lazy lap of waves, sad with love and burdened with beauty which destroyed. Like a deep-purple cloud death came, slowly, resistlessly, closing down on those who sang, clasped in each other's arms.

They lay dead at last, and up through the hovering cloud their spirits soared like gold and silver flame, woven together, and the harsh thunder of the gray sea died to a sullen boom.

*   *   *   *   *   *   *

When she rose to her feet the girl from the coolly staggered, and the brilliant, moving, murmuring house blurred into fluid color like a wheel of roses.

The real world was gone, the world of imagined

things lay all about her. She felt the power to reach out her hand to take fame and fortune.

In that one reeling instant the life of the little coolly, the lonely, gentle old father, and the days of her youth — all her past — were pushed into immeasurable distance. The pulling of weeds in the corn, the driving of cattle to pasture were as the doings of ants in a dirt-heap.

A vast pity for herself sprang up in her brain. She wanted to do some gigantic thing which should enrich the human race. She felt the power to do this, too, and there was a wonderful look on her face as she turned to Isabel. She seemed to be listening to some inner sound throbbing away into silence, and then her comprehension of things at hand came slowly back to her, and Isabel was speaking to her.

" Here's Mr. Mason coming to speak to us," interrupted Mr. Harvey.

She turned to watch him as he came along the aisle behind the boxes; her head still throbbed with the dying pulsations of the music. Everybody seemed to know Mason and greeted him with cordial readiness of hand. He came along easily, his handsome blond face showing little more expression at meeting her than the others, yet when he saw her rapt and flushed face he was touched.

" I came to see how Miss Dutcher was enjoying the concert."

Rose felt a sudden disgust with her name; it sounded vulgarly of the world of weeds and cattle.

In some way she found herself a few moments later walking out through the iron gate into the throng of promenaders back of the seats.   It was the most splendid moment of her life.   She forgot her fear of Mason in the excitement of the moment.   She walked with hands clenched tightly and head lifted.   The look in her eyes, and the burning color in her face made scores of people turn to study her.

Mason perceived but misinterpreted her excitement. He mistook her entire self-forgetfulness for a sort of vain personal exultation or rapture of social success.

She saw only dimly the mighty pillars, the massive arches, lit by stars of flame.   She felt the carpet under her feet only as a grateful thing which hushed the sound of feet.

They made one circuit with the promenaders, Mason bowing right and left, and talking disjointedly upon indifferent subjects.   He felt the tormenting interest of his friends in Rose, and drew her out of the crowd.

" Let us stand here and see them go by," he said. " You liked the music, did you ? "

His commonplace question fell upon her like the scream of a peacock amid songs of thrushes.   She comprehended by a flash of reasoning of which he could not know, that it was possible to be ennuied with glorious harmonies.   Her thought was, " Shall I, too, sometimes wish to talk commonplaces in the midst of such glories ? "

" Oh, it was beyond words ! " she said.   And then Mason was silent for a little space.   He had divined her mood at last, but he had something to say which should be said before she returned to her box.

He began at once:

"Let me say, Miss Dutcher, that while the main criticism of your work, which I made in my note this morning, must hold, still I feel the phraseology could have been much more amiable. The fact is I was irritated over other matters, and that irritation undesignedly crept into my note to you."

"I haven't received it," she said, looking directly at him for the first time.

"Well then, don't read it. I will tell you what I think you ought to do."

"Oh, don't talk of it," she said and her voice was tense with feeling. "All I have written is trash! I can see that now. It was all somebody else's thought. Don't let's talk of that now."

He looked down at her face, luminous, quivering with excitement — and understood.

"I forgot," he said, gently, "that this was your first concert at the Auditorium. It is beautiful and splendid, even to me. I like to come here and forget that work or care exists in the world. I shall enjoy it all the more deeply now by reason of your enthusiasm."

In the wide space back of the seats a great throng of young people were promenading to the left, round and round the massive pillars, in leisurely rustling swing, the men mainly in evening dress, the ladies in soft luminous colors; the heavy carpet beneath their feet gave out no sound, and only the throb of laughter, the murmur of speech, and the soft whisper of drapery was to be heard.

It was all glorious beyond words, to the imaginative country girl. It flooded her with color, beauty, youth, poetry, music. Every gleaming neck or flashing eye, every lithe young body, every lover's deferential droop of head, every woman's worshipful upturned glance, came to her with power to arouse and transform. The like of this she had not dreamed of seeing.

Nobody had told her of this Chicago. Nobody could tell her of it, indeed, for no one else saw it as she did. When Mason spoke again his voice was very low and gentle. He began to comprehend the soul of the girl.

"I've no business to advise you. I've come to the conclusion that advice well followed is ruinous. Genius seldom takes advice, and nobody else is worth advising. I took advice and went into a newspaper office twenty years ago. I've been trying ever since to rectify my mistake. I would be a literary man if I were not forced to be a newspaper man, just when my powers are freshest. I want to write of to-day. I want to deal with the city and its life, but I am forced to advise people upon the tariff. I come home at night worn out, and the work I do then is only a poor starveling. Now, see this audience to-night! There are themes for you. See these lovers walking before and behind us. He may be a clerk in a bank; she the banker's daughter. That man Harvey, in whose box you sit to-night, was a farmer's boy, and his wife the daughter of a Methodist preacher in a cross-roads town. How did they get where they are, rich, influential, kindly, polished in manner? What an epic!"

"Are you advising me now?" she asked, with a smile.

Her penetration delighted him.

"Yes, I am saying now in another way the things I wrote. I hope, Miss Dutcher, you will burn that packet without reading. I would not write it at all now."

They were facing each other a little out of the stream of people. She looked into his face with a bright smile, though her eyes were timorous.

"Do you mean manuscript and all?"

His face was kind, but he answered, firmly:

"Yes, burn it all. Will you do it?"

"If you mean it."

"I mean it. You're too strong and young and creative to imitate anybody. Burn it, and all like it. Start anew to-night."

His voice compelled her to a swift resolution.

"I will do it."

He held out his hand with a sudden gesture, and she took it. His eyes and the clasp of his hand made her shudder and grow cold, with some swift, ominous fore-knowledge of distant toil and sorrow and joy.

The lights were dimmed mysteriously, and Mason said:

"They are ready to begin again; we had better return."

He led her back to the box, and Mrs. Harvey flashed a significant look upon him, and said, in a theatrical aside:

" Aha ! at last."

Isabel said :

" Come and see us to-morrow at six — a ' powwow.' "

The music which came after could not hold Rose's attention. How could it, in the face of the tremendous changes which were in progress in her brain? What had she done? To an almost perfect stranger she had promised to burn all the work of her pen thus far.

And an hour before she had almost hated, certainly she had feared, that man. While the music wailed and clashed, she sat rigidly still, longing to cry out, to sing, and to weep. Without saying so to anyone, she had finally settled upon one great ambition which was to write, to be a great poetess. After vicissitudes and false enthusiasm she had come back to her first aspiration which she had confessed to Dr. Thatcher years before, in the little coolly school-house. And now, at the bidding of a stranger, she had made a promise to burn her work and start again !

But had not the music and the splendid spectacle before her almost determined her before he had spoken ?

She returned again and again to the wondrous gentleness which was in his voice, to the amazing tenderness which was in his eyes. The man who had held her hand that moment was not the worn, cynical man she had feared. He was younger and handsomer, too. She shuddered again, with some powerful emotion at the thought of his calm, compelling, down-thrusting glance into her eyes. His mind appeared to her to have a shoreless sweep.

R

The music rose to a pounding, blaring climax, and the audience, applauding, rose, breaking into streams and pools and whirling masses of color.

"Well, my dear, how have you enjoyed the evening?" asked Mrs. Harvey, cordially.

"Very much, indeed. I never can thank you enough."

"It has been a pleasure to feel your enthusiasm. It makes us all young again. I've asked Dr. Herrick to bring you to see us; I hope you will come."

The hearty clasp of her hand moved the motherless girl deeply, and her voice trembled with emotion as she replied:

"It will be a great pleasure to me, Mrs. Harvey."

Mrs. Harvey clutched her in her arms and kissed her.

"You splendid girl! I wish you were mine," she said, and thereafter Rose felt no fear in her presence.

"I don't care whether she's a genius or not," Mrs. Harvey said to Isabel, as they walked out to the carriage. "She's a good girl, and I like her, and I'll help her. You figure out anything I can properly do and I'll do it. I don't know another girl who could have carried off that cheap little dress the way she did. She made it look like a work of art. She's a wonder! Think of her coming from a Wisconsin farm!"

Isabel rejoiced.

"I knew you'd like her." She leaned over and said, in a low voice: "I'd like Elbert to see her."

Mrs. Harvey turned a quick eye upon her.

"Well, if you aren't a matchmaker!"

As they came out in the throng it seemed as if everybody knew the Harveys and Isabel. Out in the street the cabs had gathered, like huge beetles, standing in patient rows in the gaslight.

The bellowing of numbers, the slam of carriage-doors, the grind of wheels, the shouts of drivers, made a pandemonium to Rose, but Mr. Harvey, with the same gentle smile on his face, presented his ticket to the gigantic negro, who roared enormously:

"Ninety-two! Ninety-two!"

"Here we are!" Mr. Harvey called, finally, and handed the women in with the same unhurried action, and the homeward ride began. There was little chance for talk, though Mrs. Harvey did talk.

Rose sat in silence. This had been another moment of sudden growth. She was still conscious of great heat and turmoil in her brain. It was as if upon a seed-bed of quick-shooting plants a bright, warm light had been turned, resulting in instant, magical activity. At her door they put her down, and once more she thanked them.

"It's nothing at all, my dear; we hope to do more for you," said Mrs. Harvey. "I want you to come to dinner soon. You'll come?"

"With pleasure," Rose responded, quite as a man might have done.

CHAPTER XX

ROSE SETS FACE TOWARD THE OPEN ROAD

WHEN Rose reached her room, she found the packet of poems lying on her desk. It had come in the afternoon mail.

She sat down by the toilet-table with a burning flush on her face. A world seemed some way to lie between her present self and the writer of those imitative verses. She wished to see, yet feared to see what he had written, and taking up the packet she fingered the string while she meditated. She had not absolutely promised not to read the letter, though she had pledged herself to burn the poems.

Her life was so suddenly filled with new emotions and impulses, that she was bewildered by them. The music, the audience-room, the splendid assemblage, and some compelling power in Mason — all of these (or he alone) had changed her point of view. It was a little thing to the great city, a little thing to him probably but to her it was like unto the war of life and death.

What, indeed, was the use of being an echo of passion, a copy? She had always hated conformity; she hated to dress like other girls; why should she be without individuality in her verse, the very part wherein, as Mason had intimated, she should be most characteristically herself?

She had the chance to succeed. The people seemed ready to listen to her if she had something to say; and she had something to say — why not say it?

Rising tense with resolution, she opened the stove and dropped the packet in, and closed the door and held it as if she feared the packet might explode in her face, or cry out at her. In her poems she would have had the heroine fling it in the grate and snatch it out again, but having no grate the stove must serve, and there could be no snatching at the packet, no remorseful kisses of the charred body. It was gone in a dull roar.

She sat down and waited till the flame died out, and then drew up to her desk and wrote swiftly for an hour. She grew sleepy at last, as the tumult of her brain began to die away. Just before she went to sleep all her lovers came before her: Carl, in the strawberry-scented glade; William De Lisle, shining of limb, courtesying under the lifting canvas roof; Dr. Thatcher, as he looked that afternoon in the school-room; Forest Darnlee, with the physical beauty of William De Lisle, but vain and careless; Professor Ellis, seated at his desk in the chalk-laden air, or perched on the ladder beneath the great telescope, a man who lived in abstract regions far from sense and sound; and Tom Harris, slim, graceful, always smiling — Tom, who had the songs of birds, the smell of flowers, the gleam of sunset-water leagued with him — who almost conquered, but who passed on out of her life like a dapple of purple shadow across the lake.

And now she faced two others, for she could see that Owen was turning to her from Mary, and he had great charm. He was one of the purest-souled men she had ever known, and was enriched also by a suggestion of paganism, of mystery, as of free spaces and savage, unstained wildernesses. He could give her a beautiful home, and would not restrict her freedom. He would be her subject, not her master.

Then there was Mason — of him what? She did not know. He stood outside her knowledge of men. She could neither read his face nor understand his voice. He scared her with a look or a phrase. Sometimes he looked old and cynical, but to-night how tenderly and sympathetically he had spoken! How considerately silent he had been!

When she awoke, Mary was standing looking down at her.

"If you're going to have any breakfast, Rose, you'd better be stirring. It's nine o'clock, and everything's ready to clear away. What kind of time did you have?"

Rose resented her question, but forced herself to answer:

"Beautiful!"

"I saw you in the box. Owen and I were in the second balcony. You were just scrumptious! I wanted to throw a kiss at you." She fell upon Rose and squeezed her, quilt and all, in her long arms. "My stars! I wish I was lovely and a poet."

She felt nothing but joy over her idol's good fortune, and it made Rose feel guilty to think how resentful and secretive she had become. There was coming into her friendship with Mary something which prevented further confidence — a feeling that Mary was not a suitable confidant, and could not understand the subtleties of her position, which was correct.

With Mary, procedure was always plain sailing. Either she was in love and wanted to marry, or she wasn't. Her ideals changed comparatively little, and were healthily commonplace. Her friendships were quick, warm, and stable. She was the country girl in the city, and would be so until death. If she felt disposed, she chewed gum or ate an apple on the street like a boy, and she walked on the Lake Shore Sunday evening with Owen, unconscious (and uncaring) of the servant-girls and their lovers seated on every bench.

Rose was growing away from her friend. She perceived it dimly the first week, and now the certainty of it troubled her. Her life was too subtle, too complicated, and too problematic, for honest, freckle-faced, broad-cheeked Mary to analyze.

Then, too, there was the question of Owen. Soon Mary must see how he set face toward her, but she felt quite equal to answering him when Owen came to speak, because his appeal to her was not in the slightest degree sensuous, as Tom Harris's had been.

She spent the day in deep thought, jotting down some

lines which came to her, and writing a letter home. She filled it full of love and praise for "pappa John," as if in remorse for growing so far away from him.

That done she fell back in thought upon her group of friends; upon the concert, and upon her eventful promenade with Mason.

The world of art which she was beginning to imagine seemed so secure and reposeful, so filled with splendor of human endeavor, that nothing else seemed worth while. She drew her breath in a mighty resolution to be a part of it. Art had always seemed to her to be afar off, something European, but now she seemed to be coming in personal contact with it, and for a day she soared in exultation only to fall the day after into dreary doubt of her powers.

Her literary ideals were so hopelessly confused! She had lost the desire to write as she had been writing, and there seemed nothing left to write about. The door had closed upon her old forms of action, and yet the way Mason had pointed out to her was dark and utterly bewildering. She felt great things moving around her; themes, deeds that were enormous, but so vaguely defined, she could not lay hold upon them.

As she went down the street to Dr. Herrick's house on the night of the party, she had a feeling of having committed herself to something. She knew that Isabel had taken her case in hand, and that several young men had been invited to meet her. She could not resent this zeal of her new-found friend for it was manifestly from the heart — could not be otherwise. Of what advantage to Dr. Herrick could it be to take her up — a poor country girl?

In fact, she was puzzled by this overpowering kindness. There was so little apparent reason for it all. She could not, of course, understand the keen delight of introducing a powerful and fresh young mind to the wonders of the city. She had not grown weary of "sets" and "circles," and of meeting the same commonplace people again and again, as Mrs. Harvey had. Isabel's position was different, but she had an equal delight, more subtle and lasting, in seeing the genius (as she believed) of the girl win its way, and besides, the girl, herself, pleased her mightily.

Isabel Herrick's life was one of deep earnestness and high aims. She was the daughter of a physician in an interior city and had worked her way up from the bottom in the usual American fashion by plucky efforts constantly directed to one end. She was the head of the house of Herrick, which consisted of her young sister, a brother at college, and her aged mother, now an invalid.

She had been one of the first three girls to enter the medical school, and had been the shield and fortress to others of her sex in the storm which followed their entrance into the dissecting-room. The battle was short but decisive. Her little head was lifted and her face white as she said:

"Men — I won't say gentlemen — I'm here for business, and I'm here to stay. If you're afraid of competition from a woman you'd better get out of the profession."

In the dead silence which followed a lank country fellow stepped out and raised his voice.

"She's right, and I'm ready to stand by her, and I'll see she's let alone."

Others shouted : " Of course she's right ! " by which it appeared the disturbance was of the few and not the mass of students, a fact which Isabel shrewdly inferred. She spoke a grateful word to the lanky student, and Dr. Sanborn found his wife right there.

There was little for Isabel to discover concerning the sordid and vicious side of men. She knew them for what they were, polygamous by instinct, insatiable as animals, and yet she had been treated on the whole with courteous — often too courteous — kindness. Her dainty color and her petite figure won over-gallant footway everywhere, though she often said :

" Gentlemen, I have studied my part. I know what I am doing and I ask only a fair field and no favors."

Thatcher and Sanborn had been her close companions in the stern, hard course they set themselves ; each had said, with vast resolution to the other : " I'm not to be left behind." Thatcher had made apparently the least mark in the world, but was writing a monograph which was expected to give important facts to the medical profession. He had written to Sanborn several times : " You have the advantage of association with the ' Little Corporal.' "

They called her " Little Corporal " among themselves because her stern, sweet face had a suggestion of Napoleon in it, and besides she ordered them about so naturally and led them so inevitably in everything she undertook.

It was into the hands of the " Little Corporal " that Rose had fallen, and all Isabel's enthusiasm was roused in her behalf. Her own sister was a sweet, placid little thing, who had inherited the body, and spirit as well, of her mother, while Isabel had inherited the mind of her father in the body of her mother.

Something of this Thatcher had told Rose, part of it Isabel had imparted, and it made only one definite impression on Rose — this, that a woman could succeed if she set her teeth hard and did not waste time.

She found Isabel already surrounded by company. On every other Sunday evening she was informally " at home," and certain well-known artists and professional people dropped in to talk awhile, or to sit at her generous table. It was a good place to be, as Rose had perception enough to feel, once her first timidity had passed.

" Oh, you dear child ! I'm glad to see you. There's someone here you'll be glad to see."

Rose flushed a little, thinking of Mason.

" It's an old friend — Dr. Thatcher."

Rose clapped her hands : " Oh, is he ? I'm so glad ; it's almost like seeing the folks."

" I've asked Elbert Harvey and Mr. Mason also ; I didn't want you to think I had no friends but doctors. It must seem to you quite as if my world were made up of medicine men. But it isn't."

Thatcher greeted Rose quietly but with a pressure of

the hand which made up for his impassivity of counte-
nance.   He trembled a little as he took his seat and
saw Rose greeting Sanborn and Mason.

Fear and admiration were both present in Rose's heart
as Mason took her hand.

She forced herself to look into his face, and started to
find his eyes so terribly penetrating.

"I burned the packet," she said, with a constrained
smile.

His eyes grew softer and a little humorous.

" Did you, indeed!   Without opening?"

" Yes."

" Heroic girl!"

" Am I not?" she said over her shoulder as Isabel
dragged her toward a tall smooth-faced young fellow
who stood talking with Etta.

" Elbert, this is Miss Dutcher — Rose, young Mr.
Harvey, son of our hostess at the concert."

Young Harvey seemed much taken back as he faced
Rose, but shook hands heartily in the angular fashion
current among college men.   His mind formulated
these opinions :   " She's a stunner!   Caroline was dead
right!"   By " Caroline " he meant his mother.

Rose catalogued him at once as "another college
boy."   Paul and Etta joined them, making a handsome
group, and they were soon as much at ease as schoolmates of a year's standing, laughing, telling stories, and
fighting over the East and the West.

Rose stoutly defended the Western colleges; they
had their place, she said.

"So they have," Elbert replied, "but let them keep it."

"Their place is at the head, and that's where we'll put them soon," she said.

Elbert told a story about hazing a Western boy at Yale. He grew excited and sprang up to dramatize it. He stood on one foot and screwed up his face, while the rest shrieked with laughter, all except Rose, who thought it unjust.

Mason looked on from his low chair with a revealing touch of envious sadness. He had gone far past that life — past the land of youth and love — past the islands of mirth and minstrelsy. He was facing a cold, gray sea, with only here and there a grim granite reef gnawing the desolate water into foam.

It made him long to be part of that group again, and he valued Rose more at that moment than ever before. "The girl has imagination, she has variety. She is not a simple personality. At the concert she was exalted, rapt, her eyes deep. To-night she is a school-girl. Then it was Wagner — now it is college horse-play."

Isabel came up to sit a moment by him.

"Isn't she fine? I think I surprised young Harvey. I thought I'd like to have her meet him — he's such a fine fellow. She should meet someone else besides us old fogies."

Mason winced a little.

"Well now, that's pleasant! Do you call me an old fogy?"

She laughed:

"Oh, we're not old in years, but we're old in experience. The bloom of the grape is lost."

"But the grape is ripe, and we still have that. The bloom — what is it? A nest for bacteria."

"But it is so beautiful with the bloom on," she said, wistfully. "I'd take it again, bacteria and all. See those young people! The meeting of their eyes is great as fame, and the touch — the accidental touch of their hands or shoulders, like a return of lost ships. I am thirty-three years of age and I've missed that somewhere."

Mason lifted his eyebrows.

"Do you mean to say that the touch of Sanborn's hand does not hasten your blood?"

"I do — and yet I love him as much as I shall ever love anybody — now."

Mason studied her, and then chanted, softly:

> "Another came in the days that were golden,
> One that was fair, in the days of the olden
> Time, long ago!

You've never told me about that."

She smiled. "No, but I will some time — perhaps."

She led the way out to supper with Dr. Thatcher, and the rest followed without quite breaking off conversation, a merry, witty procession.

Rose was conscious of a readjustment of values. Dr. Thatcher had less weight in the presence of these people, but Mason — Mason easily dominated the table without effort. Indeed, he was singularly silent, but there was something in the poise of his head, in the glance of his eyes, which indicated power, and insight into life.

The young folks, led by young Harvey, took possession of the table, and laughter rippled from brief silence to silence like a mountain stream. Young Harvey aided at the chafing-dish with the air of an adept, and Isabel was almost as light-hearted in laughter as he.

Thatcher and Mason seemed to sit apart from it, and Mason found opportunity to say:

"You knew our young friend of the coolly — discovered her, in fact?"

"Yes, as much as anyone could discover her. It's a little early to talk of her as if she had achieved fame."

"Dr. Herrick thinks she's on the instant of going up higher, and so we're all hanging to her skirts in hopes of getting a rise."

Thatcher didn't like Mason's tone.

"Rose is a hard worker. If she rises any higher it will be by the same methods which put her through college." He spoke with a little air of proprietorship.

Mason felt the rebuff, but he was seeking information about Rose, and could afford to ignore it.

"She's an only child, I believe."

"Yes; her father is a hard-working, well-to-do farmer in a little 'coolly' in Wisconsin."

"It's the same old story, I suppose; he doesn't realize that he's lost his daughter to the city of Chicago. We gain at his expense."

Mason's mind had something feminine about it, and

he perceived as never before how attractive to Rose a
fine young fellow like Harvey could be. Being rich he
was lifted above worry. His activity was merely wholesome exercise, and his flesh was pink and velvety as a
girl's. He was strong, too, as it was the fashion of
college men of his day to be. He had never known
want or care in his splendid life. He was, moreover, a
good boy. Money had not spoiled his sterling nature.
It was no wonder that Rose's eyes grew wide and dark as
they rested on him. They were physically a beautiful
pair, and their union seemed the most inevitable thing
in the world.

Isabel leaned over to say :

"Aren't they enjoying themselves? I wish Mrs.
Harvey could see them."

After they had returned to the sitting-room a couple
of young artists came in with John Coburg, Mason's
room-mate on the *Star*. He was a meagre-faced fellow of extra-solemn visage, relieved by twinkling black
eyes. The artists were keen, alert-looking fellows,
with nothing to indicate their profession save their
pointed beards. One of them being lately from Paris
turned his mustaches up devilishly ; the other had fallen
away from his idols sufficiently to wear his mustaches
turned down, and allowed himself an extra width of
beard.

Rose was glad Mr. Davidson twisted his mustache ;
there was so little else about him to indicate his high
calling.

Their coming turned the current of talk upon matters

of art, which made Rose feel perfectly certain she was getting at the heart of Chicago artistic life.

Mr. Davidson inveighed against America, and Chicago especially, for its " lack of art atmosphere."

" If you've got the creative power you can make your own art atmosphere," his companion hotly said. " You always start up on that tack." Evidently it was a source of violent argument between them.

" The trouble is you fellows who paint, want to make a living too easy," Mason remarked.

" You ought to stay and do pioneer work among us," said Isabel.

" I don't consider it worth while, so far as I am concerned. I prefer Paris."

" You're not very patriotic."

" There is no patriotism in art."

" That's the regular Parisian jabber," returned his friend. " I talked all that myself. What you need is a touch of poverty. I'd like to see your people drop you in a small town where you had to make your own living for a little while."

" The hard conditions of Chicago are changing," Isabel interposed, with peaceful intent. " All that was true a few years ago is not true now. The materialism you war against no longer dominates us. We are giving a little time to art and literature."

Davidson twisted his mustache point. " It isn't noticeable yet — Oh, there's a little band of fellows starving here like rats in a garret — but what general recognition of art have you ? "

s

" What could you expect ? "

" Well, you might buy pictures."

" We do — old masters and salon pictures," said Mills, with a relenting acknowledgment of the city's weakness.

" That's it exactly ! " said Davidson. " You've no judgment here. You are obliged to take your judgment from somebody else."

So the talk proceeded. To Rose it was illuminating and epoch-making. She read in it the city's developing thought. Paris and the Rocky Mountains met here with Chicago and the most modern types of men and women.

Meanwhile Mason found opportunity to say to Thatcher, who seemed a little ill at ease :

" These little informal Sunday suppers and free-for-alls are increasing in number, and they are signs of civilization. Of course a few of the women still go to church in the morning, but that will wear off, except at new-bonnet time."

Thatcher did not reply; he thought Mason a little flippant.

Rose sought opportunity to talk about Mrs. Thatcher and Josephine.

" They're quite well."

" I wish I could see them both."

" We should be glad to welcome you back to Madison any time. But I hardly expect to see you, except on a vacation, possibly. You're a city dweller already. I can see that." He seemed sadder than she had ever known him, and his look troubled her a little.

At ten o'clock she rose to go, and young Harvey sprang up:

" Are you going ?   If you are I hope you'll give me the pleasure — my carriage —— "

" Thank you very much," she answered, quickly. " I've a friend coming for me."   Thatcher rose as if to go with her, but sat down again with a level line of resolution on his lips.

Mason and Harvey both wondered a little about that friend.   Mason took a certain delight in young Harvey's defeat, and analyzed his pulse to find out why he was delighted.   " We should mob that friend," he said to Sanborn.   " He is an impertinence, at this time."

Rose felt Isabel's arm around her as she entered the cloak-room.

" Isn't he fine ? "

" Who ? "

" Mr. Harvey."

" Oh — yes — so are the artists."   Rose began to wonder if Isabel were not a matchmaker as well as a promoter of genius.

Isabel had a suspicion of Rose's thought and she laughingly said:

" Don't think I'm so terrible !   I do like to bring the right people together.   I see so many people wrongly mated, but I don't mean — I only want you to know nice people.   You're to do your own choosing," she said, with sudden gravity.   " No one can choose for you.   There are some things I want to talk about when I can venture it."

Mason and Sanborn were the last to go and when
Isabel returned from the door, where she had speeded
the last guest, she dropped into a chair and sighed.

"It's splendid good fun, but it does tire me so!   Talk
to me now while I rest."

"Sanborn, talk!" Mason commanded.

Sanborn drew a chair near Isabel and put his arm
about her.   She leaned her head on his shoulder.

Mason rose in mock confusion.

"I beg your pardon!   I should have gone before."

Isabel smiled.   "Don't go; we're not disturbed."

"I was considering myself."

"Oh, you were!"

"Such things shock me, but if I may smoke I might
be able ——"

"Of course.   Smoke and tell me what you think of
Rose now!   Isn't it strange how that girl gets on?   She's
one of the women born to win her way without effort.
It isn't true to say it is physical; that's only part of it
— it's temperament."

Mason got his cigar well alight before he said :

"She has the prime virtue — imagination."

"Is that a woman's prime virtue?"

"To me it is.   Of course there are other domestic
and conjugal virtues which are commonly ranked higher,
but they are really subordinate.   Sappho and Helen and
Mary of the Scots were not beautiful nor virtuous, as
such terms go; they had imagination, and imagination
gave them variety, and variety means endless charm.
It is decidedly impossible to keep up your interest in a

woman who is the same yesterday, to-day, and to-mor-row — whose orbit can be predicted, whose radiance is without the shadow of turning."

" Should he be stopped ? " Isabel asked of Sanborn.

" I shouldn't like the job," Sanborn replied.   " When he strikes that line of soliloquy he's out of my control."

*   *   *   *   *   *   *

Rose again found Owen waiting in the hall, and she accepted his escort with the frankness of a sister.

" Have you waited long ? "

" No, I was just going to ring the bell when I heard your voice."

They walked on in silence.   At last he asked :

" Did you have a good time ? "

" Splendid ! " she answered.

" We missed you," he said.

Rose felt something tender in his voice and remained silent.

" I heard from my partners to-day."   He went on after a pause — " They're feeling mighty good.   Struck another vein that promises better than the one we have. I ought to go out, but I —— "   He paused abruptly. " Did you ever see the Rockies in late fall ?   Oh, they're mighty, mighty as the sky !   I wish you'd — I wish we could make up a party some time and go out.   I'd take a car —— "

She faced the situation.

" I'll tell you what would be nice : When you and Mary take your wedding-trip I'll go along to take care of you both."

Owen fairly staggered under the import of that speech, and could find nothing to say in reply. After a long pause, he pleasantly inquired, as if for the first time:

"Did you have a good time to-night?"

"Splendid! I always do when I go to Isabel's." Thereafter they walked in silence.

Rose fell to thinking of young Harvey in the days which followed. There was allurement in his presence quite different from that of any other young man she had ever known. She could not remember anything he had said, but he had made her laugh, and his face was so frank and boyish. She felt in him the grace and the charm which come from security of position and freedom from care.

He brought up to her mind, by force of contrast, her father, with eyes dimmed by the harsh winds, the dust, and the glowing sun, who was in the midst of long, dull days wandering about the house and barn, going to bed early in order to rise with the sun, to begin the same grind of duties the day following. Young Harvey's life was the exact opposite of this and to Rose it was most alluring.

Elbert admired her, she felt that as distinctly as if he had already put his feeling into words. He wanted to be near her. He had asked her to help him with the chafing-dish that night, and to pour the beer while he stirred the gluey mass of cheese. All the little signs by which a young man expresses his admiration had been used almost artlessly, certainly boyishly.

The girl who became his wife would find certain

relief from toil and worry. What a marvellous thing to be suddenly set free from all fear of hunger and every harassing thought about the future! And it was not a question of marrying an old man, or a man of repulsive appearance; it was a question of taking a bright, handsome, young man, together with his money. She felt the power to put out her hand and claim him as her own.

She liked him, too; he amused her and interested her. She admired his splendid health and his clear, laughing eyes. It seemed the easiest thing in the world—to an outsider. Isabel, she well knew, was working hard to have her see young Harvey at his best, and she felt, too, that Mrs. Harvey was taking unusual interest in her, and in her secret heart she knew she could marry into that fine family, but —

Liking was not love! She did not shiver when he clasped her hand, as she did when Mason greeted her. She feared Mason. When he came by, her judgment blurred and her eyes fell. She couldn't tell what his traits were, and she didn't know whether he was a good man or not. She hungered to see him, to hear his voice; beyond that she hardly dared consciously go.

His attitude toward her she could not understand. Sometimes he seemed anxious to please her, sometimes he seemed equally determined that she should understand how inconsequential she was in his life — and always he dominated her.

She did not once think it might be indecision in his mind — after the usual stupidity of love's victims, she thought his changes of manner due in some way to her. She had acted foolishly, or she was looking so badly he was ashamed of her.

In this condition of mind, it may be imagined, she did not do much studying or writing. She went to the library regularly, but she could not concentrate her thoughts upon her book. She grew surly and changeable with Mary, who no longer dared to talk unguardedly with her.

Mary's eyes were not glass marbles; she could see things with them, and she said gleefully to Owen one night :

" She's in love, that's what is the matter with her. I don't mind it. She'll be all right after awhile. She's short as pie-crust with me, but I know how it is myself. She's in love with some high-flyer she's met at Dr. Herrick's house."

Then she wondered why Owen made no reply.

CHAPTER XXI

MASON TALKS AGAIN

NOT seeing Mason for some days, Sanborn took a walk one night, and turned up about nine o'clock at his rooms. He found him sitting before his open-grate fire, smoking meditatively.

"Hello, Sanborn! Glad you came over." He did not rise, but Sanborn was untroubled by that.

"Got another chapter turned off?"

"Possibly. Fill up and draw up."

Sanborn obediently filled a pipe and drew up a chair.

"You look tired."

"I am. I have written a column editorial on the labor question, one on the Chinese treaty, a special article on irrigation for the Sunday issue, not counting odd paragraphs on silver, anarchy, and other little chores of my daily grind."

"That's not so bad as poulticing people."

"Bad! There's nothing any worse, and my novelistic friends are always saying, 'Why don't you turn in and finish up your novel?' What can an intellectual prostitute do?"

"Get out of the business, one would suppose."

" Well, now, that brings me to the point. In the midst of all my other worriments, I am debating whether to marry a rich girl and escape work, or a poor girl and work harder, or to give the whole matter of marriage up forever."

" These are actual cases, not hypothetical, this time ? "

Mason turned a slow eye upon him.

" I have no need to fly to hypothetical cases," he said, dryly. " In the first place, my hero — if you incline to-night to that theory of the case — my hero is equally interested in two young women. This is contrary to the story-books, but then only an occasional novelist tells the truth. I'm to be that one."

He seemed to be going off upon some other line of thought, and Sanborn hauled him back by asking a pertinent question :

" You mean to say both of these young ladies have that glamour ? "

" Oh, not at all! They did have, but it has faded in both cases, as in all previous cases, yet more seems to have remained, or else I am getting a little less exacting. In the case of the sculptress — she's the poor girl, of course — she's a genius. The first time I saw her she read a paper on ' The Modern in Sculpture' (it was good, too). She was dressed beautifully, in cheese-cloth, for all I know — I only know she put to shame her sculptured copies of Hope and Ariadne. The glamour was around her like rose-colored flame. It was about her still when I stepped up to her. She was tall, and strong as a young lioness. Her soft sweet eyes

were level with mine, and she made me ashamed of every
mean thing I had uttered in my whole life."

" Well, well! " exclaimed Sanborn.

" She was flattered and exalted to think ' the editor '
was pleased with her essay, and the rest was easy.   I
went to call on her a day or two later ——— "

" And the glamour — the glamour ? "

Mason shook his head.   " Faint!   She was in her
study, and the hard, cold light was merciless.   She was
handsome, even then, but her face had a pinched look,
and there was a heavy droop to her lips.   The color so
beautiful that night when flushed with excitement had
faded from her cheeks, and gathered in some unfortunate
way about her eyes and nose.   She was a fine woman,
but — the glamour was gone."

" What an eye for symptoms! you should have been
a physician," Sanborn put in.

" At the same time she grew upon me.   She's an
artist.   She has the creative hand — no doubt of that.
She has dreams, beautiful dreams of art.   She glows,
and dilates, and sings with the joy of it.   She could
bring into my life something of the dreams I myself had
as a youth.   She's going to make a name for herself,
without question."

" Why, that's glorious, Warren, old man ; she's just
the wife for you!   And she really inclines toward you ? "

" She does."   Then his self-crucifying humor came
in.   " That's really her most questionable virtue.   However, if Love can laugh at locksmiths, I suppose he can
laugh at a bald head.   But this is only one phase of the

matter. Like all spectators, you are informed of only one side of the banner. Let's look at the other.

"I manage to live here and support this fire, which is my only extravagance. I keep the establishment going, and a little more. I'll anticipate the usual arguments. Suppose, for a little while, it would not increase expenses. It would not do to bring a woman here, it would not be right. When children came — and I should hope for children — they should have a home in the suburbs; I don't believe in raising children in a flat. That would mean an establishment which would take every cent I could hook on to, and it would mean that the whole glittering fabric would be built upon my own personal palm."

"But she might earn something — you say she's a genius."

"She is, that's the reason she'll never make money. Holding the view I do, I could not require her to toil. I do not believe marriage confers any authority on the husband — you understand my position there?"

"Perfectly — and agree with it, to a limited extent, of course."

"Going back, therefore — I do not believe I can assume the risk involved. I'm not capable of twenty years' work at my present rate. I'd break down, some fine day, and then my little home, upheld upon my Atlas palm, would tumble. No, I can't take the risk. I'm getting too foxy; I haven't the bounce I once had. Besides, her career is to be considered. I don't believe I can afford to let her marry me."

"That's mighty kind of you," Sanborn dryly remarked.

"Thank you. I think it is an error of judgment on her part. She is younger, and as her adviser I think I must interfere and save her from the power of a vivid imagination and abounding vitality. You see, there are a great many considerations involved."

"Real love, I must repeat, would not consider."

"I wish you wouldn't repeat it, it does you an injustice. The animal passion of youth would not consider. With youth, it is marry — marry, even if within the year you are picked up by the patrol wagon, a vagrant in the streets. The love of my time is not so heedless nor so selfish; it extends to the question of the other party to the transaction."

"I suppose that should be so, but as a physician I doubt it. My observations do not run that way. Age grows like a child again, thoroughly selfish."

"Then there is the question of the 'possible woman,'" Mason resumed, and his tone was cynically humorous again. "I can't give her up. There she stands in a radiant mist always just before me like the rainbow of our childhood. I can't promise any woman to love her till death. I don't know as it would be safe to promise it even to the woman with glamour. Another might come with a subtler glory, and a better fitting glamour, and then —— "

"What then?"

"It would be all up with the first woman," he said, with a gravity of tone of which the words gave no hint.

"I'm afraid someone has already come to make pale

the beauty of the sculptress. What about the other, the rich girl you set over against the sculptress at the beginning? Mind you, I believe the whole situation is fictitious, but I'll humor you in it."

" Well, Aurelia — we'll call her Aurelia — brings up a far-reaching train of reflections, and, if you've got a patient waiting, you'd better come again."

" I'm the only patient waiting."

Mason ignored the lame old pun and proceeded :

" Aurelia lives in Springfield. You know the kind of home the wealthy politician builds in a Western town — combination of jail and court-house. I attended a reception there last winter and saw Aurelia for the first time. She was as beautiful as an acrobat —— "

" I don't want to interrupt, Mason, but I notice all your heroines are beautiful."

" They must be; my taste will not permit me to tolerate unsymmetrical heroines. I started in as an architect and I've done a little paddling in clay, and my heroines must be harmonious of structure — glamour comes only with beauty, to me."

" Largely physical, then."

" Certainly ! I believe in the physical, the healthy, wholesome physical. In the splendor of the tiger's wooing is no disease."

" Well, well, she was beautiful as an acrobat —— "

Mason looked sour. " One more interruption, and the rest of my heart-tragedy will remain forever alien to your ear."

Sanborn seemed alarmed.

"My lips are glued to my pipe."

Mason mused — ("Composed!" Sanborn thought.) "She looked as if she had been moulded into her gown. The Parisian robe and the hair piled high, were fast — undeniably theatric, but her little face was sweet and girlish, almost childish. Well, she had glamour, largely physical as you say. But like the heroes of E. P. Roe's novels, I aspired to awaken her soul. She was pleased with me apparently. I called soon after the reception — I always follow up each case of glamour. I knew she was rich, but I did not realize she commanded such an establishment.

"It was enormous. Her mother was a faded little hen of a woman, who had been a very humble person in youth, and who continued a very humble person in middle-life. The court-house in which she was forced to live, continually over-awed her, but the girl used it, entertained in it as if she had a string of palace-dwelling ancestors straggling clear back to Charlemagne."

"That's the American idea, the power of adaptation. Our women have it better developed than —— "

"She was a gracious and charming hostess, and I admit the sight of her in command of such an establishment was impressive. I thought how easily a tired editor could be absorbed into that institution and be at rest — a kind of life hospital, so to say. She was interested in me — that was certain."

"Now, Mason, I must protest. You know how high Isabel and I both hold you, but we never quite considered you in the light of a ladies' man. Your

Springfield girl must have had dozens of brilliant and handsome young men about her."

Mason smoked in silence, waiting till Sanborn's buzz ceased.

"Well, she came to the city last month, and I've been to see her a number of times; the last time I saw her she proposed to me."

Sanborn stared, with fallen jaw gaping, while Mason continued in easy flow.

"And I have the matter under consideration. I saw the coming storm in her eyes. Last night as we sat together at the piano she turned suddenly and faced me, very tense and very white.

"'Mr. Mason, why can't you — I mean — what do you think of me?'

"I couldn't tell her that night what I thought of her, for she had seemed more minutely commonplace than ever. She had trotted round her little well-worn circle of graces and accomplishments, even to playing her favorite selection on the piano. I equivocated. I professed it was not very easy to say what I thought of her, and added:

"'I think you're a fine, wholesome girl,' as she is, of course.

"'But you don't think I'm beautiful?' That was a woman's question, wasn't it? 'Yes,' I said in reply, 'I think you are very attractive. Nature has been lavish with you.'

"Then she flamed red and stammered a little:

"'Then why don't you like me?'

" ' I do,' I said.

" ' You know what I mean,' she hurried on to say — ' I want you to like me better than any other woman.'

" ' That's impossible,' I replied. It was pitiful to see her sitting there like a beggar in the midst of all her splendor. ' I like you very much. I think you're very sweet and kind and girlish.'

" She seemed to react from her boldness. Her eyes filled with tears. ' I know you think I'm *terrible* to say these things.'

" ' No. I feel that I do not deserve such trust on your part.' Then she defended me. ' Yes, you do. I couldn't have spoken to anyone else so. You're so kind and gentle.' "

" Did she say that of you ? " asked Sanborn.

" She said that."

Sanborn sighed. " I wish I could reach that phase of your character. What did you say in reply ? "

Mason apparently showed deep feeling at last.

" I told her that I was like the average man. I was taking credit to myself for not devouring her like a wolf ! She didn't listen to that. ' What can I do to make you like me ? ' she asked. She leaned toward me, her chin in her palm, thinking and suffering as her sweet little soul had never suffered before. ' I'm too simple,' she said, with a flash of startling insight. ' I don't know enough. I feel that. Can't I study and change that ? '

" ' You're changing that now,' I replied.

T

" She grew radiant for a moment.

" ' Oh, you *do* like me a little ! ' ' "

As he went on, Mason's tone grew sweet and solemn. It had singular power of suggestion, and developed more of his nature than he knew; his real gravity and tenderness and purity appeared in every word.

" There you have it," he ended. He ended by striking the ashes out of his pipe.

" I could marry her, but it wouldn't make her happy. It would make her suffer. It is not a light thing to decide. It is a very grave thing. As in the case of the sculptress I thought it an error of judgment on her part, and on my own it would be criminal."

" That's a fine bit of fiction," said Sanborn. " You're too rough on yourself, for you could do the girl a deal of good by marrying her."

" Possibly. In the case of the sculptress the problem is different. She is moving past me like a queen — splendid, supple, a smile of conscious power on her lips, the light of success in her eyes. It's a terrible temptation, I admit, this power to stretch out my hand and stay her. It makes my blood leap, but my sense of justice will not allow of it. I shall let her pass on, beautiful and rapt."

" To marry some confounded pinhead, who will make her a domestic animal, and degrade her into ' my wife, gents ' ? "

" Possibly. However, my responsibility ends where I say good-by."

" Don't shirk — don't shirk."

Mason turned on him. His voice lost a little of its coldness.

"Is a man to have no credit for letting such a glorious creature pass him, unharmed and free?"

"Why yes, certainly. But the world of art will not satisfy that girl. She's sure to marry — she *must* marry — and she is entitled to more consideration. You've got to look ahead to the time when she regrets the lack of husband and children."

"Ah, but it's a frightful thing, Sanborn, to arrest that girl, to make her a wife and mother, to watch her grow distorted, stiffened, heavy with child-bearing. I prefer to see her pass me, in order that I may remember her, rosy, radiant, moving like music and light."

"That's fine, Mason, I honor you for that spirit," said Sanborn, deeply moved. "But you must remember that I am about to be married to a beautiful woman myself, a woman who knows both sexes, knows their vices and passions. She tells me, and it fits in with what I know myself, that the woman's nature moves on from this beautiful state you've described so well, into the pain and responsibility of marriage not merely willingly, but eagerly. Half the girl's joy, which we men see in her face, is the smile of anticipated motherhood — it must be so. Isabel, as you know, is no sentimentalist; she's a woman you can talk these things to, freely. I can't state it as she did, but the substance of it was this: if the girl knew she was to be always young and childish, her youth and beauty would have no value to her — that it is the untried pain and pleasure of other years and conditions which make the beauty so radiant now."

Mason was instant in reply. "All of which merely means she makes the best of an irresistible and tragic impulse, a force which she does not originate and cannot control. Therefore I say it is a sorrowful business to hew down a temple or tear a lily in pieces."

The two men were silent again. They had reached fundamentals in their talk. Sanborn considered the whole matter an allegory, which Mason was using to veil his design to win Rose if possible. He knew the ease of his host's invention, as well as his power to present a case dramatically, and while he was moved by the expression of a noble thought, he could not think that there was any exact truth contained in the story.

Mason resumed a moment later:

"There are certain other material, minor, and prosaic considerations which must be kept in mind. Suppose I announce my engagement to Miss Aurelia; the newspapers would have a pleasant paragraph or two. Some people would say, 'What a very appropriate match.' Others would say, very knowingly, 'Well, Mason has feathered his nest.' The newspaper boys who really wish me well would say, 'Good for Mason; now he can take time to finish that great American novel he's had on hand so long!' A few shrewd fellows would say, 'Well, that ends Mason! He's naturally lazy, and with a wife and home like that he'll never do another stroke of work. Mason's like Coleridge in one thing:

he dreams great things, but never writes them. He's out of the race!'"

"There's something in that," Sanborn admitted.

"I know there is," Mason replied, without offence. "Now we'll suppose I scrape a little money together for immediate use. The old railway Baron is kind. He tolerates me for the daughter's sake. I come in contact with the relatives; already I have had a touch of them! A girl like that is not like a pebble on the seashore; she's a thread in a web of cloth, a silken thread in a breadth of shoddy, maybe. You can't marry her and have her to yourself. You come into new relations with her people as her *fiancé*. They cannot be escaped. They swarm around you. They question your motives and they comment on your person: 'He's getting bent and bald;' 'He's lazy;' 'What did she ever see in him?' They vulgarize everything they touch. They are as tiresome as the squeal of a pump, but there you are, you must meet them. The old gentleman is a man who deals in millions, reliable and conscientious. He talks to you about his business, till you say, 'business be damned.' He thereafter meets you in heavy silence. The mother is a timid soul, with an exaggerated idea of your importance as an editor. The aunts and uncles variously sniff and tremble before you."

"Meanwhile your wife has talked over all she knows, and all she says thereafter has a familiar sound. She delights in stories with many repetitions in them. Her little brain travels from the pantry to the table, from the tea-table to the children's bath-tub; its widest circuit is

the millinery store and the bargain counter. She gets
fat, that's another distressing phase of my trouble, let
me say. I seem to be gifted with a prophetic eye in
the midst of my transports —— "

"Think of you in a transport!"

"I am able to see just how each one will change,
how this pretty plumpness will get fat, how this delicate
slimness will get bony. I see how this beautiful alert
face will get beakish. In other words I am troubled
about the future, when I should be involved only in the
ecstasy of the present. In this latest case I see excessive
plumpness and chatter in ten years. I see myself bored
to death with her within ten months. She is at her best
now; in striving to win me she is like a female bird,
her plumage is at its best; she will grow dowdy when
the incentive is gone.

"There are other considerations. Aurelia, too, has
exaggerated notions of my power to earn money. She
may expect me to maintain an expensive establishment.
I can't ask anything of the political pirate, her father;
I can only put my income into the treasury. If my
power to earn money decreases, as it may, then I become an object of contempt on the part of the old
savage, who considers money the measure of ability.
Suppose at last I come to the point of borrowing money,
of going to the old man humbly, twisting my hat in my
hand: 'My dear sir, Aurelia and the children' — Pah!'"

He uttered a sound of disgust and anger and fell
silent.

Sanborn mused, "I wonder if the lovers of any other

age had any such scruples about marriage.   I guess you're right about Aurelia, but I don't believe you are about the sculptress.   I think she would make you happy."

Mason mused a moment and then went on:

" Well, now, as to that — marry her and we plunge, inside of two years, into a squalid struggle for bread and coal and a roof.   I elect myself at once into the ranks of dray-horses, and, as I said before, I chain a genius to the neck-yoke with me.   That is also out of the question."

Sanborn sought his hat.

" Well, Mason, this has been a season of plain speaking.   I'd feel pretty bad over it if I thought it was real. When you get the whole thing typewritten I should like to read it to Isabel and Rose."

Mason's face did not change, but he failed to look at his friend.   He said, quietly :

" Isabel wouldn't read it ; the girl might possibly find something in it of value.   Good-night ; you've listened like a martyr."

" Don't fail to write that out while it's fresh in your mind.   Good-night," said Sanborn.

His last glance as he closed the door fell upon a lonely figure lying in a low chair before the fire, and he pitied him.   Mason seemed " the great irresolute " which Isabel believed him to be ; helpless to do, patient to suffer.

CHAPTER XXII

SOCIAL QUESTIONS

THE social world seemed about to open to the coolly girl. At Mrs. Harvey's she called, and behold! her house was but one street removed from the Lake Shore Drive, on which she had stood that September day. It was a home of comfort rather than of wealth, not at all ostentatious, and yet its elegance troubled Rose not a little.

She knew values by instinct, and she knew there was nothing shoddy and nothing carelessly purchased in the room. The Harveys were envied by some of their wealthier neighbors for the harmoniousness of their house. They contrived to make their furniture distinguish itself from a down-town stock — which requires taste in selection, and arrangement as well.

Rose heard voices above, and soon Mrs. Harvey and Isabel came down together. Rose was glad of her friend's presence — it made things easier for her.

After hearty greetings from Mrs. Harvey they all sat down and Mrs. Harvey said:

" I'm glad you came over. We — Isabel and I — feel that we should do something for you socially. I would like to have you come over some Wednesday and

pour tea for me. It's just my afternoon at home, and
friends drop in and chatter a little while; perhaps you'd
enjoy it."

"Oh, you're very kind!" Rose said, dimly divining
that this was a valuable privilege, "but I really couldn't
do it. I — I'm not up to that."

"Oh, yes, you are. You'd look like a painting by
Boldini up against that tapestry, with your hair brought
low, the way you wore it concert night."

Isabel put in a word. "It isn't anything to scare
you, Rose. It's hardly more formal than a college tea,
only there won't be so many men. It will introduce
you to some nice girls, and we'll all make it as easy for
you as we can."

"Oh, yes, indeed; you can sit at the table with
Isabel."

"Oh, it isn't that," Rose said, looking down. "I
haven't anything suitable to wear." She went on
quickly, as if to put an end to the whole matter. "I'm
a farmer's girl living on five hundred dollars a year, and
I can't afford fifty dollar dresses. I haven't found out
any way to earn money yet, and I can't ask my father
to buy me clothes to wear at teas. You are all very
kind to me, but I must tell you that it's all out of my
reach."

The other women looked at each other while Rose
hurried through this. Mrs. Harvey was prepared at the
close:

"There, now, my dear! don't let that trouble you.
Any simple little gown will do."

" Please don't tempt me, Mrs. Harvey, until I can buy my own dresses. I can't ask my father to buy anything more than is strictly necessary."

There was a note in her voice which seemed to settle the matter.

Isabel said, " Perhaps you have something made up that will do. Won't you let me see what you have ? Certainly the dress you wore at the concert became you well."

" If you have anything that could be altered," Mrs. Harvey said, " I have a dressmaker in the house now. She could easily do what you need. She's looking over my wardrobe."

Rose shook her head, and the tears came to her eyes.

" You're very, very kind, but it wouldn't do any good. Suppose I got a dress suitable for this afternoon, it wouldn't help much. It's impossible. I'd better keep in the background where I belong."

She stubbornly held to this position and Mrs. Harvey reluctantly gave up her plans to do something for her socially.

Rose had come to see how impossible it was for her to take part in the society world, which Isabel and Mrs. Harvey made possible to her. The winter was thickening with balls and parties ; the society columns of the Sunday papers were full of " events past," and " events to come." Sometimes she wished she might see something of that life, at other times she cared little. One day, when calling upon Isabel, she said, suddenly : " Do you know how my father earns the money which

I spend for board? He gets up in the morning, before
anyone else, to feed the cattle and work in the garden
and take care of the horses. He wears old, faded clothes,
and his hands are hard and crooked, and tremble when
he raises his tea —— "

She stopped and broke into a moan — "Oh, it makes
my heart ache to think of him alone up there! If you
can help me to earn a living I will bless you. What
can I do? I thought I was right, but Mr. Mason made
me feel all wrong. I'm discouraged now; why was I
born?"

Isabel waited until her storm of emotion passed, then
she said:

"Don't be discouraged yet, and don't be in haste to
succeed. You are only beginning to think about your
place in the economy of things. You are costing your
father but little now, and he does not grudge it: besides,
all this is a part of your education. Wait a year and
then we will see what you had better do to earn a living."

They were in her library and Rose sat with her hat
on ready to go back to her boarding-house. Isabel went
on, after a time spent in thought:

"Now the social question is not so hopeless as you
think. There are plenty of select fine places for you to
go without a swagger gown. Of course, there is a very
small circle here in Chicago, which tries to be ultra-
fashionable, but it's rather difficult because Chicago men
have something else to do and won't be dragooned into
studying Ward McAllister. You'll find the people here
mostly good, sensible people, like the Harveys, who'll

enjoy you in any nice, quiet dress. You can meet
them informally at dinner or at their little Sunday
evening in. So don't you take any more trouble about
it," she ended, " and you needn't pay me for the lecture either."

Rose answered her, smiling :

" I wish I could feel — I wish I didn't care a cent
about it, but I do. I don't like to feel shut out of any
place. I feel the equal of anyone ; I was brought up
that way, and I don't like to be on the outside of anything. That's a dreadful thing to say, I suppose, but
that's the way I feel."

" I'm not going to quarrel with you about the depth
of your depravity ; but I assure you there is no circle
in Chicago worth knowing which will shut you out
because you are a poor girl. Thank heaven, we have
not reached that point yet. And now about your writing. I believe in you. I liked those verses, though I
may not be an acute critic — Mr. Mason says I'm a
conservative, and he's probably right. He says you
should write as you talk. He told me you had remark-
able power in suggesting images to the mind, but in
your verse the images were all second-hand. He be-
lieves you'll come to your own themes and style soon."

"I hope so." Her answer was rather spiritless in tone.

" There's another thing, Rose. You're going to have
suitors here in Chicago, and fine ones, too. May I talk
with you about that ? "

Rose flushed deeply and her eyes fell ; she was a little
incoherent.

"Why, yes — I don't see any reason — there isn't any need of secrecy."

Isabel studied her from a little distance.

"Rose, tell me: how is it that you didn't marry young, as so many poor girls do?"

Rose considered a moment.

"I hardly know myself."

"You had lovers, always?"

"Yes, always."

"And you had fancies, too?"

"Oh, yes, as all girls do, I suppose."

"Why didn't you marry one of these?"

"Well, for one reason, they didn't please me well enough — I mean *long* enough. They grew tiresome after awhile; and then I was ambitious, I wanted to get out into the world. I couldn't marry someone who would bind me down to the cook-stove all my life, and then I had my ideals of what a man should be — and, some way, the boys didn't interest me after awhile."

"I think I understand that. You're going to marry sometime, of course."

Rose looked down: "Why, yes, I suppose so — most girls do."

"Don't think I'm impertinent, will you, but is there any — are you bound to anyone?"

Rose lifted her face.

"No, I am as free as any woman."

"I'm glad of that, Rose. I was afraid you might be half-engaged to someone in the college or back in the valley. It makes it very fine and simple if you can enter your wider life here, free. You are sure to marry, and you ought to marry well."

Rose replied, a little disgustedly :

" I hate to think of marrying for a home, and I hate to think of marrying as a profession. Writers accuse us of thinking of nothing else, and I get sick and tired of the whole thing. I wish I was just a plain animal or had no sex at all. Sometimes I think it is a curse to be a woman." She ended fierce and sullen.

Isabel shrank a little.

" Oh, don't be too hard on me, Rose ! I didn't mean to anger you."

" I'm not angry ; the things I want to say I can't seem to say. It isn't your fault or mine. It's just fate. I hate to think of ' marrying well ' —— "

" I think I understand," Isabel said, a little appalled at the storm she had raised. " I haven't been troubled by that question because I have a profession, and have something to think about besides marriage, and still we must think about it enough to prepare for it. The world must have its wives and mothers. You are to be a wife and mother, you are fitted for it by nature. Men see that — that is the reason you are never without suitors. All I was going to say, dear, was this : you are worthy the finest and truest man, for you have a great career, I feel sure of it — and so — but no, I'll not lecture you another minute. You're a stronger woman than I ever was, and I feel you can take care of yourself."

" That's just it. I don't feel sure of that yet. I feel

dependent upon my father and I ought not to be; I'm out of school, I'm twenty-three years of age, and I want to do something. I must do something — and I don't want to marry as a — as a — because I am a failure."

"Nobody wants you to do that, Rose. But you didn't mean that exactly. You mean you didn't want to come to any man dependent. I don't think you will; you'll find out your best holt, as the men say, and you'll succeed."

Rose looked at her in silence a moment.

"I'm going to confess something," she finally said, with a laugh. "I hate to keep house. I hate to sew, and I can't marry a man who wants me to do the way other women do. I must be intended for something else than a housewife, because I never do a bit of cooking or sewing without groaning. I like to paint fences and paper walls; but I'm not in the least domestic."

Isabel was amused at the serious tone in which Rose spoke.

"There is one primal event which can change all that. I've seen it transform a score of women. It will make you domestic, and will turn sewing into a delight."

"What do you mean?" asked Rose, though more than half guessing.

"I mean motherhood."

The girl shrank, and sat silent, as if a doom had been pronounced upon her.

"That is what marriage must mean to you and to me," Isabel said, and her face had an exultant light in it. "I love my profession — I am ambitious in it, but I could bear to give it all up a hundred times over, rather than my hope of being a mother."

The girl was awed almost into whispering.

"Does it mean that — will it take away your power as a physician?"

"No, that's the best of it these days. If a woman has brains and a good man for a husband, it broadens her powers. I feel that Dr. Sanborn and I will be better physicians by being father and mother. Oh, those are great words, Rose! Let me tell you they are broader than poet or painter, deeper than wife or husband. I've wanted to say these things to you, Rose. You've escaped reckless marriage someway, now let me warn you against an ambitious marriage ——"

She broke off suddenly. "No, I'll stop. You've taken care of yourself so far; it would be strange if you couldn't now." She turned quickly and went to Rose. "I love you," she said. "We are spiritual sisters, I felt that the day you crushed me. I like women who do not cry. I want you to forgive me for lecturing you, and I want you to go on following the lead of your mysterious guide; I don't know what it is or, rather, who he is ——"

She stopped suddenly, and seating herself on the arm of Rose's chair, smiled.

"I believe it is a man, somewhere. Come now, confess — who is he?"

Quick as light the form and face of William De Lisle came into Rose's thought, and she said:

" He's a circus rider."

Isabel unclasped Rose's arm and faced her.

" A circus rider ! "

Rose colored hotly and looked away.

" I — can't tell you about it — you'd laugh and — well, I don't care to explain."

Isabel looked at her with comical gravity.

" Do you know what you've done, ' coolly ' girl ? You know the common opinion of woman's curiosity ? I don't believe a woman is a bit more curious than a man, only a woman is curious about things he isn't. I'm suffering agonies this minute. You know I'm an alienist. I've studied mad people so much I know just what sends them off. You've started me. If you don't explain at once — " She went to the door and called, " Etta ! Don't disturb me, no matter who comes."

" Now tell me about it," she said, as she sat down beside Rose and studied her with avid eyes.

" Why, it's nothing," Rose began. " I never spoke to him, and he never even saw me, and I never saw him but once —— "

" And yet he influenced your whole life ? "

Rose mused a moment.

" Yes, I can see it now — I never realized it before — he has helped me all my life."

She told of her first sight of him, of her long ride home, of her thoughts of him, reserving something, of course, and her voice grew husky with remembered emotion. She uttered more than she knew. She showed the keen little woman at her side the more

u

imaginative side of her nature. It became evident to
Isabel that the beautiful poise of the head and supple
swing of the girl's body was in part due to the suggestion of the man's perfect grace. His idealized face had
made the commonplace apparent — had led her, lifted
her.

"Why, it's all a poem!" she exclaimed at the end.
"It's magnificent; and you thought I'd laugh!" She
looked reproachful. "I think it's incredibly beautiful.
What was his name? We may meet him some
time —— "

Rose drew back and grew hot with a blush.

"Oh, no — I don't want to see him now. I'm
afraid he wouldn't seem the same to me now."

Isabel considered. "You're right! He never really
existed. He was a product of your own sweet girlish
imagination, but let me tell you — " she made a swift
feminine turn to the trivial, "You'll marry a tall, lathy
man, or a short, dumpy man. You never can marry a
handsome man. That's the way things go. Really I
must keep Doctor and Mason out of the house."

CHAPTER XXIII

A STORM AND A HELMSMAN

In quiet wise her winter wore on. In a few months the home feeling began to make itself felt, and the city grew correspondingly less appalling, though hardly less oppressive. There were moments when it seemed the most splendid presence in the world — at sunset, when the river was crowded with shipping and the great buildings loomed up blue as wood-smoke, and almost translucent; when the brick walls grew wine-colored; when the river was flooded with radiance from the western sun, and the great steamers lay like birds wearied and dreaming after a long journey.

Sometimes, too, at night, when she came out of the concert hall and saw the glittering twin tiaras of burning gold which the Great Northern towers held against the blue-black, starless sky, two hundred feet above the pavement; or when in the early evening she approached the mountainous Temple, luminous and sparkling with electric lights, lifting a lighted dome as airy as a bubble three hundred feet into the pale sapphire of the cloudless sky — the city grew lofty.

The gross, the confused in line, the prosy in color,

disappeared at such moments, and the city, always vast, took on grace and charm and softened to magnificence; became epic, expressing in prophecy that which it must attain to; expressed the swift coming in of art and poetry in the lives of the western world-builders.

She grew with it all; it deepened her conception of life, but she could not write of it for the reason that it was too near and too multiple in its appeal upon her. She strove daily to arrange it in her mind, to put it into form, and this striving wore upon her severely. She lost some of her superb color and physical elasticity because of it, and became each week a little less distinctive exteriorly, which was a decided loss, Mason told Isabel.

"She isn't losing anything very real," Isabel said. "She's just as unaccountable as ever. She goes out much less than you imagine. I take her out, and send her, all I can to keep her from getting morbid. Why don't you come oftener and help me?"

"Self-protection," said Mason.

"Are you afraid of a country girl?"

"Oh, no — afraid of myself."

"How much do you mean of that, Warren?"

"All of it."

She wrinkled her brow in disgust of his concealing candor.

"Oh, you are impossible in that mood!"

As the winter deepened Rose narrowed the circle of conquest. She no longer thought of conquering the world; it came to be the question of winning the approbation of one human soul. That is, she wished to

win the approbation of the world in order that Warren
Mason might smile and say " Well done ! "

She did not reach this state of mind smoothly and
easily. On the contrary, she had moments when she
rebelled at the thought of any man's opinion being the
greatest good in the world to her. She rebelled at the
implied inferiority of her position in relation to him and
also at the physical bondage implied. In the morning
when she was strong, in the midst of some social success, when people swarmed about her and men bent
deferentially, then she held herself like a soldier on a
tower defying capture.

But at night, when the lights were all out, when she
felt her essential loneliness and weakness and need —
when the world seemed cold and cruel and selfish, then
it seemed as if the sweetest thing in the universe would
be to have him open his arms and say " Come ! "

There would be rest there and repose. His judgment, his keen wit, his penetrating, powerful influence,
made him seem a giant to her, a giant who disdained
effort and gave out an appearance of indifference and
lassitude. She had known physical giants in her neighborhood who spoke in soft drawl, and slouched lazily in
action, but who were invincible when aroused.

She imagined Mason as a mental giant, who assumed
irresolution and weakness for reasons of his own. He
was always off duty when she saw him, and bent
more upon rest than a display of power — but once or
twice she saw him roused, and was thrilled by the
change ; that measured lazy roll of voice changed to a

quick, stern snarl, the brows lowered and the big, plump face took on battle lines. It was like a seemingly shallow pool suddenly disclosed to be of soundless depths by a wind of passion. It was over in a moment, but Mason stood revealed to her.

The lake had been the refuge of the distracted and restless girl. She went to it often in the autumn days, for it rested her from the noise of grinding wheels, and screams and yells. Its smooth rise and fall, its sparkle of white-caps, its sailing gulls, filled her with delicious pleasure. It soothed her and it roused her also. It gave her time to think.

The street disturbed her, left her purposeless and powerless, but out there where the ships floated like shadows, and shadows shifted like flame, and the wind was keen and sweet — there she regained her mental breath again. She watched the water change to wintry desolation, till it grew empty of vessels and was lonely as the Arctic sea, but always its color and reach inspired her thought.

She went out one day in March when the home longing was upon her and when it seemed that the city would be her death. She was tired of her food, tired of Mary, tired of her room. Her forehead was knotted tensely with pain of life and love.

She cried out with sudden joy, for she had never seen the lake more beautiful. Near the shore a great mass of churned and heaving ice and snow lay like a robe of shaggy fur. Beyond this the deep water spread a vivid pea-green broken by wide, irregular strips of dark purple.

In the open water by the wall a spatter of steel-blue lay like the petals of some strange flower, scattered upon the green.

Great splendid clouds developed, marvellously like the clouds of June, making the girl's heart swell with memories of summer. They were white as wool, these mountainous masses, but bottomed in violet, and as they passed the snow-fields they sent down pink-purple, misty shadows, which trailed away in splendor toward the green which flamed in bewildering beauty beyond. The girl sat like one in a dream while the wind blew the green and purple of the outer sea into fantastic, flitting forms which dazzled her eyes like the stream of mingled banners.

Each form seemed more beautiful than the preceding one; each combination had such unearthly radiance, her heart ached with exquisite sorrow to see it vanish. Spring was coming on the wing of the southern wind, and the desire to utter her passion, grew almost into pain.

It had other moods, this mighty spread of water. It could be angry, dangerous. Sometimes it rolled sullenly, convoluting in oily surges beneath its coverlid of snow, like a bed of monstrous serpents. Sometimes the leaden sky shut down over it, and from the desolate northeast a snowstorm rushed, hissing and howling. Sometimes it slumbered for days, quiet as a sleeping boa, then awoke and was a presence and a voice in the night, fit to make the hardiest tremble.

Rose saw it when it was roused, but she had yet to

see it in a frenzy. The knowledge of its worst came to her early in May. The day broke with the wind in the northeast. Rose, lying in her bed, could hear the roar of the breakers; never before had their tumult penetrated so far. She sprang up and dressed, eager to see the lake in such a mood. Mary responded sleepily to her call, saying it would be there after breakfast.

Rose did not regret her eagerness, though it was piercingly cold and raw. The sea was already terrific. Its spread of tawny yellow showed how it had reached down and laid hold on the sand of its bed. There were oily splotches of plum-color scattered over it where the wind blew it smooth and it reached to the wild eastern sky, cold, desolate, destructive.

It had a fierce, breathing snarl like a monster at meat. It leaped against the sea-wall like a rabid tiger, its sleek and spotted hide rolling. Every surge sent a triangular sheet of foam high above the wall, yellow and white, and shadowed with dull blue; and the wind caught it as it rose, and its crest burst into great clouds of spray, which sailed across the streets and dashed along the walk like rain, making the roadway like a river; while the main body of each up-leaping wave, falling back astride the wall, crashed like the fall of glass, and the next wave meeting it with a growl of thunderous rage, struck it with concave palm, with a sound like a cannon's exploding roar.

Out of the appalling obscurity to the north frightened ships scudded at intervals with bare masts bending like fire-trimmed pines. They hastened like homing pigeons which do not look behind.   The helmsmen stood grimly at their wheels, with eyes on the harbor ahead.

The girl felt the terror of it all as no one native to the sea can possibly do.   It seemed as if the bounds of the flood had been overcome, and that it was about to hurl itself upon the land.   The slender trees standing deep in the swash of water, bowed like women in pain ; the wall was half hidden.   The water and the land seemed mingled in battle.

Rose walked along the drive, too much excited to go back to her breakfast.   At noon she ate lunch hurriedly and returned to the shore.   There were hundreds of people coming and going along the walk; young girls shrieking with glee, as the sailing clouds of spray fell upon them.   Rose was angry to think they could be so silly in face of such dreadful power.

She came upon Mason, dressed in a thick mackintosh coat, taking notes rapidly in a little book.   He did not look up and she passed him, wishing to speak, yet afraid to speak.   Near him a young man was sketching.

Mason stood like a rock in his long, closefitting rain-coat while she was blown nearly off her feet by the blast. She came back against the wind, feeling her soul's internal storm rising.   It seemed quite like a proposal of marriage to go up and speak to him — yet she could not forego the pleasure.

He did not see her until she came into his lee, then he smiled, extending his hand.   She spoke first :

" May I take shelter here? "

His eyes lightened with a sudden tender humor.

" Free anchorage," he said, and drew her by the hand
closer to his shoulder.   It was a beautiful moment to
her, and a dangerous one to him.   He took refuge in
outside matters.

" How does that strike your inland eyes?"   He
pointed to the north.

" It's awful.   It's like the anger of God."   She spoke
into his bowed ear.

" Please don't think I'm reporting it," he explained.
" I'm only making a few notes about it for an editorial
on the needs of harbors."   Each moment the fury
increased, the waves deepened.   The commotion sank
down amid the sands of the deeper inshore water, till it
boiled like milk and wine.   Splendid colors grew into it
near at hand ; the winds tore at the tops of the waves,
and wove them into tawny banners which blurred in the
air like blown sand.   On the horizon the waves leaped
in savage ranks, clutching at the sky like insane sea-
monsters, frantic, futile.

" I've seen the Atlantic twice during a gale," shouted
the artist to a companion, " but I never saw anything
more awful than this.   These waves are quicker and
higher.   I don't see how a vessel could live in it if
caught broadside."

" It's the worst I ever saw here."

" I'm going down to the South Side ; would you like
to go ? " Mason asked of Rose.

" I would, indeed," she replied.

Back from the Lake Shore the wind was less powerful
but more uncertain.   It came in gusts which nearly up-

turned the street-cars. Men and women scudded from shelter to shelter like people of a leaguered city avoiding cannon shots.

"What makes our lake so terrible," said Mason, in the car, "is the fact that it has a smooth shore — no indentations, no harbors. There is only one harbor here at Chicago, behind the breakwater, and every vessel in mid-lake must come here. Those flying ships are seeking safety behind it like birds. The harbor will be full of disabled vessels."

As they left the car a roaring gust swept around a twenty-story building with such power that Rose would have been taken off her feet had not Mason put his arm about her shoulders.

"You're at a disadvantage," he said, "with skirts." He knew she prided herself on her strength, and he took no credit to himself for standing where she fell.

It was precisely as if they were alone together; the storm seemed to wall them in, and his manner was more intimate than ever before. It was in very truth the first time they had been out together, and also it was the only time he had assumed any physical care of her. He had never asserted his really great muscular power and mastery of material things, and she was amazed and deeply pleased to know his lethargy was only a mood and that he could be alert and agile at need. It made his cynicism appear to be a mood also; at least, her heart was made wondrously light in thinking so.

They came upon the Lake Shore again, near the Auditorium. The refuge behind the breakwater was full of

boats, straining at anchor, rolling, pitching, crashing
together.   Close about the edge of the breakwater, ships
were rounding hurriedly, and two broken vessels lay
against the shore, threshing up and down in the awful
grasp of the breakers.   Far down toward the south the
water dashed against the spiles, shooting mast high above
the wall, sailing like smoke, deluging the street, and
lashing against the row of buildings across the way.

Mason's keen eye took in the situation.

" Every vessel that breaks anchor is doomed !   Nothing can keep them from going on shore.   Doubtless
those two schooners lost anchor — that two-master is
dragging anchor."   He said, suddenly, " She is shifting
position, and see that hulk ! "

Rose for a moment could not see it.   It lay flat on
its side, a two-master, its sails flapping and floating on
the waves.   Its anchor still held, but it had listed its
cargo, careened, and so lay helpless.

" There are men on it ! " cried someone.   " Three
men — don't you see them ?   The water goes over
them every time ! "

" Sure enough !   I wonder if they are going to let
them drown, here in the harbor ! "

Rose grew numb with horror.   On the rounded side
of the floating hulk three men were clinging, looking
like pegs of tops.   They could only be seen at intervals,
for the water broke clear over their heads.   It was only
when one of them began to move to and fro that the
mighty crowd became certainly aware of human beings
still clinging to the hull.

It was an awful thing to stand helplessly by, and see those brave men battle, but no life-boat or tug could live out there. In the station men wept and imprecated in their despair — twice they tried to go to the rescue of the beleaguered men, but could not reach them.

Suddenly a flare of yellow spread out on the wave. A cry arose:

" She's breaking up! "

Rose seized Mason's arm in a frenzy of horror.

" O God! can't somebody help them? "

" They're out of reach! " said Mason, solemnly. And then the throng was silent.

" They are building a raft! " shouted a man with a glass, speaking at intervals for the information of all. " One man is tying a rope to planks . . . he is helping the other men . . . he has his little raft nearly ready . . . they are crawling toward him —— "

" Oh, see them! " exclaimed Rose. " Oh, the brave men! There! they are gone — the vessel has broken up."

On the wave nothing now swam but a yellow spread of lumber; the glass revealed no living thing.

Mason turned to Rose with a grave and tender look.

" You have seen human beings engulfed like flies —— "

" No! no! There they are! " shouted a hundred voices, as if in answer to Mason's words.

Thereafter the whole great city seemed to be watching those specks of human life, drifting toward almost certain death upon the breakwater of the south shore. For miles the beach was clustered black with people. They stood there, it seemed for hours, watching the slow approach of that tiny raft. Again and again the waves swept over it, and each time that indomitable man rose from the flood and was seen to pull his companions aboard.

Other vessels drifted upon the rocks. Other steamers rolled heavily around the long breakwater, but nothing now distracted the gaze of the multitude from this appalling and amazing struggle against death. Nothing? No, once and only once did the onlookers shift their intent gaze, and that was when a vessel passed the breakwater and went sailing toward the south through the fleet of anchored, straining, agonized ships. At first no one paid close attention to this late-comer. Mason lifted his voice.

" By Heaven, the man is *sailing !* "

It was true; steady, swift, undeviating, the vessel headed through the fleet. She did not drift nor wander nor hesitate. She sailed as if the helmsman, with set teeth was saying :

" By God! If I must die on the rocks, I go to my death the captain of my vessel ! "

And so, with wheel in his hand and epic oaths on his lips, he sailed directly into the rocky walls, over which the waves ran like hell-hounds ; where half a score of wrecks lay already churning into fragments in the awful tumult.

The sailing vessel seemed not to waver, nor seek nor

dodge — seemed rather to choose the most deadly battle-place of waves and wall.

" God ! but that's magnificent of him ! " Mason said to himself.

Rose held her breath, her face white and set with horror.

" Oh, must he die ? "

" There is no hope for him. She will strike in a moment — she strikes ! — she is gone ! "

The vessel entered the gray confusion of the breakers and struck the piles like a battering ram ; the waves buried her from sight ; then the recoil flung her back ; for the first time she swung broadside to the storm. The work of the helmsman was over. She reeled — resisted an instant, then submitted to her fate, crumpled against the pitiless wall like paper and thereafter was lost to sight.

This dramatic and terrible scene had held the attention of the onlookers for nearly a quarter of an hour — once more they searched for the tiny raft. It was nearing the lake-wall at another furious point of contact. An innumerable crowd spread like a black robe over the shore waiting to see the tiny float strike.

A hush fell over every voice. Each soul was solemn as if facing the Maker of the world. Out on the point, just where the doomed sailors seemed like to meet their death, there was a little commotion. A tiny figure was seen perched on one of the spiles. Each wave, as it towered above him, seemed ready to sweep him away, but each time he bowed his head and seemed to sweep through the gray wall.　He was a negro, and he held a rope in his hands.

As they comprehended his danger and his daring, the crowd cheered him, but in the thunder of the surf no human voice could avail.　The bold black could not cry out, he could only motion, but the brave captain of the raft understood — he was alone with the shipwrecked ones.

In they came, lifted and hurled by a prodigious swell. They struck the wall just beneath the negro and disappeared beneath the waves.

All seemed over, and some of the spectators fell weeping ; others turned away.

Suddenly the indomitable commander of the raft rose, then his companions, and it was perceived that he had bound them all to the raft.

The negro flung his rope and one man caught at it, but was swept out of reach on a backward leaping billow.　Again they came in, their white, strained, set faces and wild eyes turned to their intrepid rescuer. Again they struck, and this time the negro caught and held one of the sailors, held him while the foam fell away, and the succeeding wave swept him over the spiles to safety.　Again the resolute man flung his noose and it was caught by the second sailor, whose rope was cut by the leader, the captain, who was last to be saved.

As the negro came back, dragging his third man over the wall, a mighty cry went up, a strange, faint, multi-

tudinous cry, and the negro was swallowed up in the
multitude.

*   *   *   *   *   *   *

Mason turned to Rose and spoke: "Sometimes men
seem to be worth while!"

Rose was still clinging to his arm as they walked
away.   Mason did not speak again for some time.

"We have suffered in vain," he said at last, "and you
are cold and stiffened with long standing.   Let me put
you in a cab and ——"

"Oh, no, thank you!   The walk will do me good."

"Perhaps you are right.   I'll go with you to the car,
and then I must go to my desk for six hours of hard
work.   Put this behind you," he said, tenderly.   "It
does no good to suffer over the inevitable.   Forget those
men!"

"I can't!   I shall never forget them while I live.   It
was awful!"   She shuddered, but when she looked into
his face she nearly cried out in astonishment at the light
in his eyes.   His voice was solemn as he said:

"It had its grandeur.   They went to their death like
men.   They have taught me a lesson.   Hitherto I have
drifted — henceforth *I sail!*"   He bent to her with
a mystical smile.

She drew away in a sort of awe as if she looked
unworthily upon a sacred place.   He misunderstood her
action and said, "Don't be afraid.   I have something
to say to you, but not here; perhaps I'll write it.
When do you go?"

"On Saturday."

x

"I will write you soon. Good-by."

She watched him as he moved away into the crowd, powerful, erect — the desk-man's droop gone out of his shoulders. What did he mean?

She was standing waiting for a chance to board a State Street car when Elbert Harvey came pushing along against the wind, fresh and strong and glowing with color like a girl.

"Oh, I've been looking for you, Rose," he cried, breathlessly. "I was at your house. They said you were over on the lake front and so — See here! You're all wet and cold. I'm going to get a carriage."

He would not be gainsaid, and she was really glad to escape the crowd in the car. He said: "I'm going to take you home to get warm."

She allowed herself to be driven to the door before she realized what it might be taken to mean, but it was then too late to insist upon being driven home, it would do no harm to see Mrs. Harvey for a moment — and then she was so tired — too tired to resist.

Mrs. Harvey met her in the hall, smiling and scolding:

"Why you reckless girl! Have you been down town? Elbert, where did you get her?"

"I found her on the street waiting for a car — shivering, too."

"Why, you're all wet! Come up to my room and change your shoes."

The warm air and the glow of the beautiful rooms

seemed to narcotize Rose, and she allowed herself to be led away like a sleepy child. It was delicious to be so attended. Mrs. Harvey took her to her own room, a room as big and comfortable and homey as herself, and there she put Rose down before the grateful fire and rang for her maid.

"Annette, remove Mademoiselle's shoes and give her some slippers."

The deft girl removed Rose's wraps, then her shoes, while Mrs. Harvey knelt by her side and felt of her stocking soles.

"They're wet, just as I expected." She said, joyfully, "Take them off!"

"Oh, no! They'll dry in a minute."

"Take them off, Annette," commanded Mrs. Harvey. "Oh, what lovely feet and ankles!" she said, and so betrayed her not too subtle design to Rose.

Rose was passive now, and yielded to the manipulations of the two women. They all had a gale of fun over the difference between Mrs. Harvey's stockings and her own, and then they brought out a fantastic pair of slippers and a beautiful wrap, which Mrs. Harvey insisted upon putting about her.

Elbert knocked on the door.

"Can't I come in and share the fun, Caroline?"

"In a moment!" she replied, and finished tucking the robe about Rose. "Now you may."

Elbert came in, radiant, unabashed, smiling, almost grinning his delight. He had changed his dress to a neat and exquisitely fitting dark suit, and he looked very handsome indeed. His cheeks were like peaches, with much the same sort of fuzz over them.

He took a place near the fire where he could see Rose, and he signalled to his mother at the earliest chance that she was stunning.

Rose lay back in the chair with the robe drawn about her, looking the *grande dame* from the crown of her head to the tasselled toes of her slippers. She might almost have been Colombe on the eve of her birthday.

It was delicious, and she had neither heart nor resolution at the moment to throw off this homage. She knew that Mrs. Harvey was misreading her acquiescence, and that every moment she submitted to her care and motherly direction, involved her, enmeshed her. But it was so delicious to be a princess and an heiress — for an hour.

The whole situation was intensified when Mr. Harvey's soft tender voice called from below.

" Where *is* everybody ? "

" Come up ; here we are ! There's somebody here you'll want to see."

Mr. Harvey came in smiling, looking as calm and contained as if he were just risen from sleep. He was almost as exquisitely dressed as his son.

" Well ! Well ! This is a pleasure," he cordially exclaimed. " What's the meaning of the wrap; not sick ? "

" Elbert picked her up on the street, wet and shivering, waiting for a car, and brought her home."

"Quite right. We're always glad to see you. Did you give her a little cordial, Caroline? In case of cold —— "

Rose protested. " I'm not sick, Mr. Harvey, only tired. I've been out all the day watching the dreadful storm. I saw those ships go on the rocks. Oh, it was dreadful! "

" Did you see the three men on the raft? " asked Elbert.

Rose shuddered. How far away she was from that cold, gray tumult of water. Of what manner of men were they who could battle so heroically for hours in the freezing sleet?

" Well, now, we won't talk about the storm any more," Mrs. Harvey interposed. " It does no good, and Rose has had too much of it already. Besides, it's almost dinner-time, Mr. Harvey. Go dress! "

There was not a thread ruffled on Mr. Harvey's person, but he dutifully withdrew. He had passed a busy day, and had transacted business which affected whole states by its influence, yet he was quiet, cordial, exquisite.

" What does this mean, my dear? " he asked of Mrs. Harvey, who followed him out.

" It may mean a great deal, Willis," she said. " All I know is Elbert brought her home, his eyes shining with delight."

" Not to be wondered at," Mr. Harvey replied. " I'm only afraid of actresses," he added, a little incoherently, but his wife understood him.

Elbert was not lacking in adroitness. He did not

presume on his position during his mother's absence. He remained standing in the same position.

"How do you like coddling? Now, you see what I get when I dare to sneeze. Caroline will coddle any-one into regular sickness if you let her."

"I was chilled, but I am not sick in the least."

"You'd better straighten up and shout at her when she comes in, or she'll be for sending your dinner up to you, and I don't want that."

"Oh, I must go home now."

"Not till after dinner."

"I'm not — dressed for dinner."

"There's nobody here but ourselves. You *must* stay."

Everyone seemed determined to press her into a false position, and there was so little chance to throw the influence off.

She rose out of her cloak, and when Mrs. Harvey came back she was standing before the fire with Elbert — which seemed also to be significant.

"Caroline, don't coddle Rose any more; she's all right."

Mrs. Harvey accepted this command, because it argued a sense of proprietorship on her son's part.

Elbert took her down to dinner and placed her near him. They continued in intimate talk during the meal. A couple of elderly ladies, sisters of Mr. Harvey, occupied places at the table sitting in meek and shadowy way, as if carefully subordinating themselves. They had the air of dependent beings and Rose perceived how difficult it was to eat the bread of charity and be free.

She felt it her duty to rouse herself to talk, and took a small part in the jolly patter between Elbert and his mother. Their companionship was very charming — so charming one almost forgot the irreverence expressed by Elbert's use of " Caroline."

After dinner Mrs. Emma Seymour Gallup, whom Rose had met two or three times but who always demanded a new introduction, came whisking in on her way to some party. She wore everything in decidedly the very latest crimp. Her sleeves did not fit ; her hips seemed enormous ; her bonnet seemed split on the middle of her head, and was symmetrically decked with bows of ribbon and glitter and glimmer. Her real proportions were only to be divined at the waist, all else was fibre-cloth and conjecture.

Her eyes were bright and her face cold and imperious. She had once before chilled Rose with a slighting nod and an insulting shift of shoulder. She was plainly surprised to see the girl in the bosom of this family, and seized upon the only plausible explanation with instant readiness. She had a beautiful smile, and Rose could not help seeing that she could be very charming after all.

" Ah ! How do you do Miss Dutcher ! I am very glad to see you again ! "

" Thank you," Rose replied, simply.

" You're quite well ? — but then I know you're well," Mrs. Gallup went on, assuming still greater knowledge of her. " Did you see the storm ? Wasn't it dreadful ! I saw it all quite securely from Mrs. Frost's window. How cozy you all look. I wish I could stay, but I just

dropped in to ask you to take a seat in my box on
Saturday night. Bring Miss Dutcher — Mr. Gallup
will be delighted to meet her."

All that she said, and more that she implied, enmeshed
Rose like the folds of an invisible intangible net.

Mrs. Harvey calmly accepted, but Rose exclaimed:
"Oh, you're very kind, but I am going home on
Saturday morning!"

"How sad! I should have liked to have you come."

After she was gone Rose sprang to her feet. "I
must go now," she said, and there was a note in her
voice which Mrs. Harvey accepted as final.

As they went upstairs Rose was filled with dread of
some further complication, but Mrs. Harvey only said:

"I love you, my child. I wish you were going to
stay here always."

She left the way open for confidences, but Rose was
in a panic to get away and kept rigid silence.

In the carriage she contrived to convey to Elbert her
desire to be left alone, and he manfully kept back the
words of love which were bubbling in his good, frank
soul. He was saddened by it but not made hopeless.
It would have been a beautiful close to a dramatic day
could he have kissed her lips and presented her to his
mother as his promised wife — but it was impossible for
even his volatile nature to break into her sombre, almost
sullen, silence; and when he said "Good-night, Rose!"
with tender sweetness she replied, curtly, "Good-night!"
and fled.

She hurried past Mary to her own room and lay for

hours on her bed, without undressing, listening to the howl of the wind, the grind of cars, and the distant boom of the breakers. There was a storm in her heart also.

She thought of that lovely and gentle home, of the power wealth would give her, of the journeys into the world, of trips to Europe, to the ocean, to Boston and New York and London. It could give her a life of ease, of power, of grace, and charm. Oh, how beautiful it all was, but ——

To win it she had to cut off her old father. He never could fit in with these people. She thought of his meeting with the Harveys with a shudder. Then, too, she would need to give up her own striving toward independence, for it was plain these people would not listen to her continued effort. Even if they consented, she would be meshed in a thousand other duties.

And then she thought of Mason toiling at his desk down there in the heart of the terrible town, and the look on his face grew less and less imperious and more wistful and pleading. This day she had caught a new meaning from his eyes — it was as if he needed her; it seemed absurd, and she blushed to think it, but so it seemed. That last look on his face was the look of a lonely man.

His words came to her again and again: " *Hitherto I have drifted — henceforth I sail!* "

That night she pushed away the splendid dream of a life of ease and reached out for comradeship with a man of toil, of imagination, and hidden powers.

CHAPTER XXIV

MASON TAKES A VACATION

As Mason walked away from the lake that terrible day it seemed as if he had ceased to drift. The spirit of that grim helmsman appeared to have entered into him. Life was short and pleasures few. For fifteen years he had planned important things to do, but had never done them — feeling all the time the power to write latent within him, yet lacking stimulus. From the very first this girl had roused him unaccountably. Her sympathy, her imaginative faculty, as well as her beauty, had come to seem the qualities which he most needed.

Could he have gone to his own fireside at once, the determining letter would have been written that night, but the routine of the office, the chaff of his companions, took away his heroic mood, and when he entered a car at twelve o'clock he slouched in his seat like a tired man, and the muscles of his face fell slack and he looked like a hopeless man.

After Rose went home he seemed to Sanborn to be more impassible than ever. As for Mason himself, it seemed as if some saving incentive — some redeeming grace, had gone out of his life. He had grown into the habit of dropping in at Isabel's once a week, and Isabel had taken care that Rose should be often there on the same evening; and so without giving much thought to it he had come to enjoy these evenings as the most regenerating pleasures of his sombre life.

It was such a delight to come up out of the vicious, pitiless grind of his newspaper life and sit before a fire, with the face of a radiant girl to smile upon him. Her voice, with its curiously penetrating yet musical quality, stirred him to new thoughts, and often he went home at ten or eleven and wrote, with a feeling of exultant power, upon his book. After she left the city he wrote no more; he smoked and pondered. When he called upon Isabel and Sanborn he continued to smoke and to ponder.

He had not abandoned his allegory in talking with Sanborn, and Sanborn and Isabel together could not get at his real feeling for Rose.

Sanborn one day daringly asked.

" Mason, why don't you marry the 'coolly girl,' and begin to live ? "

" It would be taking a mean advantage of her. She's going to be famous one of these days, and then I should be in the way."

" Nonsense ! "

" Besides, she probably would not marry me; and if she would, I don't think I could keep up the pose."

" What pose ? "

" Of husband."

"Is that a pose?" Sanborn smiled.

"It would be for me," Mason said, rather shortly.
He was thinking once more of the letter he had promised to write to Rose, but which he had never found
himself capable of finishing.

*   *   *   *   *   *   *

Isabel and Sanborn were married just before leaving
the city on their summer vacation in July.

Sanborn said he had the judge come in to give him
legal power to compel Isabel to do his cooking for him,
and Isabel replied that her main reason for submitting
to a ceremony was to secure a legal claim on Sanborn's
practice.

The wedding was very quiet.   Society reporters
(who did not see it) called it "an unique affair."   But
Mason, who did see it, said it was a very simple process,
so simple it seemed one ought to be able to go through
it one's self.   To which Sanborn replied: "Quite right.
Try it!"   And both invited him to their home at
Oconomowoc.

They had a little cottage on the bank of the lake,
and Sanborn came up on Saturdays with the rest of the
madly busy men who rest over Sunday and overwork
the rest of the week.   Mason went up late in July, and,
though he gave no sign, he was nearing a crisis in his
life.   He had gone to the point of finishing his letter to
Rose — it was lying at that moment in his valise waiting
to be posted — but it was a long way from being over
with.   It was a tremendous moment for him.   As he
approached the deciding moment the deed grew improb-

able, impossible. It was a very beautiful life there on
the lake, with nothing to do but smoke and dream, but
one evening he had the impulse to ask Isabel's advice,
and after dinner invited her to sail with him in order to
be quite alone with her.

There was some joking by Sanborn about the impro-
priety of such a thing on Isabel's part, and many offers
to man the boat, which, Mason said, sprang from jeal-
ousy. "I consider I am doing you people a kindness in
not letting you bore each other into black hatred." It
ended in the two friends drifting away over the lake,
while Sanborn called after them threats of war if they
were not at the wharf at nine — sharp!

They talked commonplaces for a time, while the sky
flushed and faded and the lake gradually cleared of its
fisher boats. Slowly the colors grew tender and a subtle.
An impalpable mist rose from the water, through which
the boat drifted before an imperceptible breeze.

The two sailors lay at ease, Mason at the rudder.
The sail stood up light and airy and soundless as a but-
terfly's wing. It pointed at the sparse stars as if with
warning finger.

The hour and the place were favorable to confidences.
As the dusk deepened, a boat-load of young people put
off into the lake, singing some wailing sweet song.
They were far enough away to be unobtrusively imper-
sonal. A plover was faintly calling from the sedgy
shore on the other side.

"One should be forever young," said Mason, brood-
ingly.

Isabel replied : " Once I heard a cow low, and a robin laugh, while a cricket chirped in the grass. Why should they have moved me so ? "

Mason mused a moment. " The cow was maternity pleading for its young; the robin's laugh suggested a thousand springtimes, and the cricket prophesied the coming of frost and age. Love and loss are in the wail of yonder song, the loneliness of age in yonder piping bird, and the infinite and all-absorbing menstruum of death in the growing dusk."

" And the light of man's optimism in the piercing out of the stars."

" It may be so," he replied, uncertainly.

They drifted on in silence. There was a faint ripple at the prow and that was all. At last Mason roused himself to say his word.

" All these intangible essences and powers are no apparent reason why I should do so foolish a thing — but they have influenced me. To-day I wrote to our coolly girl — I hope to say *my* coolly girl."

Isabel caught her breath.

" Warren, did you ? I'm very glad. If I could reach you I'd shake your hand."

" I don't rejoice. This thing which boys and girls find easy I find each year more difficult, quite equal to the revolution of the earth — perhaps the girl will save me from myself."

" She'll save you *for* yourself, and you'll be happy."

" It is impossible to say," he said, sombrely. " I have warned her fairly. Once I should not have warned the woman of my choice. Am I gaining in humanity or losing? Please lower your head, I am going to tack."

The boat swung about like a sleeping gull, and the sail slowly filled, and the ripple at the prow began again.

After a pause Mason went on, in a calm even voice:

" The world to me is not well governed, and I hesitate about marriage, for it has the effect, in most cases, of perpetuating the human species, which is not as yet a noble business. I am torn by two minds. I don't appear to be torn by even one mind, but I am. I am convinced that Rose has imagination, which is in my eyes the chief thing in a wife. It enables her to idealize me " — there was a touch of his usual humor in that — " and fills me with selfish desire to possess her, but it is sad business for her, Isabel. When I think of her I am of the stature of a thief, crouching for concealment."

The two in the boat were no longer young. They had never been lovers, but they seemed to understand each other like man and wife.

" I am old in knowledge of the world — my life has ground away any charm I might have once possessed. For her sake I hope she will refuse."

She perceived he was at the end of his confidence, and she began speaking. " I promised you a story once," she began, " and I'm going to tell it now, and then we'll return to Rose."

She spoke in a low voice, with a little catching of the breath peculiar to her when deeply moved. It made her voice pulse out like the flow of heavy wine. She faced him in the shadow, but he knew she was not regarding him at all. Just how she began he didn't quite hear — perhaps she was a little incoherent.

"Oh, those days when I was seventeen!" she went on. "Everything was magical. Every moonlit night thrilled me with its possibilities. I remember how the boys used to serenade me, and then — I was a mediæval maiden at my barred window and they were disguised knights seeking me in strange lands by their songs.

"You know what I mean. I tingled with the immense joy of it! They sang there in the moonlight, and I tiptoed to the window and peeped out and listened and listened with pictures and pictures tumbling in and out of my head.

"Of course it was only the inherited feminine rising up in me, as you would say — but it was beautiful. It just glorified that village street, making it the narrow way in a Spanish city."

There was silence again. Mason softly said: "Bend your head once more."

When the boat swung around and the faint moon and the lights of the town shifted, Isabel went on.

"One of the boys who came on those midnight serenadings became my hero — remember, I was only seventeen and he was twenty! We used to meet on the street — and oh! how it shook me. My heart fluttered so I could not speak, and at first I had to run past him. After a time I got composed enough to speak to him."

Her voice choked with remembered passion, but after a little pause she went on:

" All this, I know as well as you, is absurd —— "

" It is very beautiful," he said. " Go on! "

" He was tall and straight, I remember, with brown hair. He was a workman of some kind. I know he used to show me his powerful hands and say he had tried to get the grime from them. They were splendid, heroic hands to me. I would have kissed them if I dared. It was all incredible folly, but I thought I was loving beneath my station, for I was a little grandee in the town. It pleased me to think I was stooping — defying the laws of my house. He never tried to see me at home — he was good and true — I can see that now, for I remember just how his big clear eyes looked at me. He didn't talk much, he seemed content to just look at me."

" Well, that went on for weeks. He used to follow me to church, as the boys do in country towns, but I used to go to different places just to see if he would find out and be there to meet me at the door. He never offered to speak to me or take my arm, but he stood to see me go by. Do you know, if I go into a country church to-day, that scent of wilted flowers and linen and mingled perfumes almost makes me weep."

" I understand."

Her voice was lower when she resumed.

" Well, then the dreadful, the incredible happened. He did not meet me any more, and just when I was wild with rage and humiliation came the news of his illness — and then I suffered. O God! how I suffered! I couldn't inquire about him — I couldn't see him. I had kept my secret so well that no one dreamed of my loving

Y

him so. The girls thought that he followed me and that I despised him, and when they jested about him I had to reply while my heart was being torn out of me. I spent hours in my room writhing, walking up and down, cursing, in a girl's way, myself and God—I was insane with it all."

She drew a long breath, but it did not relieve her. Her voice was as tense as before when she spoke again. The helmsman leaned to listen, for he could hardly hear.

"Then one day he died—Oh, that awful day! I sat in my room with the curtains down. I couldn't endure the sunlight. I pretended to be sick. I was numb with agony and yet I could do nothing. I couldn't even send a rose to lay on his coffin. I couldn't even speak his name. I could only lie there like a prisoner gagged and on the rack—to suffer—suffer!"

The shadow of the sail covered the woman like a mantle. It was as if the man listening had turned away his face from her sacred passion. She was more composed when she spoke again.

"Well, it wore itself out after a time. I got hungry and ate once more, though I did not suppose I ever should. I came down to my family a week later, a puzzle to them. They never thought to connect my illness with the death of an obscure machinist, and then in the same way I crept gradually back into society— back into the busy life of a popular young girl. But there was one place where no one ever entered. I never told anyone of this before. I tried to tell Dr. Sanborn about it once, but I felt he might not under-

stand; I tell you because — because you can understand and because you may be influenced by it and
understand your wife when she comes to you. These
days come to many women at seventeen, and, though
we can't spare them out of our lives, it doesn't mean dis-
loyalty to our present ideals. I think you understand?"

"Very well, indeed," he said. "I have such
memories myself."

"Then I resolved to be a physician. I felt that he
would not have died if he had been treated properly;
the connection was obscure but powerful enough to
consecrate me to the healing profession. Then I met
Dr. Sanborn. I love him and I couldn't live without
him, but there is that figure back there — to have
him and all that he means go out of my life would
take part of my heart away." Her voice had appeal
in it.

"You understand me? It was all girlish and innocent, but it was my first passion, and I can't spare it.
Rose may have such a memory. It has nothing to do
with to-day, with her present ideals. It is not dis-
loyalty — it is —— "

"The love of love," said Mason. "I thank you for
your trust in me. Rose is what she is, not what she
has been." And then in perfect stillness the boat
swung around and drifted toward the shore, where a
ruby lantern was swinging. Isabel turned and her voice
was tremulous with earnestness.

"Warren, Rose loves you — not as she loved when a
girl, but as a woman loves. I think I understand your

hesitancy— and I say you are wrong. You need her and you will do her good. You will develop her."

"She will suffer through me."

"That's a part of our development."

The boat was nearing the wharf, and Sanborn's hearty voice came from the shore :

"See here ! Isn't it pretty late for a pair of rheumatic old folks to be out sailing ? It's 9.30 o'clock."

"The breeze failed us," Isabel answered, as Mason took her hand to help her ashore.

"And the night was so beautiful," said Mason. Before she loosed his hand Isabel shook it hard and now Mason understood. He mailed the letter that night, and Rose held his future in her hand.

CHAPTER XXV

ROSE RECEIVES A LETTER

ROSE went directly from that storm in the city to the calm and apparent peace of the country, and it helped her to make a great discovery. She found every familiar thing had taken on a peculiar value — a literary and artistic value. It was all so reposeful, so secure. A red barn set against a gray-green wooded hillside was no longer commonplace. " How pretty ! " she thought ; " I never noticed that before."

A little girl wrapped in a shawl was watching cattle in the field ; a dog sat near, his back to the misty drizzle. Rose saw it and put herself in the place of that child, chilled and blue of hand, with unfallen tears upon her cheeks.

A crow flying by with ringing, rough cry made her blood leap. Some cattle streamed up a lane and over a hill ; their legs moving invisibly gave them a gliding motion like a vast centipede. Some mysterious charm seemed imparted to everything she saw, and, as the familiar lines of the hills began to loom against the sky, she became intolerably eager to see her father and the farm. She hoped it would be a sunny day, but it was raining heavily when she got out at the station.

He was there, the dear, sweet, old soul smiling, almost tearful. He had an umbrella and couldn't return her hug; but he put his arm about her and hurried her to the carriage, and in a few moments they were spattering up the familiar road.

Instantly it seemed as if she had never been away. She was a little girl again; the horses shook their heads, impatient of the rain; the pools in the road were green as liquid emerald, and were dimpled by the pelting drops. The wheels flung segments of mud into the air, but the horses drove ahead sullenly, almost desperately, unmindful of the splash and splatter.

Rose took keen delight in it all. She had been shut away from nature so long, it seemed good to get back into even the stern mood of a May storm. The great, reeling masses of gray cloud delighted her, and the ringing cry of frogs seemed delicious orchestration. Everything was fresh, cold, almost harsh. How arid and artificial the city life seemed in the freshness of green fields!

It was a pleasure to return to the barnyard, to get back into the kitchen where her aunt was phlegmatically working away at supper-getting. She wiped her hands on her apron, and said "How-de-do!" as if Rose were a neighbor just dropped in for a call.

The life all seemed heroically dull, but the coolness, repose, and sanity of nature was elemental, as if she had risen into the rainy sky or sunk into the depths of the ocean. It was deathly still at times. And dark, dark and illimitable, and freshly sweet that first night shut down over the valley.

She went to sleep with the soft roar of the falling rain near her window; and the faint puffing in of the breeze brought to her the delicious smell of the rain-washed leaves, the acrid, pungent odor of poplars, the sweet smell of maples, the fragrance of rich loam — she knew them all.

By force of contrast she thought of Mason and his life in the city. The roar of traffic: the thunder of great presses; the nights at the opera or the theatre, all had enormous significance and value to her, but how remote it all was! In the country the city seemed unreal; in the city the country seemed impossible.

She awoke at the cry of a jay in the maples, and then as she listened she heard a mourning-dove sob from the distance. Robins were laughing merrily, an oriole whistled once and flew away, and hark! yes, a thrush was singing, sitting high in some tree-top, she knew.

The rain was over; the valley was flooded with sunshine. Oh, so beautiful! — flooded with light like the love of God. She sprang up with joyous energy. Life's problem was not without solution if she could enjoy — both city and country alike.

Indeed her joy of the country seemed doubled by her winter in the city — each day on the valley was made marvellous by that storm on the lake. In the days which followed, rhymes formed in her mind upon subjects hitherto untouched by her literary perception.

Things she had known all her life, familiar plants, flowers, trees, etc., seemed haloed all at once by a supernatural radiance.

The clouds on the hills, the buzz of bees in the clover, the sabre swing of poplar-trees against the sky, moved her to song, and she wrote daily with marvellous ease. She flung herself prone on the bank by the spring, and strove to mix and be one with the wind and the trees. She thought of her childish crooning over Carl that day his head lay in her lap, and its significance came to her and voiced itself in music.

She traced out every path wherein her feet had trod as a child, and the infinite suggestions and terror and high beauty of life and death came upon her. She seemed to summon up and analyze all her past, as if she were about to end one life and begin another. These wonderful moods and memories in some unaccountable way co-ordinated themselves in lines of verse, and the restless, vigorous heart of the girl felt the splendid peace which comes when the artist finds at last the form of art which is verily his.

The body of her work grew, and she longed for Mason's opinion upon it, and yet she feared to send it, it seemed so different from other verse. At times she felt sure of its passionate and imaginative quality, and made up selections to send him, but ended always by putting them away again.

She had his picture in her room, and sometimes she sat down to write with his sadly inscrutable face before her. She could see in it (as she studied it here in her home) the lines of varied and restless thought which make up the face of one who largely comprehends American civilization in the light of experience.

That face represented to her the highest type of intellectual manhood, and something more. It was refined and infinitely subtle compared with the simple, almost ox-like faces of the men about her. It was sad, too, as her father's face in repose was sad, but the sadness was different. There was patient, resigned sadness in her father's eyes and lips; in Mason's, bitter, rebellious, perhaps despairing sadness, and something else, too — youth taking hold upon the hopeless sorrow of the whole world.

And yet she knew how sweetly those lips could smile, and she had known the gentleness and purity hid in those eyes.

She thought less of his fine, erect bearing, and yet she liked to remember him as he walked down the street that day of the storm. He had physical power and dignity, but his face and eyes were etched in minutest detail upon her brain. The life companionship of such a man came to seem more and more impossible for her to attain to. The common little details of her life seemed to lower her. She fell back into inelegant habits and careless speech, and every time she realized these faults, they put Mason far off and high above her. Her verse lost its brilliancy, its buoyancy, and became dark and bitter at such times.

Every day she hoped to hear from him. He had promised to write, and he had hinted at something very important which he designed to put into his letter. She knew that she had no definite claim upon him, and yet her last letter had contained one question, not of any importance only as it gave him a chance to reply if he felt like it.

Then the question came: "What of my winter in the city? What has it done for me? Is not life as insoluble as ever — success as far away as ever?"

Could she live here in the country any easier because of her stay there; did it not, in fact, make life harder?

It was in thinking about these things and Mason's letter, which did not come, that her new-found rapture in nature began to cool down. She began to spend more time in her room, thinking of him, and wondering what his attitude toward her really was.

She had moments at last when his face seemed cynically smiling at her. What did he care for an awkward country girl like her? He pitied her, that was all. He wanted to help her, and had tried, and finding her dull, had given her up and forgotten her. He knew scores of beautiful women, actresses, artists, millionaires' daughters; it was absurd to suppose that a girl from the coolly could be of any special interest to him; and to win his love, that was impossible.

She had not the personal vanity which makes so many pretty and brainless women think themselves irresistible to any man, and a fair return for any man's name and fame. Her comeliness she made little of in the question.

She hoped on week by week for a reply, but none

came, and in her letters to Isabel she asked for news about " all my friends," meaning Mason especially.

Isabel wrote, saying they had invited Mr. Mason up to stay a few days at their cottage, and that Elbert Harvey had asked after her, and couldn't she come down ?

By the middle of July she had begun to pass days without writing at all — and then the letter from Mason came! John brought it to her with a smile: " Guess this must be a love-letter ; it's a big one ! "

She took it from his hand, with a keen, swift premonition of its importance. It was indeed a heavy letter — almost a packet.

She went to her room with it and took a seat by the window, quite deliberately, though her hands shook as she opened the envelope. Her senses seemed some way to acquire unnatural keenness, like a scared animal's. She heard every voice about the barn-yard, and she felt the wind on her cheek like a live thing beating its slow wings. The letter opened simply :

" DEAR MISS DUTCHER :

" I must begin by asking pardon for not writing before, but as a matter of fact I have not found this letter easy to compose. It represents a turning-point in my life, and contains an important decision, and I have never been less sure of my judgment than now.

" This letter may be considered an offer of marriage. It is well to say that now, and then all the things which come after, will be given their proper weight. Let me state the debit side of the account first, and if you feel that it is too heavy you can put the letter down and write me a very short answer, and the matter will be ended.

"First, I say to you: whoso weds me weds sorrow. I do not promise to make you happy, though I hope my influence will not be always untoward. I cannot promise any of the things husbands are supposed to bring. I cannot promise a home. My own living is precarious, dependent upon my daily grind of newspaper work. For though I hope to achieve a success with my novel, successes with novels do not mean much money. I do not feel either that I shall ever be free from money cares; luxury and I are to continue strangers.

"I cannot promise to conform to your ways, nor to bend to your wishes, though I will try to do so. I cannot promise to assume cordial relations with your relatives, nor accept your friendships as binding upon me.

"I cannot promise to be faithful to you until death, but I shall be faithful so long as I fill the relation of husband to you. I shall not lead a double life, or conceal from you any change in my regard toward you. If at any time I find a woman whom I feel I should live with, rather than with you, I shall tell you of her with perfect frankness. I *think* I shall find you all-sufficient, but I do not know. Men and women change, grow weary of cares, of bonds, of duties. It may be that I shall become and continue the most devoted of husbands, but I cannot promise it. Long years of association develop intolerable traits in men and women very often.

"On the other hand, let me say I exact nothing from

you. I do not require you to cook for me, nor keep house for me. You are mistress of yourself; to come and go as you please, without question and without accounting to me. You are at liberty to cease your association with me at any time, and consider yourself perfectly free to leave me whenever any other man comes with power to make you happier than you are with me.

"I want you as comrade and lover, not as subject or servant, or unwilling wife. I do not claim any rights whatever over you. You can bear me children or not, just as you please. You are a human soul like myself, and I shall expect you to be as free and as sovereign as I, to follow any profession or to do any work which pleases you. It is but just to say that I have never been a man of loose habits. No woman has any claim upon me for deed or word. I have thought at various times that I could marry this woman or that woman, but I have never before made a proposition of marriage to any woman.

"I have written you in good, set terms what you may expect of me. I am not a demonstrative man by nature, and my training from childhood has made me saving of words of endearment. My love for you must be taken largely for granted after it is once stated, for I regard the word 'love' as a jewel not to be carelessly tossed from hand to hand.

"Doubtlessly I shall make a dull companion — of that I cannot judge for myself. I have written frankly because I believed it would prejudice you in my favor. Had I believed otherwise, doubtless I should have written in terms of flattery and deceit, for of such is man when seeking woman in marriage."

This was characteristic of his speech; she seemed to hear his voice as she read it. He must needs mock at himself somewhere even in his proposal. However, he ended in clearer tone.

"If you return an affirmative answer I shall be very happy to come up and spend the rest of my vacation at your father's home — provided it is agreeable to you."

Rose sat rigidly still in her chair, her hands in her lap, holding the letter.

It had come again, this question of marriage, and this time it appealed to her whole nature — to her intellectual part as well as to her material self; an offer of companionship uttered this time by a voice which had no tremor in it.

How strange it all was! How different from the other proposals she had received; apparently cold and legal, yet under the lines she felt something deep and manly and passionate, because she was only a coolly girl, and he was a man of the great intellectual world; a man who changed public opinion by the power of his editorial pen. He was greater than that. In his presence she felt as if he were a man of national reputation living quietly under an assumed name.

A feeling of pride rose in her heart. Warren Mason had selected her from among the women of the world! He loved her so much that he had written her this strange letter, which pleaded for her under its rigid

order of words.   She held the letter to her lips as if to
get at its most secret meaning, and then dropped it as if
it were a husk.   No matter what it said, she knew the
spirit of the man to be grand and noble.

She wrote a few lines, then fell again into thought
upon the terms of his letter.   She hardly comprehended
the significance of its minor statements, so filled was she
with the one great fact.   She was poor, and unknown,
and yet he had chosen her!

There was something sad in the letter, too — like his
face it was inscrutable, intricate, but (she believed) noble
in intention.   The freedom of action which he claimed
for himself did not trouble her, for she felt his love
steady and strong beneath it.   His word " comrade "
pleased her, too.   It seemed to be wholesome and sweet,
and promised intellectual companionship never before
possible to her.

Oh, to be the wife of such a man! to have his daily
help and presence; it was wonderful, it could not be
true!   Yet there lay the letter in her lap, and there the
firm, calm, even signature.   She rose to her feet and her
heart dilated with joy, and her head was that of a newly
crowned princess.   Oh, the great splendid world out there!

She took up her letter suddenly and went downstairs
and out into the yard in search of her father.   He was
sitting by the bees, with dreamy eyes.   He spent a great
deal of his time there watching their ceaseless coming
and going.

" Father, I want you to hitch Kitty to the buggy
for me."

"Why, of course. Where are you goin', Rose?"

"I'm going to the Siding to post a letter. Oh, pappa John!" she cried, suddenly, putting her arms round him, "I'm going to be married."

John did not instantly comprehend her passion; he was slower to move, but he said:

"Why, Rosie! When? Who to?"

"To a man in Chicago, Mr. Warren Mason, a great editor. I'm just writing to him to come."

John began to feel the solemnity of the thought.

"Does he live in Chicago?"

"Yes." She understood his thought. "But we'll come and see you, summers, just the same, pappa John."

"Well, I'll take the letter down."

"No, I must take it myself," she said, smilingly, holding the letter behind her like a child.

There was something fine in carrying the letter to the post-office herself. It seemed to hasten Warren's coming. The spirited horse carried her at a steady trot up hill and down, and soon the railway track was in sight. The singing wires on their poles instructed her; why not telegraph her answer? The clerk might suspect Warren to be her lover, but what did she care now? She mentally formed this message:

"Come up to-morrow if you can, please. Rose."

But as she approached the desk she shrank from handing it in. It seemed too plainly a love-message. She mailed her letter in the post-office and fell to calculating when it would reach him. He could not possibly come till the second day, whereas if she telegraphed he might arrive in the morning. This thought strengthened her resolution; going over to the window she placed the message firmly before the operator, who knew her and admired her deeply.

" Please send that at once, Mr. Bingham."

The operator smiled and bowed, and when he read the message he looked up at her keenly, but did not smile.

" Any answer ? " he asked.

" No, probably not," she replied. " Will it go right out ? "

" Immediately."

As she turned away to ride home her soul took wing. A marvellous elevation and peace came upon her. It was done. Life held more than promise now, it contained certainties. Her chosen one of Israel was coming!

z

CHAPTER XXVI

MASON AS A LOVER

THE telegram came to Mason as he sat on the porch of the Herrick cottage. He read it, and his eyes smiled, but his feeling was not one of amusement. The significance of that impulsive message struck deep, and his blood responded to it as if it were the touch of a hand.

It settled all doubt in his mind concerning Rose. She was as free and self-reliant as he thought her, the severe terms of his proposal had not repelled her, and yet that she loved him in a right human and very passionate way did not seem to him possible.

He had, also, other misgivings. He regretted that he had not delineated more fully in his letter the unlovely side of his character. "She is young and beautiful," he thought, "and will want to see life. She will value social affairs — I am done with them. She will want words of tender protestation, flattery perhaps, which I cannot give.

"My habits are fixed. I like my silent pipe at night after dinner. I shall undoubtedly get more and more disinclined to social duties as time goes on.

"In ten years I shall be forty-eight years old, when

338

she is just in her splendid June season. She will find
the difference between our ages wider than now. She
will be a wife. I can free her when she asks it, but I
cannot give her back her buoyant girlhood. I can give
her perception and comprehension of the world and of
life, but I cannot make her young again. I may die
after a few years, leaving her a mother with a hazardous
future. Then she will be doubly cursed.

"Again, this marriage may ruin and interrupt her career. With some women marriage, especially maternity,
seems to take away their power as artists, and to turn
them into cooks and nurses; meritorious vocations of
course, but —— "

All night long he alternately mused and dozed upon
the problem. He roused up at early daylight with a
feeling of doom upon him. He had made a mistake.
He was not fitted to be a husband — he was a poor thing,
at best, who had not had energy enough to get out of a
groove nor to demand adequate pay for grinding in his
groove. He lacked "push," and had dreamed away the
best years of his life, at least such parts of the years as
he had saved from the merciless drive of his paper. He
was pulp, squeezed dry.

He groaned, and a curse came upon his lips, and his
forehead knit into a tangle of deep lines. His paper
had used him. It had sucked the blood of his heart.
The creative energy of his brain had gone into the im-
personal columns of the editorial page — to what end?
To the end that the Evening Star Publishing Company
should be rated high in Bradstreet. Had any human

being been made better by anything he had written in those columns ? Politics ? Good God ! he had sold his soul, his blood, the grace of his limbs, the suppleness of his joints, the bloom of his enthusiasms, to put this or that damned party into power.

And now, when a beautiful young woman, singing her way to fame, had sent for him, he must go to her, cynical, thin-haired, stiff in joints, bent in shoulders, and reeking with the smell of office life and, worst of all, worked out, his novel not yet written, and his enthusiasm turned to indifference and despair.

The problem of the age that morning made him savage. He looked out of the window at the farm-houses gleaming in the early light, at the smoke curling up into the still air, at the men going to milk the cows.

" The damn fools ! " he said in his heart. " They don't know enough to vegetate any more than I had sense to know I was becoming a machine. Rot and rot ! So we go like leaves to the muck-heap." The porter rushed in and shook him.

" Almos' to Bluff Siding, sah."

This put a little resolution into his blood, and he dressed rapidly, with little thought for anything else. Once or twice he looked out at the misty blue hills, cool and fresh with recent rains. As the porter came to get his grip a few minutes later, Mason wondered how he should meet his Rose, with a hand-shake or a kiss ? How would she meet him ?

As the train slowed down he saw her at the platform. She sat in a carriage waiting for him. A sudden flashing thought lit his brain: "There sits my wife!" It startled him. The tremendous significance of that phrase made his brain dizzy for a moment.

She was trimly dressed, he noticed, as he came toward her, and she held her horse firmly — he liked her for that, it showed self-mastery. As for him, he felt more uncertainty of footing than ever before in his life, and tried to throw off the stoop in his shoulders.

As he came forward, she flushed, but her steady eyes met his unwaveringly. He looked into their clear obscurity of depth, wherein were purity and all unworldly womanly ways.

She held out her hand, firm and strong, and he took it in his. Outwardly it was merely a friendly greeting, yet something subtler than light came from her to him. He did not speak for an instant, then he said:

"This is good of you! I did not expect this great pleasure."

Her voice trembled as she said:

"I wanted to be the first to greet you, and besides, pappa wouldn't know you."

He smiled for the first time.

"That's true. But it's very early — quite in the small hours."

"Oh, that's nothing; I'm a farmer's girl, you know. But put your valise in, we must be off."

How strong and supple she looked! and how becoming her silk waist and straw hat! She could drive, too. Someway she seemed quite another sort of person here in her own land and in her own carriage. She was so much more composed. "She has imagination," he repeated to himself.

They turned into the road before he spoke again.

"So this is your 'coolly'?"

"No, this is our valley. The coolly is over there where you see that cloud shadow sliding down."

He looked about slowly at the hills and fields.

"It's very fine; much finer than Oconomowoc and Geneva."

"We like it — pappa and I."

They were both talking around the bush, as the saying goes, but he finally said:

"I was very glad to receive your telegram. Am I to take it as an affirmative answer?"

She said with effort:

"I wanted you to see how poor and humble we all are before — before I ——"

He studied her profile. Her lips quivered, and a tear glistened through the veil.

"On my part," he said, "I regretted that I did not further set forth my general cussedness and undesirability.— How well you drive!" he said, by way of relieving the stress of the moment.

He took command now, and there were no more tender allusions. He sniffed the smell of the grass and the wayside trees, and remarked upon the cattle, and inquired the names of several birds whose notes reached across the field.

"Do you know, I'm no wild lover of the country, and I don't admire the country people unreservedly.

There are exceptions, of course — but my experience
with them has not been such as to make them heroic
sufferers, as the new school of fiction sets 'em forth.
They are squalid enough and poor enough, heaven
knows, but it is the squalor of piracy — they do as well
as I should under the same circumstances, no doubt."

Rose looked at him narrowly, as if to find his real
thought. He stopped abruptly at her glance.

" I beg your pardon for boring you; but these dis-
agreeable phases of my character should be known to
you. I'm full of whims and notions, you'll find."

She looked away and a moment later said: " There
is our farm; that house in the grove is ours."

" Cattle I hate, so I hope your father will not expect
me to be interested in stock."

This was the first time he had mentioned her father,
and it moved her unaccountably. It would be so dreadful if he should not understand her father. His per-
verse attitude toward her and toward the country had
brought her from exalted singleness of emotion down to
a complexity of questionings and forebodings.

As they whirled into the yard Mason saw a new
house of the ambitious pork-pie order, standing in a
fairly well-kept sward, with a background of barns,
corn-cribs, pigsties, and beehives. A well-to-do farm-
stead of the more fortunate sort, and the thought that
the man coming out of the barn to meet them was to be
his father-in-law struck him like a gust of barn-yard air.
Really could it be that he had made this decision ?

As the man came nearer he appeared a strong-armed,

gentle-faced farmer of sixty. His eyes were timid, almost appealing. His throat was brown and wrinkled as leather. His chin-beard was a faded yellow-gray, and his hands were nobbed and crooked in the fingers. He peered at Mason through dimmed eyes.

"Father," said Rose, and her voice trembled a little, "this is Mr. Mason."

John Dutcher put up his hand heartily.

"How do you do, sir?" His timid smile touched Mason, but there was something else in the man which made him return the hand-clasp.

"I am glad to see you Mr. Dutcher," he said, and his tone was so genuine it brought a gush of tears to the daughter's eyes. Her lover understood her father after all.

"Won't you 'light out, sir?" continued John, with elaborate hospitality.

"Well, yes, I think I will," said Mason, and Rose's spirits shook off their cowls.

Suddenly she heard every bird singing, the thrush in the poplar top, the catbirds in the willows, the robin on the lawn; the sun flooded the world with magical splendor. It was morning in the world and morning in her life, and her lover was walking up the path by her side.

It was splendid beyond belief to show him to his room, to bring him water and towels and to say from the doorway, with a smile:

"Breakfast is ready!"

The picture that she made lingered pleasantly on

Mason's interior eye.   She was so supple of form and so radiant of color, and so palpitant with timid joy.

She was alone at the table when he came in.   She explained as she showed him his seat, " Father and my aunt had breakfast long ago."

Mrs. Diehl brought the coffee in and bowed awkwardly to Mason.   The whole thing seemed like a scene in a play to him.   It was charming, all the same, to sit alone at the table with such a girl; it was just the least bit exciting.   His hand shook a little, he noticed.

As he took his cup of coffee from her he said, whimsically :

" I expect to wake up soon."

" Does it seem like a dream to you too ? "

" Well, it isn't my every-day life, I must confess.   I keep expecting to hear the trained quartette in the wings."

To her he seemed handsomer and more refined than in the city.   He seemed simpler, too, though he was still complex enough to keep her wondering.   The slope of his shoulders and the poise of his head were splendid to her.   It could not be possible that he was here to see her; to be served by her; to spend the days with her; to be her husband if she should say so.

And yet she retained her dignity.   She did not become silly nor hysterical as a lesser woman might have done.   She was tremulous with happiness and wonder, but she sat before him mistress of her hands and voice.   Her very laughter pleased him ; if she had giggled — heavens, if she had giggled !

John for his part went busily, apparently calmly,

about his work. Mason was pleased at that; it showed astonishing reserve in the man.

Again that keen sweet feeling of companionship — wifehood — came to Rose as they walked out side by side into the parlor. He had come to her; that was the marvellous thing! She was doing wifely things for him; it was all more intimate, more splendid than she thought!

They took seats in the "best room" and faced each other. It was their most potential moment. Breakfast was eaten and the day was before them, and an understanding was necessary.

"Now, I can't allow you to be hasty," Mason said. "I'll tell you what I think you had better do; defer your answer until two weeks from to-day, when I shall return to the city. That will give us time to talk the matter over, and it will give you time to repent."

A little shadow fell over her and the sunlight was not quite so brilliant. The incomprehensible nature of the man came to her again, and he seemed old, old as a granite crag, beyond song, beyond love, beyond hope.

Then he smiled: "Well now I'm ready to go see the sights; any caves, any rocking bowlders, any water-tower?"

She took up the cue for gayety: "No, but I might take you to see the cemetery, that is an appropriate Sunday walk; all the young people walk there."

"The cemetery! No, thank you. I'm a believer in crematories. I'll tell you what we'll do. After you've hung out the wash-boiler to dry we'll go down under the trees, and I'll listen to some of your verse. Now, that is a tremendous concession on my part. I hope you value it to the full."

"I do, indeed."

"You do? good! We'll put the matter in movement at once."

"The dew is still on the grass," she said, warningly.

"So it is. I thank you for remembering my growing infirmities. Well, let's go out and see the pigs. As I told you, I hate cattle and swine, they act out so frankly the secret vices of man — but, never mind, I'll go out and have it out with your father."

The moment he began in that tone she was helpless.

They moved out into the barn-yard, but John was not in sight.

"I guess he's with his bees," Rose said. "He likes to sit out there and watch them when he is resting."

They peered over the fence, and their eyes took in a picture they will never forget while they live. John Dutcher sat before his bees in the ripe bloom of the grass, his head bowed in his hands. He was crying for his lost daughter.

There came a gripping pain in the girl's throat, the hot tears rushed to her eyes, and she cried, in a voice of remorseful agony:

"Father — pappa John!"

He lifted his head and looked at her, his eyes dim with tears, his lips quivering.

The girl rushed through the gate, and Mason turned and walked away like a man discovered thieving from an altar.

CONCLUSION

THE WIND IN THE TREE-TOPS

MASON freshened magically under Rose's sweet and self-contained companionship. She did not coddle him, nor bore him by attentions, but seemed to do the right thing instinctively. She assumed command over him in certain ways — that is, she insisted on his taking long walks and drives with her — though he sturdily refused to climb hills. "Bring me to them gradually," he said, "for I am Egyptian."

One Sunday afternoon he consented to try an easy one and they started out — she in radiant, laughing exultation, he in pretended dark foreboding of the outcome.

She led the way with swift, steady swing of skirts, her smiling face a challenge to him when he fell too far behind. He never ceased to admire her powerful, decisive movement and her radiant color, though he said nothing about it to her. She stopped at a spring which came silently to light beneath an overhanging sandstone. There was no dipper, and Rose, with a new daring, dropped on her knees and dipped some of the cool, sweet water in her palm.

"Do you thirst, Sir Guy?"

He kneeled beside her with a comical groan, and drank from her hand.

"Thanks, a sweeter draught from fairer hand was never quaffed."

Rose was highly elated at the success of her trick. She dipped another palm full. He shook his head.

"With your permission I'll use my hat brim."

"I'll show you how to do it," she said. And flinging herself down full length on the ground, and resting her palms on two flat stones, she drank from the pool, like an Indian.

"There!" she cried, triumphantly. "That's the way to drink. All my life I've done this way at this spring — when there wasn't anyone to see."

Mason felt a wild charm in this. Most women he knew would have tumbled to pieces doing such a thing, while Rose sprang up a little flushed, but with no other sign of exertion.

There was something primeval, elemental, in being thus led by a beautiful woman through coverts of ferns and hazel. Every shadow seemed to wash away some stain or scar of the city's strife. He grew younger.

"I almost like this sort of thing," he said.

They came at last to the smooth slope of the peak where grass stood tall in bunches on a gravelly soil, and wild flowers of unusual kinds grew. As they mounted now, the landscape broke over the tree-tops, and the valleys curved away into silent blue mist.

On every side low wooded ridges lay, with farms spread like rugs half-way up their deep green clearings.

On the farther slope a pasture came nearly to the summit, and the tinkle of a bell among the bushes sounded a pastoral note. A field of wild grasses just to the left glowed with a beautiful pink-purple bloom.

" Isn't it beautiful ? " asked Rose.

Mason dropped full length on the grass before replying.

" Yes, it is lovely — perfectly pastoral. Worthy a poem."

" I've written three, right on this spot," she said, a little shyly.

He seemed interested.

" Have you ? Haven't one with you ? "

" No."

" Always go armed. Now here's a golden opportunity gone to waste."

She smiled, archly.

" I can repeat one though."

" Can you ? Better yet ! Begin ! "

She sat down near him, but not too near, and began, in a soft, hesitant voice, to repeat a poem which was full of feminine sadness and wistfulness. As she went on Mason turned his face toward her, and her eyes fell and her voice faltered.

" That's glorious ! " he said. " Go on."

The wind swept up the slope and through the leaning white bodies of the birches with a sadness like the poem. The wild barley bowed and streamed in the wind like an old man's beard ; the poem struck deep into secret moods, incommunicable in words — and music came to carry the words. The girl's eyes were sweet and serious, and the lovely lines of her lips shifted and wavered.

Mason suddenly reached out and took her right hand. Her voice died out and her eyes met his. He drew her hand toward him and laid his lips upon her strong white wrist.

"You're a poet," he said. "You have found your voice, and I — I love you because you are a poet and because you are a beautiful woman."

At the touch of his bearded lips upon her arm, the whole world reshaped itself for Rose. His praise of her poem — her victory over him as a critic was great, but his final words drowned in fierce light the flame of her art's enthusiasm.

Once more a man's voice came to her, filled with entreaty and command, but in this case she had no reservations. It was well, it was inevitable, and it was glorious to set her face toward wifehood and fame with such a man as companion, friend, and lover.

*   *   *   *   *   *   *

A few weeks later, Mason came down from his room with a grim look on his face. He stepped out on the porch and stood there feeling the change in the air. The wind was from the north, cool and dry. The sky was softened by a thin white veil of mist. The woodpecker was uttering a new note. The air was touched with the faint smell of wood-smoke. The orioles and robins were silent, the crickets sounding the passing of the day. The summer was over.

Rose came out, and he put his arm about her.

"Hark!" he commanded. "Do you hear the wind in the tree-tops? It brings me the roar of the city this morning. I hear the grind of cars, the roar of mills, the throb of presses; the city calls me and I must go. My vacation is over. I must say good-by to-night."

"It's very beautiful up here now," she said, a little wistfully. "The sumac is beginning to turn and the hills are like jewels."

"Oh, yes, it is beautiful," he said, smiling a little. "But down there life is — infinite novelty, ceaseless change. As you love the country, so I love the city. It is a greater pleasure to me to meet men than trees, and concerts are more than winds in the pines. Artist souls, poets, people who do and think, are there, and so I must go."

"When shall I go?" she asked.

"When you please," he said. "I have no commands. You are perfectly free to do as you like. I need you always now."

"Then I will go to-night," she said, firmly.

He turned his eyes upon her in a look she never forgot.

"My dearest girl, do you realize what you are doing? Do you realize that you are entering upon a dubious line of action — that you are inviting pain and sorrow and care, that you are leaving girlhood and leisure behind — that you are entering gates that never swing outward? Do you know this — once more and finally, do you realize all this?"

She stood tall before him stronger than he; that he

acknowledged. She knew him at last since that touch of his lips to her arm, since that look in his eyes — and she said : "I realize it all, and I choose it."

The janitor of the Berkley flats stood transfixed as he became aware of a young woman just behind Mason, but being natively polite he concealed his astonishment by bowing low.

"Williams," said Mason with an air of apology, "I have gone and done it. This is my wife," (Williams bowed definitely to Rose). "I promise not to do it again if you won't mind — and if you keep it from the fellows for a day or two."

"Cehtinly not, sah, of co'se not, Misto Mason."

"And send Annie up; she may be of some use to Mrs. Mason."

"All right, sah. You'll find everything in ohder, sah."

As Rose went up the stairway she heard Williams chuckle softly.

At the door Mason turned, dangling a key on his finger.

"Mistress of my heart — here is the key to my poor home. Therewith I surrender my dominion like Boabdil the Moor."

Rose took the key gently, for under Mason's playful words ran a perceptible note of sadness. He was surrendering a part of his freedom to her — the sacrifices were not all on her side. Without a word she turned the key in the lock and he threw the door open.

2 A

" Enter, my ' bread-dispenser.' "

She gave a little cry of surprise. The apartment, glowing with light and with warmth, reflected Mason's mind as in a magic mirror. Books — everywhere books, that was the first impression. Next the pictures and odd pieces of sculpture claimed her interest, and photographs of poets, actors, and musicians, and then more books and easy chairs and pipes.

After another keen glance Rose uttered her pleasure. " Oh, how cozy ! It is ever so much more interesting and lovely than I imagined it."

" Thanks, dreadfully," replied Mason, gloomily. " I took years to get these things together."

She came and put her hand in his. " And you thought I'd change all this ! " she softly said in reproach.

As they took seats before the fire Mason settled down into his favorite arm-chair with a sigh of content ; " Home once more ! " Then he looked up at Rose and replied to her question. " Well, as we faced Judge Wilson I had that fear, but as I sit here it seems as if neither my life nor this room could ever change ; it seems as if you were merely a visitor. Now that is honest, but let me tell you something further, my lady." He took her hand between his strong smooth palms. " I used to be lonely here, but when I look at you I know I shall never be lonely again."